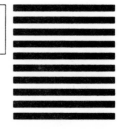

UNIX Utilities

OTHER McGRAW-HILL BOOKS OF INTEREST

Hancock and Krieger, The C Primer

McGilton and Morgan, Introducing the UNIX System

Morgan and McGilton, Introducing UNIX System V

UNIX Utilities

Ramkrishna S. Tare

AGS Computers, Inc.
Mountainside, New Jersey

McGraw-Hill Book Company

New York St. Louis San Francisco Auckland Bogotá Caracas
Colorado Springs Hamburg Lisbon London Madrid Mexico Milan
Montreal New Delhi Oklahoma City Panama Paris San Juan
São Paulo Singapore Sydney Tokyo Toronto

Library of Congress Cataloging-in-Publication Data

Tare, Ramkrishna S.
    UNIX utilities.

        1. UNIX (Computer operating system) 2. Utilities
(Computer programs) I. Title.
QA76.76.063T38   1987   005.4'3   87-17045
ISBN 0-07-062879-3
ISBN 0-07-062884-X

UNIX is a trademark of Bell Laboratories.
WRITER's WORKBENCH and Spell are trademarks of AT&T.
VAX is a registered trademark of Digital Equipment Corp.
INFORMIX is a registered trademark of Relational Database Systems, Inc.
UNIFY is a registered trademark of Unify Corp.
SQL is a registered trademark of International Business Machines Corp.
Scribe is a trademark of UNI-LOGIC.
POSTSCRIPT is a registered trademark of Adobe Systems Inc.

1234567890 DOC/DOC 8921098

ISBN 0-07-062879-3 {HC}

ISBN 0-07-062884-X {PC}

The editors for this book were Theron R. Shreve and Stephen M. Smith, the designer
was Naomi Auerbach, and the production supervisor was Richard A. Ausburn.

Printed and bound by R. R. Donnelley & Sons Company.

TO MY PARENTS

Shrimati Yashoda

and

Shri Surya

Colophon

This book was typeset using the rich document preparation tools of the UNIX system and printed on a POSTSCRIPT printer. The entire manuscript was prepared using *troff*, *pic*, *eqn*, and *tbl*. The power and elegance of these tools in conjunction with file manipulation and project management utilities offered by the UNIX system created a very sophisticated and congenial environment for typesetting and maintaining the various bits and pieces of this project. The POSTSCRIPT language was also used to design the title page. The book uses several font types including Times Roman, Times Italic, Helvetica Bold, ZapfChancery MediumItalic, Courier, and Courier Bold.

Contents

Preface

This book is about UNIX utilities; it teaches you how to use the most popular of the numerous utilities that are available in the UNIX environment. This book does not teach you how to get started with UNIX. It is for those who wish to program in the UNIX environment. It can also serve as a supplementary textbook for a course in UNIX.

There are numerous versions of UNIX available on the market today. While programming at the system level is increasingly becoming unportable across versions, the UNIX utilities which are discussed in this book hardly vary across versions. Furthermore, the utilities discussed are available on most UNIX versions. The primary purpose of this book is to simplify utilities that may look cryptic and advanced in the reference manuals. The material presented here can save a lot of programming efforts. If the reader reads just one chapter and uses it in the UNIX software development environment, the cost of this book will have been recovered several times over. The numerous examples given here are not intended to demonstrate any particular programming style.

I strongly believe that this book can be best utilized by having access to a UNIX system. The exercises at the end of the book provide practical examples of the use of the utilities. The user should try these examples in order to gain confidence in the use of the utilities. After you have completed studying a chapter or a utility, read the UNIX reference manual and try to use all the options available.

I have grouped the utilities in chapters based on their usage. When I read a book, I rarely read it in sequence. I expect the same from you, and accordingly you may skip from one chapter to another in any sequence; however, please try to maintain the sequence within a chapter. Chapter 5 discusses database management systems (DBMS) which are available in the UNIX environment. Most of these are sold separately. However, Ingres is widely available on most machines running Berkeley Software Distribution (BSD) version 4.2, so I have used it to demonstrate most of the features of a UNIX-based DBMS.

Chapter 1 discusses basic file manipulation tools. These are the most commonly used utilities. Lack of knowledge of these utilities should be remedied at all cost. The focus of Chapter 2 is the discussion of the various debugging tools available. They are primarily intended for programmers who use high-level languages like C or Pascal for programming. Chapter 3 discusses tools for developing language processors and compilers. These utilities are primarily intended for the compiler writer, but *yacc* and *lex* are widely used outside the world of compilers. The novice user is often intimidated by the use of compiler jargons like grammar and parsing techniques. This chapter does not assume any knowledge of parsing techniques or compiler design. Chapter 4 discusses utilities that are available for maintaining and developing systems and programs. UNIX is becoming increasingly popular in the world of data processing, therefore Chapter 5 is devoted entirely to the discussion of DBMS available in the UNIX environment. Chapter 6 explains the tools that are available for text processing. This book was written using some of these tools. In Chapter 7 I have discussed data communication utilities. Chapter 8 discusses the various tools that are available to the technical writer. It includes some of the tools that were used for writing this book. Finally, Chapter 9 discusses miscellaneous utilities which are very useful but which could not be classified in the other chapters.

I used UNIX utilities extensively during the writing of this book. *Awk* was used to generate the table of contents. The book itself was phototypeset using *troff*, *pic*, *eqn*, and *tbl*. Numerous macros were required to generate appropriate page layouts, number sections automatically, move figures and tables which could not be accommodated on the remaining part of the page, and so on. There were situations where these macros were not sufficient. These situations gave birth to more than one version of *troff* macros. The Source Code Control System (SCCS) was used to retrieve the required version needed by specific chapters. The table of contents and the index were maintained using *make*. Finally, the Writer's Workbench was used to detect spelling errors and provide some useful suggestions for my writing.

It is a pleasure to acknowledge the help and guidance provided by many friends and colleagues during the writing of this book. I wish to thank Dr. Larry Medsker of Purdue University for his help in reviewing the proposal for the book. Martha Desmond, Chandra Kintala, Hai-Yann Hwang, Chris Ramming, and Yu-Lien Yen of Bell Laboratories, Rick Greer and John Snyder of AT&T Corporation, Dave Falgun of Lechman Assoc., Anil Pal of Auxco Computers Inc., Ulka Rodgers, Stuart Dutfield, and Rasta Mansoor helped in reviewing the technical accuracy of the text. Henry McGilton, coauthor of *Introducing the UNIX System*, a McGraw-Hill publication, provided some invaluable suggestions. In addition, I have to thank Nikki Herbst for her help in copy editing the manuscript and verifying the examples so meticulously. The inevitable errors, if any, are, however, strictly mine! I also wish to express my thanks to Florry Brenner and the management of AGS Computers, Inc., for their encouragement and to all my friends for their pleasant and egoless support, in particular Neil Torino, Cheng Yeh, Vidyadhar Rao, Judith Ferguson, and Harpreet Singh Chawla. Finally, this book would not have been possible without the help and cooperation of Jeremy Robinson, Theron Shreve, and Stephen Smith of McGraw-Hill Book Co.

A few personal notes before I begin: Years ago, I entered the computer field by chance, thanks to the advice of Dr. M. N. Seetharamanath of the department of computer science at the Indian Institute of Technology. Since then I have been fortunate to work on software development with many senior programmers and other professionals who have taught me more than any book has. In particular, P. C. Narayan of Telco, India, taught me a great deal. I have worked as a CAD programmer, have programmed extensively in ALGOL and FORTRAN while working in the Burroughs environment, and have even had my share of COBOL. I have taught graduate and undergraduate courses at the New Jersey Institute of Technology. I have worked as a consultant at AT&T Communications and Bell Laboratories. All these experiences have added to my knowledge about computers, programming, and programmers and have helped me to write this book. I enjoyed completing this project, though most of it was done during late hours and weekends. I hope it provides you with a more productive UNIX environment.

Enjoy the book!

Ramkrishna S. Tare

Introduction

Whatever you can do, or dream you can do,
begin it.
Boldness has genius, power and magic in it.
Begin it now.

Goethe

Let me welcome you to the world of UNIX utilities! This book was written to make cryptic utilities easy to understand. The targeted audience is primarily those who have already started working in the UNIX environment. Some common terms are widely used in this book. The next paragraphs give brief explanations of these terms.

Shell: The shell is also a utility! It is started when you log into the system. It first displays a prompt and then waits for the user to type a command line. It is responsible for analyzing this line, searching for the appropriate program file, and initiating the execution.

Shell comments: All lines starting with the character # are considered comment lines by the shell. In addition, if the shell encounters this character in a line, it views the rest of the line as a comment line.

Standard input and output: Most UNIX programs are written to read from a default file. This default input file is also referred to as the standard input. Similarly, the default output file is referred to as the standard output. All error messages are written to the standard error. Unless redirected, as explained later, the standard input, standard output, and standard error files are associated with your terminal.

Redirection: The default input and output files can be changed by using input-output redirection. The > character is used to redirect standard output and the < character is used to redirect standard input. For example, the command *comm* can be made to read from a file called inpfile and write to a file called outfile by using the command *comm < inpfile > outfile.*

Pipe: The output of one command can be made the input of another command by connecting the two commands with a pipe (|). For example, *comm1 < inpfile|comm2 > outfile* will have the command *comm1* read from the file inpfile and feed the output to the command *comm2*. The command *comm2* will store its output in the file outfile.

Filter: Any program that can read from the standard input and write to the standard output is called a filter. Normally, the output of a filter depends on its input.

Cat: The command *cat* is used very widely in this book. This simple command can be used to display the contents of a file or to concatenate two or more files.

Login id: When your terminal is connected to a computer running the UNIX system, the system will display a prompt `login:` on the terminal. The user types in the assigned login id and the system then asks for the password with another prompt. Users on the system are referred to by their login id's.

Vi: It is the most popular screen editor available in the UNIX environment.

Regular expressions: Regular expressions are used by many UNIX utilities. They provide a way to specify patterns to be matched. The shell also uses these expressions to generate file names. Regular expressions use a group of characters, known as metacharacters, which are interpreted differently from other characters. The interpretation of the metacharacters varies across utilities.

Options: Most UNIX utilities accept options on the command line. These options are usually specified using the − (minus) sign. Options increase the flexibility of the utilities. There are some options which do not need the minus sign, some which do not need any sign, and some which are preceded by a + (plus) sign. If an option discussed in this book does not function correctly on the UNIX version that you have access to, then you may find it necessary to display the on-line documentation for the command to get the correct option for that command on your local UNIX system.

On-line help: On-line help is available on most UNIX systems. The documentation of any command can be printed using the *man* command. For example, to get a full documentation of the *sed* command, type *man sed.*

UNIX Utilities

1 File Processing

UNIX offers a wide range of tools for examining the contents of a file. These tools have some common features and many incongruous options. They can read a standard input file and write to the standard output. Such utilities, often called filters, are powerful enough to serve the data processing needs of small databases and files; however, they provide only sequential access and can be slow for search operations. They do not modify the contents of the input file but will simply write the result to the standard output. The following sections show how these utilities can become a powerful arsenal for both casual and serious UNIX users.

1.1 Head and Tail

Head is used to display the specified number of records from the top of a selected file. The most commonly used option is the one that specifies the number of records to be displayed. If you do not have *head* on your system, then you probably have a *more* or a *pg* command which will let you do a *head* and something more! *Tail* does the same as *head* but in the reverse direction: it displays the specified number of lines from the end of the file. In most UNIX versions, *tail* allows only a limited number of lines to be displayed. This limit depends primarily on the record size of the file to be displayed. Here is an example of *head* usage:

```
head -5 file1
John    23      123-38-9073
Michael 23      321-12-8921
James   25      142-32-4564
Paul    26      231-34-1212
Tom     23      123-12-1245
```

In the above example we have used an option to display the first five lines. By default, *head* displays the first 10 lines of selected files.

1.2 More and Pg

More and *pg* are used to examine the contents of a file. These utilities can be used to display a file one screenful at a time or a specified number of lines at a time. Thus

```
more bigfile
```

can be used to display the file bigfile one screenful at a time, while

```
more -10 bigfile
```

can be used to display the file 10 lines at a time. They also provide a mechanism to search for regular expressions. Most options are common to both *pg* and *more*. *More* is more popular and commonly used on the Berkeley Software Distribution (BSD) version while *pg* is normally available on the System V version of UNIX. They provide numerous command line options and search features. We will look at the most commonly used features of these utilities.

1.2.1 Examining a File

To examine a file, use the command along with the name of the file to be examined, as follows:

```
more somefile
```
or
```
pg somefile
```

Either of these commands will display the first screenful of the file. *More* and *pg* will then wait for the user response. If you are using *pg*, a carriage return in response to the prompt will display the next screenful. If you are using *more*, entering a space character in response to the prompt will display the next screenful. A ˆD (control D) will display the next 11 lines or half a screenful. To skip some lines while using *more*, specify the number of lines to be skipped followed by the letter *i*, and *more* will position itself after the specified number of lines. *Pg* allows you to scroll backward and forward with the *l* command. A negative number preceding this command can be used to specify the number of lines to be scrolled backward. A positive number with the + sign will scroll the file forward and and an unsigned number will display a screenful beginning at the specified line. In addition, the $ command in *pg* can be used to display the last screen of the file.

1.2.2 Searching for Regular Expressions

Pg and *more* also enable us to search for regular expressions in the file. In *pg*, the command *i/regular expression/* is used to search forward for the *i*th occurrence of the regular expression. The command *i?regular expression?* is used to search backward for the *i*th occurrence of the regular expression. In *more*, the command *i/regular expression* is used to search forward for the *i*th occurrence of the regular expression. In *more* there is no command to search backward.

1.2.3 Escaping to the Shell

More and *pg* allow us to escape to the shell and execute a UNIX command by the use of *!command*, where *command* is any UNIX command.

1.2.4 Examples of More and Pg Usage

Here are some examples of *more* and *pg* usage:

```
man cat|more -200 > catman
```

will store the first 200 lines of the manual page of the *cat* command in the file catman.

```
pg -1 file1
John      23        123-38-9073
1/^J/
James     25        142-32-4564
```

In the above session we invoke *pg* to peruse file1 one line at a time and then display the next line which starts with the letter *J*.

On-line help for using these commands is available by using the *h* command.

1.3 Cut

Each record of a file can be considered as a collection of characters or fields. The fields may be separated by any field separation character. Data processing requirements often make an extraction of only certain character positions or fields from a file. *Cut* is the UNIX utility that provides these capabilities. The syntax of *cut* is as follows:

```
cut -f list [-d char] file1 file2...
         or
cut -c list file1 file2...
```

List is a comma-separated list of integers or range of integers. For example, 1,3-5,7 would project the first, third, fourth, fifth, and seventh positions. The first form is used to cut specified fields from a file using the field separator *char*. The second form is used to cut columns based on character positions. The only option required for a *cut* by character positions is the −*c* option which specifies a list of character positions to be projected. Here is an example of a *cut* by character positions:

```
cat file1
John,P  23       123-38-9073     75
Phil,R  23       321-12-8921     59
Mike,T  25       142-32-4564     32
Rick,L  26       231-34-1212     65
Jack,T  23       123-12-1245     90


cut -c1-4,10-15 file1
John    123-3
Phil    321-1
Mike    142-3
Rick    231-3
Jack    123-1
```

The file named file1 has four fields separated by a tab character which has been expanded in the display. A cut by field positions is more commonly used. Let us look at another example in which we will cut a list of fields from the same file:

```
cut -f1,3-4 file1
John,P  123-38-9073     75
Phil,R  321-12-8921     59
Mike,T  142-32-4564     32
Rick,L  231-34-1212     65
Jack,T  123-12-1245     90
```

The default field separator is a tab but it can be changed by using the $-d$ option on the command line. In the following example the fields are separated by a blank character:

```
cat file1
John,P 23 123-38-9073 75
Phil,R 23 321-12-8921 59
Mike,T 25 142-32-4564 32
Rick,L 26 231-34-1212 65
Jack,T 23 123-12-1245 90


cut -f2,1,3 -d" " file1
John,P 23 123-38-9073
Phil,R 23 321-12-8921
Mike,T 25 142-32-4564
```

```
Rick,L 26 231-34-1212
Jack,T 23 123-12-1245
```

When specifying the field delimiter, only characters which have a special meaning to the shell have to be enclosed in quotes; otherwise quoting is not required. *Cut* will give an error diagnostic if the line length is greater than 1023 characters.

1.4 Paste

Paste is used to paste several files together. It is similar to the UNIX utility *cat* except that while *cat* concatenates files vertically, *paste* concatenates files horizontally. The number of records in the output file is equal to the number of records in the longest input file. The syntax of the *paste* command is as follows:

paste *[-s] [-d char] file1 file2 ...*

The output file contains a record for each record in the longest input file. These records are concatenated together with their newline characters replaced by tab characters, except for the records of the last file which retain their newline characters. The tab character can be replaced by another character by using the −*d* option. The file names can be substituted by the − (minus) characters. This indicates that the records of the file must be read from the standard input. A −*s* option is useful for reading lines from the same file and pasting them together. Here are some examples of the use of *paste*:

```
cat f1
a
b
c
d
cat f2
1
2
3
4
5
6
```

Example 1

```
paste f1 f2
a        1
b        2
c        3
d        4
         5
         6
```

Example 2

```
paste -d" " f1 f2
a 1
b 2
c 3
d 4
 5
 6
```

Example 3

```
paste -s f1
a        b        c        d
```

Example 4

```
cat f1 | paste - -
a        b
c        d
```

In example 1, *paste* was used to simply paste horizontally the records of the two files f1 and f2. The newline character of file f1 was replaced by the tab character. In example 2, we pasted f1 and f2, but this time the newline character of file f1 was replaced by a blank character. This was specified by the −*d* option. In example 3, we used the records in the same file f1 to be pasted together into one record. In the last example, the input consisted of two files. Records for both files were taken from the standard input. This option is used to convert a file of *n* records into a file containing *n/x* records, where *x* is the number of minus signs on the command line. The first record contains the first *x* records pasted together as described earlier, the second record contains the next *x* records from the input file, and so on.

1.4.1 Using Cut and Paste Together

Cut and *paste* can be used together to restructure the columns of a file. Let us move the first column of file file1 to the end of the record. This can be done as follows:

```
cat file1
John,P 23 123-38-9073 75
Phil,R 23 321-12-8921 59
Mike,T 25 142-32-4564 32
Rick,L 26 231-34-1212 65
Jack,T 23 123-12-1245 90

cut -f1   -d" " file1 > file2
cut -f2-4 -d" " file1 > file3
paste -d" " file3 file2 > file1

cat file1
23 123-38-9073 75 John,P
23 321-12-8921 59 Phil,R
25 142-32-4564 32 Mike,T
26 231-34-1212 65 Rick,L
23 123-12-1245 90 Jack,T
```

In this example, we first cut the first field of file1 and stored it in file2. Next, we cut the remaining fields of file1 and stored this segment in file3. We then pasted file3 and file2 and redirected the output into file1. The new file1 is now restructured as desired.

1.5 Od: Unraveling the Hidden

One of the frustrating things in programming is to display nongraphic characters in a file. Attempts to display a file which has these characters can create problems, as these characters may alter some of the terminal settings. *Od* helps us to display these characters in various formats. The syntax of *od* is as follows:

od [-bcdosx] [file] [[+]offset[.][b]]

Let us try to dump the contents of a directory file using *od*. The directory file in the UNIX System V consists of a 16-byte entry for each file. The first two bytes store the i-number of the file. The i-number is used to locate an inode for the file being accessed. The remaining 14 bytes store the name of the file. If you try to *cat* the directory file, you will see strange characters because the first two bytes of a file entry may not represent graphic ASCII characters. Let us use *od* to dump one such directory file:

```
ls dirfile
s.t.c
dummy.c
a.out
core
test.c
od -c dirfile
0000000   \0   b    .  \0  \0  \0  \0  \0  \0  \0  \0  \0  \0  \0  \0  \0
0000020    6   a    .   .  \0  \0  \0  \0  \0  \0  \0  \0  \0  \0  \0  \0
0000040   \0 211    s   .   t   .   c  \0  \0  \0  \0  \0  \0  \0  \0  \0
0000060  003 340    d   u   m   m   y   .   c  \0  \0  \0  \0  \0  \0  \0
0000100  036   @    a   .   o   u   t  \0  \0  \0  \0  \0  \0  \0  \0  \0
0000120   \0 206    c   o   r   e  \0  \0  \0  \0  \0  \0  \0  \0  \0  \0
0000140  001   f    t   e   s   t   .   c  \0  \0  \0  \0  \0  \0  \0  \0
0000160
```

The −c option instructs *od* to interpret the bytes in ASCII. The first column indicates the character position in octal; thus the first row starts with 0000000, indicating that the first character is at position 1. The second row starts with the octal number 0000020, or decimal 16, indicating that the first character in the second row is at position 17. The ASCII graphic characters are printed appropriately. If the character does not have a graphic representation, then it is printed as a C escape character or a three-digit octal number. The first two bytes of each file entry have some characters which are nongraphic, as may be expected. The \0 represents the NULL character in C escape format.

When *od* is invoked with the −d option, two adjacent bytes are clubbed together and their decimal equivalent is printed as an integer value. Here is the output of *od* with the −c and the −d options on the same directory file:

```
od -cd dirfile
0000000    00098   11776   00000   00000   00000   00000   00000   00000
            \0  b    .  \0  \0  \0  \0  \0  \0  \0  \0  \0  \0  \0  \0  \0
0000020    13921   11822   00000   00000   00000   00000   00000   00000
             6  a    .   .  \0  \0  \0  \0  \0  \0  \0  \0  \0  \0  \0  \0
0000040    00137   29486   29742   25344   00000   00000   00000   00000
            \0 211   s   .   t   .   c  \0  \0  \0  \0  \0  \0  \0  \0
0000060    00992   25717   28013   31022   25344   00000   00000   00000
           003 340   d   u   m   m   y   .   c  \0  \0  \0  \0  \0  \0
0000100    07744   24878   28533   29696   00000   00000   00000   00000
           036  @    a   .   o   u   t  \0  \0  \0  \0  \0  \0  \0  \0
0000120    00134   25455   29285   00000   00000   00000   00000   00000
            \0 206   c   o   r   e  \0  \0  \0  \0  \0  \0  \0  \0  \0
0000140    00358   29797   29556   11875   00000   00000   00000   00000
           001  f    t   e   s   t   .   c  \0  \0  \0  \0  \0  \0  \0
0000160
```

The second row shows the ASCII character representation and the first row displays the same characters with their decimal equivalent. For example, ASCII characters \0 and b represent binary values 00000000 and 01100010. If we club them together, we get 0000000001100010. This number, with the most significant bit at the left side, represents the decimal number 98. This number is shown above the two characters it represents. If the bit order on the machine is different, the decimal number displayed will be different. There are certain software packages which create files with integer data stored in their binary representation. Data in these files can be examined by using *od* −*d*. The −*b* option dumps the characters in their octal representation. The −*o* option dumps two characters clubbed together as a word in their octal representation. The −*x* option gives the hexadecimal representation, and the −*s* option is identical to the −*d* option except that it interprets the most significant bit as a sign bit.

Od also offers a feature to look at only a certain segment of the file. This feature can be used by specifying the byte offset from where *od* is to start reading the file. This offset is interpreted as an octal number. If this offset is followed by a . (dot) then it is interpreted as a decimal number. If a *b* is specified along with the offset, then the offset is multiplied by 512. Finally, if data is piped into *od* and an offset is desired, then a + must be specified. Here are some examples of using *od* with an offset. Try to compare the results with earlier outputs from the same file.

```
od -c dirfile 10
0000010   \0  \0  \0  \0  \0  \0  \0  \0   6   a   .   .  \0  \0  \0  \0
0000030   \0  \0  \0  \0  \0  \0  \0  \0  \0 211   s   .   t   .   c  \0
0000050   \0  \0  \0  \0  \0  \0  \0  \0 003 340   d   u   m   m   y   .
0000070    c  \0  \0  \0  \0  \0  \0  \0 036   @   a   .   o   u   t  \0
0000110   \0  \0  \0  \0  \0  \0  \0  \0  \0 206   c   o   r   e  \0  \0
0000130   \0  \0  \0  \0  \0  \0  \0  \0 001   f   t   e   s   t   .   c
0000150   \0  \0  \0  \0  \0  \0  \0  \0
0000160
od -c dirfile 10.
0000010   \0  \0  \0  \0  \0  \0   6   a   .   .  \0  \0  \0  \0  \0  \0
0000026   \0  \0  \0  \0  \0  \0  \0 211   s   .   t   .   c  \0  \0  \0
0000042   \0  \0  \0  \0  \0  \0 003 340   d   u   m   m   y   .   c  \0
0000058   \0  \0  \0  \0  \0  \0 036   @   a   .   o   u   t  \0  \0  \0
0000074   \0  \0  \0  \0  \0  \0  \0 206   c   o   r   e  \0  \0  \0  \0
0000090   \0  \0  \0  \0  \0  \0 001   f   t   e   s   t   .   c  \0  \0
0000106   \0  \0  \0  \0  \0  \0
0000112
```

In the first example, *od* started reading the file from offset 8, which is the decimal equivalent of octal 10. In the second example we have specified the offset as a decimal number by the use of a . (dot); therefore *od* started reading the file from offset 10. *Od* continues dumping the data until it reaches the end of the file.

1.6 Join: Joining Data in Two Files

Join is a utility that supports the relational database operator *natural join*. It enables extraction of data from two files having a field that is defined over some common domain. While this definition may sound theoretical, it is worthwhile to understand what it means. Let us consider two files, suppliers and parts. The suppliers file has three fields, representing supplier number, supplier name, and part number of the part supplied. The parts file also has three fields, representing part number, part name, and part description. If you needed to create a file having supplier name and part name, it would be necessary to make a comparison of the two files based on information in the part number column of each file. Since the part numbers in both files have the same type and represent the same object, we can say that the part number fields in the two files are defined over the same domain. The comparison of the two files based on the field defined over the same domain can therefore be made by using the *join* utility. The syntax of *join* is:

join *[options] file1 file2*

File1 and file2 are the two input files. These files have to be sorted by the field on which a comparison is to be made. Each output line is made up of the common field followed by a line of file1 followed by a line of file2. This output can be modified by using the various options that *join* is equipped with. Here is an example to create a file having supplier name and part name.

```
cat suppliers
S0101:PRS, Inc:p123
S0230:Tare, Inc:p123
S1213:Unicomp Corp.:p223
S0202:Strakers, Inc:p23
S3030:Ritecore, Inc:p234

cat parts
p123:Resistors:multi
p223:Boards:brown
p234:Gloves:blue

join -j1 3 -j2 1 -o 1.2 2.2 -t: suppliers parts
PRS, Inc:Resistors
Tare, Inc:Resistors
Unicomp Corp.:Boards
Ritecore, Inc:Gloves
```

The output shows how the records are joined over the common fields. There is no output record corresponding to the supplier record *S0202:Strakers, Inc:p23* because there is no parts record for part number *p23*. If there are records with duplicate keys in the same file, the join is performed on all the duplicate key records. Since we have two records in the suppliers file with the same part number *p123*, we also have two records with part name *Resistors* in the output.

This example employs the most commonly used options of *join*. The *−j* option is used to specify the common fields on which the join is to be made: *−j1 3* means join on the third field of the first file, *−j2 1* means join on the first field of the second file. The *−o* option is used to specify a list of fields to be output. The list contains blank-separated field specifiers in the form *m.n*, where *m* is the file number and *n* is the position of the field in the file. Thus, *−o 1.2* means output the second field in the first file. The *−t* option is used to specify the field separator character, a colon in this example. By default, the field separators are blank, tab, or newline characters. Multiple blanks and tabs count as one field separator.

It is possible to create output records for unpairable lines in the input files. This is particularly helpful when the purpose of the *join* is to append some data from one file to another without losing any records. *Join* provides the −*a n* and −*e str* options to output records for unpairable lines. The −*a n* option produces a line for each unpairable record in file *n*, where *n*=1 or 2. The −*e str* option replaces the empty fields for the unpairable file by the string specified by *str*. If we require a suppliers parts file with the part name attached if known and the string *NA* attached if it is not known, here is how we would request it:

```
join -a1 -e NA -j1 3 -j2 1 -o 1.1 1.2 1.3 2.2 -t: suppliers parts
S0101:PRS, Inc:p123:Resistors
S0230:Tare, Inc:p123:Resistors
S1213:Unicomp Corp.:p223:Boards
S0202:Strakers, Inc:p23:NA
S3030:Ritecore, Inc:p234:Gloves
```

Join is very helpful when we need to attach information from one file to another file when the two files are of different lengths and/or are sorted by different fields. A *cut* and *paste* works as long as the two files have exactly the same number of records sequenced exactly the same on the common field.

1.7 Sed: A Stream Editor

Sed is a noninteractive editor that can be used to edit files which are too large for *ed*. This is possible because *sed* does not read the entire file into a buffer, rather it reads only a few required lines at a time. *Sed* is a filter because it does not change the original file: it reads the input file and creates a new file which is sent to standard output by default. *Sed* can be invoked as follows:

```
sed [-n] [[-e command]...] [-f] [file]
```

The −*e* option is used to specify that there are multiple commands in the *sed* command string. This is not required if we have only one *sed* command. Let us get started with some simple *sed* scripts.

1.7.1 Getting Started

The minimum requirements to run *sed* are an input file and a command to let *sed* know about the tranformations that should be applied on this file to create an output file. Let us run *sed* to change all occurrences of *"and,"* to *"and"* in the input file file1 and then output only the changed lines.

```
cat file1
It follows,then,that the divine, being good,
is not, as most people say,
responsible for everything that happens to mankind,
but only for a small part;
for the good things in human life are far fewer than
the evil, and, whereas the good must be ascribed to heaven only,
we must look elsewhere for the cause of evils.*

sed  -n s/and,/and/p file1
the evil, and whereas the good must be ascribed to heaven only,
```

We used the $-n$ option to specify that only those lines selected for printing (p) should be output. By default, *sed* will print all lines in the input file. Edited lines will replace the original lines in the input file. The *s/and,/and/p* string is the *sed* command string. The *s* instructs *sed* to do a pattern substitution. This is followed by the string to be searched for, which is enclosed in slashes, and then by a string that should replace the searched pattern. The final *p* instructs *sed* to print the edited lines. If the $-n$ option was not given, we would get both the edited line as well as the entire input file, as follows:

```
sed s/and,/and/p file1
It follows,then,that the divine, being good,
is not, as most people say,
responsible for everything that happens to mankind,
but only for a small part;
for the good things in human life are far fewer than
the evil, and whereas the good must be ascribed to heaven only,
the evil, and whereas the good must be ascribed to heaven only,
we must look elsewhere for the cause of evils.
```

If the *sed* editing command was not terminated by the *p* option we would get only the edited file as the output:

The Republic of Plato, translated by Francis Comford, 1945.

```
sed s/and,/and/ file1
It follows,then,that the divine, being good,
is not, as most people say,
responsible for everything that happens to mankind,
but only for a small part;
for the good things in human life are far fewer than
the evil, and whereas the good must be ascribed to heaven only,
we must look elsewhere for the cause of evils.
```

1.7.2 Sed Commands

Sed commands have the general syntax

line1,line2 [edit commands] [opt commands]

This instructs *sed* to apply the edit commands and the optional (opt) commands on the input file but only on the segment of the file from line number *line1* to line number *line2*. *Line1,line2* can be substituted by just one line number, in which case the following command operates only on that particular line of the input file. It is also possible to use pattern matching to select the lines. This is done by enclosing the pattern in slashes for selecting the lines. For example, the command */John/s/tare/Tare/* substitutes the string *Tare* for *tare* only in those lines which have the string *John* in them. If the line specification is missing, the edit commands are applied to all the lines in the file. The most commonly used edit commands are shown in Table 1.1.

TABLE 1.1 Commonly Used Edit Commands

Command	Explanation
s	Substitute one string with another string.
a	Append newlines in the file.
i	Insert newlines in the file.
d	Delete lines from a file.
c	Change lines from a file to user-specified lines.
p	Print the specified/edited lines.
w	Write selected lines into a specified file.

1.7.3 Examples of Sed Usage

All of the following examples assume the same input file, file1, which was used in the previous examples. Let us use *sed* to display lines 3 to 4 of file1:

```
sed -n 3,4p file1
responsible for everything that happens to mankind,
but only for a small part;
```

Let us create a file with the third and fourth lines deleted:

```
sed  3,4d file1
It follows,then,that the divine, being good,
is not, as most people say,
for the good things in human life are far fewer than
the evil, and, whereas the good must be ascribed to heaven only,
we must look elsewhere for the cause of evils.
```

Here is an example that deletes lines containing the string *the*:

```
sed /the/d file
is not, as most people say,
responsible for everything that happens to mankind,
but only for a small part;
```

The program presented below handles more than one *sed* command on the command line. It substitutes the occurrence of the string *the* with the null string. It also deletes lines with occurrences of the word *for*.

```
sed -e s/the// -e /for/d file1
It follows,n,that the divine, being good,
is not, as most people say,
  evil, and, whereas the good must be ascribed to heaven only,
```

In the above example we had to use the −*e* option because we have more than one command. In this example we see that the string *the* is still present in the output, though our command was to substitute this string by a null string. Here is what happened: Unless we specify a global substitution, the substitution takes place on only the first occurrence of the string *the* in a line.

The second and any subsequent occurrences of the string will not be changed. In order to do a global substitution, we have to use the optional command *g*. Here is how we can do it:

```
sed -e s/the//g -e /for/d file1
It follows,n,that  divine, being good,
is not, as most people say,
 evil, and, whereas  good must be ascribed to heaven only,
```

1.7.4 Sed Commands from a File

We have so far used only the *−e* and the *−n* command line options. The *−f* option is used to store the edit commands in a file and then inform *sed* to take the edit commands from this file. This option is particularly helpful if the edit commands are long; it is also useful for appending or inserting newlines. The *sed* command below performs the same task as the previous *sed* command; however, this time the *sed* edit commands are stored in a file.

```
cat editfile
s/the//g
/for/d
sed -f editfile file1
It follows,n,that  divine, being good,
is not, as most people say,
 evil, and, whereas  good must be ascribed to heaven only,
```

Multiple options can also be used, as shown in the following example:

```
sed -n -f optfile file1
It follows,n,that the divine, being good,
for  good things in human life are far fewer than
 evil, and, whereas the good must be ascribed to heaven only,
we must look elsewhere for  cause of evils.
```

1.7.5 Appending and Inserting New Lines

In *sed*, appending of new lines is done with the *a* command. This command appends lines after the specified line number. Like all other *sed* commands, if a line number is not specified, the append command operates on all lines. The *a* command has to be followed by a backslash (\). The lines to be appended are then specified after the command line. Each line except the last line must be terminated by a backslash character. Let us add a line containing underscores after each line in the input file.

```
cat addfile
a \
------------------------------------------------------------
sed -f addfile file1
It follows,then,that the divine, being good,
------------------------------------------------------------
is not, as most people say,
------------------------------------------------------------
responsible for everything that happens to mankind,
------------------------------------------------------------
but only for a small part;
------------------------------------------------------------
for the good things in human life are far fewer than
------------------------------------------------------------
the evil, and, whereas the good must be ascribed to heaven only,
------------------------------------------------------------
we must look elsewhere for the cause of evils.
------------------------------------------------------------
```

The new lines added are not affected by subsequent deletes, as shown here:

```
cat add_del
a\
-----------
1,3d
head -4 file1 | sed -f add-del
-----------
-----------
-----------
but only for a small part;
-----------
```

The addition of new lines does not affect the line number counter in the same *sed* command file. In the above *sed* command we have not specified a line number; therefore the lines were appended after every record in the input file. Note how the command to delete the first three lines does not affect the newly added lines. The insert (*i*) command is identical to the append command except that the lines are inserted before the specified line number.

1.7.6 Writing Output to Files

It is possible to write the output of selected or edited lines to a file by using the *w* command. Let us output the first two lines of the input into a file called firsttwo, lines having the string *the* into a file called thefile, and finally, substitute the string *good* with the string *nice* and output the result into a file called nicefile. The *sed* command below performs these tasks:

```
cat writefile
1,2w firsttwo
/the/w thefile
s/good/nice/w nicefile
```

```
sed -n -f writefile file1
```

```
cat firsttwo
It follows,then,that the divine, being good,
is not, as most people say,
```

```
cat thefile
It follows,then,that the divine, being good,
for the good things in human life are far fewer than
the evil, and, whereas the good must be ascribed to heaven only,
we must look elsewhere for the cause of evils.
```

```
cat nicefile
It follows,then,that the divine, being nice,
for the nice things in human life are far fewer than
the evil, and, whereas the nice must be ascribed to heaven only,
```

1.7.7 Use of Regular Expressions In Sed

UNIX filters thrive on the use of regular expressions and *sed* is no exception to this rule. Until now we have selected lines for operations to be performed by *sed* commands by explicitly specifying the line numbers or by specifying a string so that the *sed* commands could operate on lines having this string. We can extend this line selection capability by specifying a regular expression. The *sed* commands would then operate on lines which have a string that matches the regular expression. *Sed* regular expressions are either text characters which match verbatim or operator characters which have special interpretations. Operator characters are

```
"\ [ ] ^ - ? . * + ( ) $ /
```

Table 1.2 explains the special meaning associated with eight of the available operator characters. These characters will suffice for most purposes and are more than enough to get started. Meanings for the remaining operator characters can be found in the UNIX system documentation.

TABLE 1.2 Sed Operator Characters in Regular Expressions

Character	Meaning	Examples
.	Matches any character except a newline character.	#.* matches a string starting with a # character until the end of a line. Typically used for removing comment lines.
$	Used at the end of an expression to indicate that a string should match the regular expression preceding this operator only if it occurs at the end of a line.	p$ matches any lowercase letter p occurring at the end of a line.
"	Used to match a string containing operator characters. The special meaning of the operator characters is turned off.	"Tip*Top" matches the string *Tip*Top*.
\	Also used to turn off the special meaning of an operator character. This character can be followed by a number to give an octal representation.	Tip*Top matches the string *Tip*Top*. \40 matches a single blank.

TABLE 1.2 Sed Operator Characters in Regular Expressions (contd.)

Character	Meaning	Examples
//	Matches the last regular expression compiled.	
*	Matches zero or more occurrences of the preceding element of an expression.	bc*d matches strings like bd, bcd and bccd.
[ ]	Used to specify character classes. Within a character class, three characters have special meanings. The −(minus) character is used to indicate a range of characters. It loses its special meaning if it occurs at the beginning of a character class. The ^ character is used to indicate the complement set of characters, i.e. all characters specified except those in the character class. The \ character is used as explained above.	[A−Za−z_][A−Za−z0−9]* matches any C variable name. [^0−9] matches all characters except the digits 0 to 9. [0\−9] matches the three characters 0, 9 and −.
^	If this character occurs outside a character class and at the beginning of an expression, it matches the expression only if it starts after a newline character.	^"New line" matches the string *New line* only if it starts on a newline.

Here are some examples of the use of regular expressions for specifying lines:

Example 1
```
sed -n /^It/p file1
It follows,then,that the divine, being good,
```

In this example, only lines which began with the word *It* were selected. The next example uses the [] operator characters to match lowercase letters. The −*n* option is used once again to output only lines selected for printing.

Example 2
```
sed -n /p[a-z]/p file1
is not, as most people say,
responsible for everything that happens to mankind,
but only for a small part;
```

Here a line was selected if it had a word with the letter *p* followed by any other lowercase letter.

Example 3
```
sed -n /" "p[a-z]/p file1
is not, as most people say,
but only for a small part;
```

In this example, a line was printed only if it had a word that was preceded by a blank character and that began with the letter *p*. In both example 2 and example 3, the selected word had to be at least a two-letter word and the second letter had to be a lowercase letter.

Example 4
```
sed -n s/,$//p file1
It follows,then,that the divine, being good
is not, as most people say
responsible for everything that happens to mankind
the evil, and, whereas the good must be ascribed to heaven only
```

In example 4, we deleted all line-terminating commas and printed the edited lines. With these examples we conclude the discussion of *sed*.

1.8 Egrep

Egrep is a utility which can search for patterns or regular expressions in a file. It is simple to use and comes in three flavors, grep, egrep, and fgrep. The predecessor of *egrep* is *grep*. *Egrep* is an extension of *grep* and can handle more powerful regular expressions. *Fgrep* is a subset of *egrep* that can handle only strings of fixed size, and it is faster to use to search for such strings. In this book we will discuss the use of *egrep*.

1.8.1 Getting Started with Egrep

Egrep can be invoked as follows:

```
egrep [options] [regular expression] files
```

It is always safe to enclose the regular expression in single quotes to protect it from the shell. For the purpose of illustrating the use of *egrep*, we will use the same input file, inpfile, in all the examples. Here is a very simple *egrep* command:

```
cat inpfile
```
And if a man is temperate and free from the love of money, meanness, pretentiousness, and cowardice, he will not be hard to deal with or dishonest. So, as another indication of the philosophic temper, you will observe, from youth up, he is fair-minded, gentle, and sociable.

```
egrep 'So,' inpfile
```
deal with or dishonest. So, as another indication of the

In this example we displayed only those lines in which the string *So,* appeared. *So,* is a very simple regular expression that we were looking for. Like *sed*, *egrep* also has some special characters that allow *egrep* to form regular expressions. The interpretation of these characters is identical to the operator characters in *sed* and is explained in Table 1.2. The following examples show how *egrep* can be used to search for regular expressions in a file:

Example 1
```
egrep '-$' inpfile
```
philosophic temper, you will observe, from youth up, he is fair-

Example 2
```
egrep ',.*,.*,' inpfile
```
meanness, pretentiousness, and cowardice, he will not be hard to
philosophic temper, you will observe, from youth up, he is fair-

Example 3
```
egrep '(^[A-Z])|([a-z]$)' inpfile
```
And if a man is temperate and free from the love of money,
meanness, pretentiousness, and cowardice, he will not be hard to
deal with or dishonest. So, as another indication of the

Example 1 printed lines which end with a minus. Example 2 printed lines
which have more than two commas in them. Finally, example 3 displayed
lines which either start with an uppercase letter or end in a lowercase letter.
Note the use of the ( ) operator characters to group regular expressions.

1.8.2 Command Line Options with Egrep

Egrep provides several command line options. The most useful ones are listed
in Table 1.3.

TABLE 1.3 Egrep Command Line Options

Options	Description
−v	Print lines which do not match the regular expression.
−c	Do not print any lines but give the count of the number of lines that matched the regular expression.
−i	Do not distinguish between lowercase and uppercase letters.
−n	Print the line numbers along with the lines.
−e	Print lines which begin with a − (minus).
−f	Get regular expression from a file which is specified after this option.

Here are some examples which use command line options:

Example 1
```
egrep −e '−$' −v inpfile
```
And if a man is temperate and free from the love of money,
meanness, pretentiousness, and cowardice, he will not be hard to
deal with or dishonest. So, as another indication of the
minded, gentle, and sociable.

Example 2:
```
egrep -c '.' inpfile
2
```

Example 3:
```
egrep -n ',.*,.*,' inpfile
2:meanness,  pretentiousness, and cowardice, he will not be hard to
4:philosophic  temper, you will observe, from youth up, he is fair-
```

Example 4:
```
cat exprfile
,.*,.*,

egrep -n -f exprfile inpfile
2:meanness,  pretentiousness, and cowardice, he will not be hard to
4:philosophic  temper, you will observe, from youth up, he is fair-
```

In example 1, *egrep* printed lines which do not end in a − (minus). Example 2 gave a count of . (periods) in the input file. Example 3 displayed lines which have at least three commas. In example 4, *egrep* performed the same function as in example 3 but the regular expression was taken from the file exprfile.

Though we have showed the use of *egrep*, the usage of *grep* and *fgrep* are identical except that the regular expressions are restricted. In particular, *fgrep* should be used if the size of the string to be searched is fixed. For this purpose it is documented to be more efficient than *egrep*.

1.9 Awk

Awk is a pattern scanning and processing language. It is undoubtedly the most popular and the most powerful filter available in the UNIX environment. It is particularly helpful because it supports field-oriented processing. It also has capabilities for matching on regular expressions. *Awk* has many built-in functions and supports many conventional arithmetic expressions. *Awk* statements and expressions are C-like. *Awk* supports scalar variables and arrays, has many built-in variables, and has a wide range of operators. *Awk* does not need any declarations of variables. The data type of the variable is inferred from its context. *Awk* has been updated recently to extend its capabilities as a high-level language. If some of the features of *awk* discussed here do not work on your system, you probably have an old version of *awk*.

1.9.1 Invoking Awk

Awk can be invoked as follows:

> **awk** *[-Fsep]* ' *pattern {action}*
> > *pattern {action}*
> > .
> > .
> > ' *filenames*
>
> or
>
> **awk** *[-Fsep]* *−f pattern-action-file filenames*

Awk checks to see if the input records in the specified files satisfy the *pattern* and, if there is a match, then executes the action associated with it. If the pattern and action sequences are long, it is convenient to store them in a file, referred to in the syntax as *pattern-action-file*, and then invoke *awk* with a *−f* option as shown in the second form. The field separator can be specified by the *−F* option as shown above where *sep* is the field separator string. By default, *awk* fields are separated by white space.

Patterns are defined as follows:

> BEGIN
> END
> /regular expression/
> relational expression
> pattern && pattern
> pattern || pattern
> (pattern)
> !pattern
> pattern, pattern

Actions consist of a list of zero or more statements separated by semicolons or newline characters. Braces can be used to group statements. *Awk* supports the following statements:

> if (expression) statement [else statement]
> while (expression) statement
> for (expression;expression;expression) statement
> break;
> continue;
> next;

exit
variable = expression
print [expression] > [expression]
print [expression] | [expression]
for (var in array) statement

1.9.2 Getting Started with Awk

A common use of *awk* is to select some records based on a value in some field. Fields can be referred to in *awk* by prefixing the field number with a dollar sign $. Thus $1 refers to the first field, $2 refers to the second field, etc. $0 refers to the entire record. Let us look at a small file containing student name, major, and age and then run a sample *awk* program on it:

```
cat students
John,P   Physics  20
Rick,L   Mechanical  21
Jack,T   electrical  23
Larry,M  Chemical   22
Phil,R   Electrical  21
Mike,T   mechanical  22
Paul,R   Chemical   23
John,T   Chemical   23
Tony,N   Chemical   22
James,R Electrical  21

awk '$3 > 22 { print $1 }' students
Jack,T
Paul,R
John,T
```

In this example, we printed the first field of all records where the third field was greater than 22. The pattern is *$3 > 22* and the action consists of one statement: *print $1*. The pattern can be categorized as a relational expression.

Now let us print out the names of all students whose major is electrical. Since we know that when the data was entered, *Electrical* was also entered as *electrical*, we have to make use of regular expressions to do the searching. Here is the *awk* command:

```
awk '$2 ~ /[Ee]lectrical/ { print $1} ' students
Jack,T
Phil,R
James,R
```

The relational operator ~ is used for matching regular expressions. !~ means that the condition is satisfied if the regular expression is not matched. The complete set of regular expressions supported by *awk* is shown in Table 1.4.

TABLE 1.4 Regular Expressions in Awk

Element	Meaning
c	Matches any nonspecial character c.
\c	Matches c even if c is a special character.
.	Matches any character but newline.
^	Matches beginning of line or string.
[xyz..]	Matches any of the specified characters. A −(minus) may be used to specify a range, e.g. [a−z] matches any lowercase letter. A ~ may be used to negate the character class.
ex1|ex2	Matches either the regular expression ex1 or the regular expression ex2.
ex+	Matches one or more occurrences of the regular expression element ex.
ex*	Matches zero or more occurrences of the regular expression element ex.
ex?	Matches zero or one occurrence of the regular expression element ex.
(ex)	Matches the regular expression element ex. It can be used for grouping in order to resolve ambiguities in regular expressions.

Here are some examples of regular expression usage in *awk*:

Example 1
```
awk '$0 ~ /^J.*/ {print $0} ' students
John,P   Physics     20
Jack,T   electrical  23
John,T   Chemical    23
James,R  Electrical  21
```

Example 2
```
awk '$1 !~ /[A-Zb-z]*a[A-Zb-z]*/ {print $0}' students
John,P   Physics     20
Rick,L   Mechanical  21
Phil,R   Electrical  21
Mike,T   mechanical  22
John,T   Chemical    23
Tony,N   Chemical    22
```

In the first example, we displayed all fields of all records where the record began with the letter *J*. In the second example, we displayed all fields of all records where the first field did not have a single lowercase letter *a* in it.

1.9.3 Awk Operators

Apart from the two relational operators, ~ and !~ that *awk* uses for matching regular expressions, it also has six other relational operators. They are <, <=, >, >=, !=, and ==. These relational operators have the same meaning as the C relational operators. Awk also supports the logical operators ||, &&, and ! to signify a logical OR, a logical AND, and a logical negation, respectively. The operators +, -, /, *, %, ^=, +=, -=, /=, %=, *=, ++, and -- have the same meanings as in C. Exponentiation can be done by the use of the operator ** or ^ in the proper context. Finally, the operator $ is used to refer to a field, as indicated earlier.

1.9.4 Using Awk Statements

So far we have been using the capabilities of the *pattern* section of *awk* for selecting records. *Awk* also provides statements that can be used for selecting records and performing operations on the contents of these records. The statements that *awk* supports are listed in Section 1.9.1. Let us look at an example of *awk* that uses some of these statements:

```
cat awkprog1
{sum += $3
 ++no
}
END {printf "The average of the ages is %.2f\n", sum/no}
```

```
awk -f awkprog1 students
The average of the ages is 21.80
```

The *awk* program listed above calculates the average of the third field of the file, student age. We have used the variable *no* to keep count of the number of input records. The variable *sum* is used to keep track of the sum of the third fields from all the records input. The pattern END is a special pattern. Statements associated with this pattern are executed after the end of the input file is reached. Similarly, the pattern BEGIN can be used to execute statements before reading any records from the file. We used the *printf* statement to print the result. This statement is almost identical to the *printf* statement in C. It provides a way to print output in a format specified by the first double-quoted argument.

1.9.5 Awk Defined Variables

Awk defines a number of variables that have special meaning. These variables provide access to values that are very commonly used. *NR* is one such variable. It keeps track of the number of the record that is currently being processed. It will have a value of zero if it is accessed in statements associated with the BEGIN pattern. If it is accessed in the action associated with the pattern END, then it will have a value corresponding to the number of records in the input file. Let us rewrite the earlier examples to calculate the average age of the students, using the variable *NR*:

```
cat awkprog2
 {sum += $3
 }
END {printf "The average of the ages is %.2f\n",sum/NR}
awk -f awkprog2 students
The average of the ages is 21.80
```

Other variables defined by *awk* are listed in Table 1.5.

1.9.6 More on Awk Statements

Awk statements provide us with many features. In the next few examples we will see how these statements can be used. We have seen two versions of the

TABLE 1.5 Awk Variables

Variable	Description
FILENAME	Name of the current file being read
NR	Number of records read so far
NF	Number of fields in current record
RS	Input record separator
ORS	Output record separator
OFS	Output field separator
FS	Input field separator
OFMT	Output format for numbers (default: %.6g)
FNR	Record number in current file
	(Same as NR unless more than 1 input file)

awk print statements. One provides unformatted output and the other provides formatted output. In the previous examples, this output was written to the standard output. It is possible to write the output of the print statements to files other than the standard output. The *awk* program listed below would create two files. The first file, named Jfile, would contain the data of all students whose name starts with the letter J. The second file, Pfile, would contain data of all students whose name starts with the letter P:

```
awk '{ if ($1 ~ /^J/) printf "%s\n", $0 > "Jfile"
       if ($1 ~ /^P/) printf "%s\n", $0 > "Pfile"}' students

cat  Jfile
John,P  Physics  20
Jack,T  electrical  23
John,T  Chemical  23
James,R Electrical  21

cat Pfile
Phil,R  Electrical  21
Paul,R  Chemical  23
```

Notice that the *if* statement has been used to select records where the first field starts with the required letter. It is also possible to do this selection by specifying the appropriate regular expression in the pattern section of the *awk* program.

Awk also provides some functions that can be invoked in the same way that functions are used in programming languages. The most commonly used functions are shown in Table 1.6.

TABLE 1.6 Commonly Used Awk Functions

Function	Description
length(string)	Returns the length of *string*
substr(string,st,l)	Returns substring of *string*
	starting at position *st* and of length *l*
index(str1,str2)	Returns position of string *str2* in *str1*
	If not found returns 0
sprintf(fmt,expr-list)	Returns a string formatted according to
	format *frmt* using the values in the expression list
int(num)	Returns the truncated integer value of *num*
cos(x)	Returns the cos of *x*, *x* is in radians
exp(x)	Returns the exponential of *x*
sin(x)	Returns the sine of *x*, *x* is in radians
sqrt(x)	Returns the square root of *x*

It is also possible to define and use your own functions. In the next example, we will make use of *awk* functions to create a file having the initials of each student, followed by a three-character abbreviation of the student's major, followed by the student's age. We will sort this file before outputting it and do all this using *awk*.

```
awk '{ pos = index($1,",");
       lname = substr($1,pos+1,1);
       fname = substr($1,1,1);
       major = substr($2,1,3);
       name  = fname lname;
       printf "%s\t%s\t%s\n", name,major,$3 | "sort";
       }' students
JP     Phy     20
JR     Ele     21
JT     Che     23
JT     ele     23
LM     Che     22
MT     mec     22
PR     Che     23
PR     Ele     21
RL     Mec     21
TN     Che     22
```

The first *awk* statement located the position of the comma in the first field.

The second *awk* statement used this position to get the inital letter of the last name and stored it in the variable *lname*. The third statement got the first letter of the first field, student first name, and stored it in *fname*. Similarly the next statement fetched the three-character abbreviation of the student major from the second field. Then *fname* and *lname* were concatenated using the next statement to give us the two-character abbreviated name. The final statement output the result into a pipe. The *sort* command read from this pipe, sorted the input, and provided the final sorted result.

1.9.7 Arrays in Awk

Awk supports one-dimensional arrays. Array elements may be numeric or nonnumeric. The latter facility is particularly helpful for string processing. Since the size of the array is not fixed but can grow indefinitely, the statement *for (var in array) stat* executes the statement *stat* for each defined element of the array.

Here is an example of array usage in *awk*. Let us try to get the distribution of students in each major:

```
cat awkprog
{ if ($2 == "electrical") $2 = "Electrical";
  else if ($2 == "mechanical") $2 = "Mechanical";
  else if ($2 == "chemical")   $2 = "Chemical";
  else if ($2 == "physics")    $2 = "Physics";
  major[$2]++
}
END {
  for (i in major)
  printf "There are %d student(s) majoring in %s\n",
                                     major[i],i
}


awk -f awkprog students
There are 4 student(s) majoring in Chemical
There are 3 student(s) majoring in Electrical
There are 1 student(s) majoring in Physics
There are 2 student(s) majoring in Mechanical
```

Notice that we changed the second field so that it uniformly starts with an uppercase letter. Thus it will suppress the distinction between majors like *Electrical* and *electrical*. The statement *major[$2]++* increments the count of the major referred by $2. Finally, at the end of the file, we print each element of the defined array *major* along with its subscript. The element itself has the count and the subscript is the string representing the major.

1.9.8 Command Line Arguments and Parameters

Usage of arguments and parameters make *awk* programs flexible and powerful. Parameters are variable values that can be set during the invocation of *awk*. Command line arguments are arguments that can be specified while invoking *awk* and can be accessed in the *awk* program as the shell positional argument. Let us write an *awk* program to calculate the area of a circle, a square, or a rectangle given the required parameters. For example, if we store the *awk* program in a file named area, we can invoke the program as *area circle 12* to calculate the area of a circle with radius 12 units, as *area square 12* to calculate the area of a square with side 12 units or as *area triangle 5* to calculate the area of a triangle with side 5 units. The program is listed below:

```
cat area
awk ' BEGIN {pi = 3.14
if ("'$1'"=="circle")
    printf "Area of the circle is %d\n", pi * '$2' ** 2;
else if ("'$1'"=="square")
    printf "Area of the square is %d\n", '$2' ** 2;
else if ("'$1'"=="triangle")
    printf "Area of the triangle is %d\n", '$2' ** 2 * 0.5
    }'


area triangle 12
Area of the triangle is 72
```

The single quotes in the above example were required to protect the *awk* program from the shell. The positional parameters were excluded from the quotes because it was desired that the shell interpret them.

Let us now rewrite the *awk* program to perform the same task. This time we will use parameters instead of positional command line arguments. Here is the *awk* program:

```
cat awkprog
BEGIN {
  pi = 3.14;
  if (figure=="circle")
    printf "Area of the circle is %d\n", pi* param **2
  if (figure=="square")
    printf "Area of the square is %d\n", param**2
  if (figure=="triangle")
    printf "Area of the triangle is %d\n", param**2*0.5
}
awk -f awkprog figure=circle param=3
Area of the circle is 28
```

As you can see from this program, *awk* variables can be initialized on the command line. In older versions of *awk*, these values are not assigned to the respective *awk* variables in the statements associated with the BEGIN pattern.

1.9.9 Awk: Closing Thoughts

In the preceding sections we have shown selected features of *awk*. A language as powerful as *awk* cannot be covered in its entirety in a few pages. Awk has been used for a variety of purposes ranging from database management systems (DBMS) to language processors and data processing tasks. If you are not a C programmer and do not wish to learn C, yet you need to do some processing that cannot be done by the other utilities, *awk* may just be the tool you are looking for. Give it a try, you will love it!

1.10 Other Commonly Used Filters

UNIX offers a multitude of filters; it would take a whole book to discuss all of them. Some of the other widely used file processing utilities are discussed briefly in this section. The *bdiff* utility shows us the differences between two files. It displays the result of its comparison in the form of *ed* commands. It is possible to get the second file from the first file by applying these *ed* commands to the first file. *Diff* also displays the lines in the two files which create the differences in them.

```
cat file1              cat file2
file1a                 file1a
file1fr                file1b
file1b                 file1d
file1c                 file1e
file1d                 file1f
file1e                 file1fn
file1f                 file1g
file1g                 file1h
file1h


diff file1 file2
2d1
< file1fr
4d2
< file1c
7a6
> file1fn
```

In this example the differences between file1 and file2 are displayed. The <
refers to the affected lines which are in the first file. The > refers to the
affected lines which are in the second file. *Ed* commands used are *c, a,* and
d, which refer to changes, additions, and deletions to be made to the first file.
The number after the command refers to the second file; thus, the first line of
the display informs us that the second line of the first file has to be deleted.
The next line < *file1fr* is the line to be deleted. Similarly, the next two lines
inform us that line number 4 from file1 is also to be deleted. Finally, the last
two lines tell us that a newline *file1fn* has to be added to file1 after line
number 7.

Two files can also be compared using the *cmp* command. This command
compares two files and prints the character position from the beginning of the
file of the first difference encountered, as shown in the following example:

```
cat cmpf1
pqrs
abcd
cat cmpf2
lmno
abed
cmp cmpf1 cmpf2
cmpf1 cmpf2 differ: char 1, line 1
```

```
cmp -l cmpfl cmpf2
      1 160 154
      2 161 155
      3 162 156
      4 163 157
      8 143 145
```

The −*l* option can be used to get a long listing of all differing characters. The output specifies the byte number in decimal and the differing bytes in octal. Clearly the differing bytes in file cmpf1 and cmpf2 are at positions 1, 2, 3, 4, and 8. Do not forget to count the newline byte!

Another file comparison utility is *comm*. This utility requires that the input file be sorted. The output is in the form of three columns. The first column contains lines that exist only in the first file listed on the command line, the second column lists lines that are found only in the second file listed on the command line, and the third column has lines that are common to both files. If file comm1 is:

```
cat comm1
1
2
3
4
5
```

and file comm2 is

```
cat comm2
1
2
4
7
```

then a *comm* on these two files will display:

```
comm comm1 comm2
                1
                2
3
                4
5
        7
```

Yet another utility for comparing two files is *sdiff*. It uses the output of *diff* to produce a more readable report of the differences between the two files. Let us use *sdiff* to report the differences between the two files comm1 and comm2. Here is the output:

```
sdiff -w 20 comm1 com2
1               1
2               2
3          <
4               4
5          |    7
```

The files are listed side-by-side. Records which differ are marked with a vertical bar (|). A record which exists in the first file but not in the second file is marked with the < character and a record which exists in the second file but not in the first file is marked with the > character. The −*w* option is used to control the width of the output record. The default width is 130 characters. Only records from the first file of identical records can be made to output by the use of the −*l* option. Outputting of identical records can be suppressed by the use of the −*s* option. This option results in an output similar to the output of the *diff* command.

Tr is a utility that is available for translating occurrences of a set of characters in a file to another set of characters. It also allows for deletion of characters and squeezing of adjacent occurrences of the same character into a single character. Here are some examples of *tr* usage:

```
cat inpfile
asdfasdf      asdfasdf      asdfsdaf
adsf asdfasdf aaadsf asdf
```

Example 1:
```
tr −ds  "df" " " <inpfile
asas asas assa
as asas aaas as
```

Example 2:
```
tr "as" "pq" < inpfile
pqdfpqdf      pqdfpqdf      pqdfqdpf
pdqf pqdfpqdf pppdqf pqdf
```

In example 1, we used the $-d$ and $-s$ options. The $-d$ option is used to delete all occurrences of the characters in the first string. In the example the first string is made up of two characters, d and f. The $-s$ option allows us to squeeze multiple adjacent occurrences of the characters in the second string to a single character. Since our second string consists of a single character which is a blank, all adjacent blanks are squeezed into a single blank character.

In example 2, the character p is substituted for the character a and the character q for the character s.

Split is a utility that is used to break big files into smaller files. The size of the small files can be specified explicitly or a default value of 1000 bytes is used. The files created are named xaa, xab, xac, ..., xzz. Although x is the default prefix, it can be changed by specifying the desired prefix on the command line. Let us split the file *splfile* into small files of four records each, specifiying the prefix *new*:

```
cat splfile
1
2
3
4
5
6
7
8
9
0


split -4 splfile new

cat newaa        cat newab        cat newac
1                5                9
2                6                0
3                7
4                8
```

Split can be used for various purposes. It is especially useful when a file is too large to be edited and most of the editing is to be done in one segment of the file. *Split* can be used to separate the segment, which can then be edited. The new updated file can be created by simply *cat*ing the old segments and the updated segment in the correct sequence.

Sort and *uniq* are two other utilities which are very commonly used in the UNIX environment. *Sort* can be used to sort and/or merge input files. Once the files are sorted, *uniq* can be used to remove duplicate records or to get counts of each unique record occurrence. Other options are also available to output only repeated or nonrepeated lines in the input file.

1.11 Summary

In this chapter, the various tools for manipulating the contents of a file were discussed. Some tools can operate only on the whole record, while others like *awk* can manipulate individual fields within a record. Most of these tools also support a search on regular expressions. It is important to recognize that these tools can be used by users without any knowledge of programming. Further, UNIX provides a congenial environment for using these tools in conjunction with each other. Indeed, with some knowledge of shell programming and with the use of the pipeline mechanism, users can design their own tools using the utilities discussed in this chapter as building blocks.

2 Debuggers

Debuggers are used extensively in programming environments to assist in debugging programs. This may include running a program under the control of the programmer or examining the core image dumped by the system. The core image is normally examined after an abnormal termination of any program. Messages like *Bus error - core dumped* are very common in the UNIX environment. Novice users are frequently baffled by such messages. This chapter explains the various tools that are available on the UNIX operating system to help programmers develop programs which are free from bugs. Various examples are used to explain the use of these debuggers to debug programs written in the C language; however, some of these tools can also be used for debugging programs written in other languages, such as FORTRAN 77 and Pascal. Other uses of the debuggers are also highlighted. This chapter explains the use of *dbx*, *adb*, *sdb*, and *ctrace*.

2.1 Dbx

Dbx is a debugger that is available primarily on the BSD version of UNIX. It has fairly high-level commands and is very user friendly compared to *adb*.

2.1.1 Getting Started

Consider the following program:

```
1  #include <stdio.h>
2  main()
3  {
4      int i,j,k;
5      printf("Input the value of j : ");
6      scanf("%d",j);
7      i=4;
8      k=2;
9  }
```

(The line numbers are not part of the program but are shown here and in some
other programs in this chapter to make it easy to understand the working of
the debuggers.) Compile and run the program.

You will be first prompted for the value of *j*. If you input an integer, say
12, you will encounter the familiar message *Bus error - core dumped*. What
went wrong? Well, there are very few statements in the above program, so
you can easily see that the error was due to a missing ampersand (&) before *j*.
In large programs, however, this inadvertence may not be very obvious. Let us
look at how *dbx* will allow you to find the above problem.

Compile the program using the −*g* option in the *cc* command. This option
will retain the symbol table and additional debugging information that is used
by the debugger. Run the program exactly as you did before. When you get
the *Bus error - core dumped* message, run *dbx*. *Dbx* takes two arguments.
The first argument is the name of the object code file. This defaults to a.out if
it is not specified explicitly. The second is the name of the core file. This
option is rarely required unless you are trying to debug a program after a core
dump and have renamed the core file to something other than core. Running
dbx would give you the following prompt:

```
dbx
dbx version of 9/26/83 10:42 (ucbmonet).
Type 'help' for help.
reading symbolic information ...
(dbx)
```

The first problem is to locate the statement having the bug. *Dbx* provides the *where* command to locate the problem as follows:

```
(dbx) where
_innum(0x7fffeaec, 0x64, 0x752e, 0x1, 0x1d80, 0x7fffea8c) at 0x5b4
_doscan(0x1d80, 0x1c46, 0x7fffeaec) at 0x1f0
scanf(0x1c46, 0x0) at 0xc6
main(0x1, 0x7fffeb24, 0x7fffeb2c), line 6 in "temp.c"
(dbx)
```

The above display indicates that the error was at line 6 in file temp.c. It further indicates that the problem occured in the function *scanf*. *Dbx* also displays the names of the other functions that *scanf* invoked during execution.

Consider the following program, which performs four simple tasks in four different functions. The four tasks are addition, subtraction, multiplication, and division of two numbers. We could have passed the values of the variables *add_res*, *div_res*, *sub_res*, and *mul_res* rather than their address; however, the purpose of this program is only to show the use of the debugger! There is a bug in the program. In the *div* function, which performs the division, we have assigned the result to the address of the variable *res* rather than assigning it to the variable itself. Let us see how *dbx* can help us in locating the error.

```
1   #include <stdio.h>
2   main(argc,argv)
3   int argc;
4   char *argv[];
5   {
6       int num[2],add_res,div_res,sub_res,mul_res;
7       num[0]=atoi(argv[1]);
8       num[1]=atoi(argv[2]);
9       add(num,&add_res);
10      div(num,&div_res);
11      sub(num,&sub_res);
12      mul(num,&mul_res);
13  }
14  add(num,res) /** add the two numbers **/
15  int num[2],*res;
16  {
17      *res = num[0] + num[1];
18      printf("The result of addition is %d",*res);
19  }
```

```
20  div(num,res) /** divide the two numbers **/
21  int num[2],*res;
22  {
23    res = num[0] / num[1];
24    printf(" of division is %d",*res);
25  }
26
27  sub(num,res) /** subtract the two numbers **/
28  int num[2],*res;
29  {
30    *res = num[0] - num[1];
31    printf(" of subtraction is %d",*res);
32  }
33  mul(num,res) /** multiply the two numbers **/
34  int num[2],*res;
35  {
36    *res = num[0] * num[1];
37    printf(" of multiplication is %d\n",*res);
38  }
```

Compile the program with the −*g* option and run it:

```
a.out 21 -2
Memory fault - core dumped
```

Invoke *dbx* to debug the program. The first step is to locate the problem. This can be easily done with the *where* command; however, let us take a different approach this time. Let us try to trace the values of variables *add_res* and *div_res*. Run *dbx* as usual and use the *trace* commands as shown below:

```
dbx a.out core
dbx version of 9/26/83 10:42 (ucbmonet).
Type 'help' for help.
reading symbolic information ...
(dbx)trace add_res
(1) trace add_res in main
(dbx)trace div_res
(3) trace div_res in main
(dbx)run 21 0
initially (at line 7): add_res = 0
initially (at line 7): div_res = 0
```

```
after line 17: add_res = 21
floating point exception in div at line 23
    23    res = num[0] / num[1];
(dbx)
```

The *trace* commands set the trace feature on. This facilitates the tracing of specified variables as they change their values during the execution process. The command *run 21 0* runs the program and displays the various values that the traced variables get during the execution, including their initial values. In the execution of the above program, the variable *add_res* gets a new value at line 17. The value of *div_res* never changes. Instead we get a floating point exception at line 23, and this line is displayed. The bug has been located! The following are some of the other variations of the *trace* command:

trace *[in procedure/function]*
trace *[source-line-number]*
trace *expression* **at** *source-line-number*

Examine the following program, which is a very elementary form of *fgrep*, as it prints all lines matching a given string:

```
 1   /* An elementary form of fgrep */
 2   #include <stdio.h>
 3   main(argc,argv)
 4   int argc;
 5   char *argv[];
 6   {
 7       char line[35];
 8       int eof;
 9       while (getline(line) > 0) /** for each line **/
10       if ((search(line,argv[1])) >= 0)/*search for the string*/
11               printf("%s",line);
12   }
13   getline(line) /** return the next line **/
14   char line[35];
15   {
16       int character,line_length=0;
17       while (((character=getchar()) != EOF) && (character != '\n'))
18               line[line_length++] = character;
19       if (character != EOF)
20               line[line_length++] = '\n';
21       line[line_length] = '\0';
```

```
22      return(line_length);
23  }
24  search(line,pattern)  /** search for the string in the line **/
25  char *line,*pattern;
26  {
27      int i,j,k;
28      j = strlen(line) - strlen(pattern) + 1;
29      for (i=0;i<j;++i)
30              if (strncmp(&line[i],pattern,strlen(pattern))==0)
31                      return(0);
32      return(-1);
33  }
```

Now let us compile this program and run it:

```
cat test.d
main123
123456mai
mainmain12
3456m1ain
main234na

a.out main < test.d
main123
mainmain12
main234na
```

So far so good. Now let us try to run the program with another input file:

```
cat test2.d
It follows,then,that the divine, being good,
is not, as most people say,
responsible for everything that happens to mankind,
but only for a small part;
for the good things in human life are far fewer than
the evil, and, whereas the good must be ascribed to heaven only,
we must look elsewhere for the cause of evils.

a.out the  < test2.d > the_file
Memory fault - core dumped
```

Bug! Well, let us try to debug it by using *dbx*:

```
dbx a.out core
dbx version of 9/26/83 10:42 (ucbmonet).
Type 'help' for help.
reading symbolic information ...
(dbx) where
 main(argc = 2037149295, argv = 0x7f000a2c, 0x7fffe98c, 0x7fffe98c,
 0x7fffe98c, 0x7fffe98c, 0x7fffe98c, 0x7fffe98c, 0x7fffe98c,
 0x7fffe98c, 0x7fffe98c, 0x7fffe98c, 0x7fffe98c, 0x7fffe98c,
 0x7fffe98c, 0x7fffe98c, 0x7fffe98c, 0x7fffe98c, 0x7fffe98c,
 0x7fffe98c, 0x7fffe98c, 0x7fffe98c), line 10 in "temp.c"
 exit.o      (0x7fffe98c, 0x7fffe98c, 0x7fffe98c, 0x7fffe98c,
 0x7fffe98c, 0x7fffe98c, 0x7fffe98c, 0x7fffe98c, 0x7fffe98c,
 0x7fffe98c, 0x7fffe98c, 0x7fffe98c, 0x7fffe98c, 0x7fffe98c,
 0x7fffe98c, 0x7fffe98c, 0x7fffe98c, 0x7fffe98c, 0x7fffe98c,
 0x7fffe98c) at 0x61656820 exit.o data address 0xa
 too low (lb = 0x1400)
(dbx) stop at 10
 (1) stop at 10
(dbx) run the < test2.d
 stopped in main at line 10
    10          if ((search(line,argv[1])) >= 0)/*search for the string*/
(dbx) print line
 "It follows,then,that the divine, be"
(dbx)stop at 19
 (3) stop at 19
(dbx) status
 (1) stop at 10
 (3) stop at 19
(dbx) delete 1
(dbx) status
 (3) stop at 19
(dbx) run the < test2.d
 stopped in getline at line 19
    19          if (character != EOF)
(dbx) print line
 "It follows,then,that the divine, being good,k(k^B"
(dbx) quit
```

In the above example, we have demonstrated many features of *dbx*. Let us examine each one of them. First, we tried to locate the problem by using the *where* command. This was useful in finding that the problem was in line 10, but that was all the *where* command could tell us. To inspect the problem further, we set what are known as breakpoints. Breakpoints suspend the execution of the program at the lines where they are set. In *dbx*, breakpoints can be set by using the *stop* command. In the above example, we first set a breakpoint at line 10 because we knew that the core was dumped at that statement.

The next logical thing to do after a *stop* is to rerun the program. This is done by the *run* command. The syntax of the *run* command is exactly like a UNIX command line with arguments and redirection of files. In the example under consideration, *the* is an argument and *test2.d* is the input data file. When we give the *run* command, the program starts executing and stops at the breakpoint. At this point *dbx* waits for more commands. Typically, one would like to examine the values of various variables at the breakpoints. The values of the variables can be examined by using the *print* command. In the above example, we found that the value of the variable *line* was "*It follows,then,that the divine, be*". Of course, something had gone wrong. *Line* should have the value *It follows,then,that the divine, being good,*; therefore, we knew that the problem was somewhere before the statement in line 10. Line 9 invokes the *get_line* function. To check to see if this function worked, we needed to set some more breakpoints. We therefore set a breakpoint at line 19. We can check the status of various breakpoints by using the *status* command and can delete a breakpoint by using the *delete* command. We reran the program with the new breakpoint. After checking the value of the variable *line* at line 19, we knew that the problem was with the *while* statement at line 17. Indeed, we have declared our *line* variable too small to accommodate the first line in the data file!

2.1.2 Running a Program under Dbx Control

Let us look at another program to understand some additional features offered by *dbx*. This program computes the square root of a number which is given to it as the first argument. After having compiled the program, let us run it under *dbx*. Remember that we do not need a core dump to run *dbx*.

```
dbx a.out
dbx version of 9/26/83 10:42 (ucbmonet).
Type 'help' for help.
reading symbolic information ...
(dbx) list 1,20
      1    #include <stdio.h>
```

```
 2    main (argc,argv)
 3    int argc;
 4    char *argv[];
 5    {
 6            float abs(),number,precision=.001,initial=1.0;
 7            number=atoi(argv[1]);
 8
 9            while (abs(initial * initial - number) >= precision)
10                    initial = (number/initial + initial) / 2.0;
11            printf("The square root is %.02f",initial);
12    }
13    float abs(number)
14    float number;
15    {
16            if (number < 0)
17                    return(-number);
18            else
19                    return(number);
20    }
```
(dbx) **stop at 9**
(1) stop at 9
(dbx) **run 16**
stopped in main at line 9
```
 9            while (abs(initial * initial - number) >= precision)
```
(dbx) **step**
stopped in abs at line 15
```
15    {
```
(dbx) **step**
stopped in abs at line 16
```
16            if (number < 0)
```
(dbx) **cont**
stopped in main at line 9
```
 9            while (abs(initial * initial - number) >= precision)
```
(dbx) **print initial**
8.5
(dbx) **next**
stopped in main at line 10
```
10                    initial = (number/initial + initial) / 2.0;
```
(dbx) **next**
stopped in main at line 9
```
 9            while (abs(initial * initial - number) >= precision)
```
(dbx) **cont**
stopped in main at line 9

```
    9              while (abs(initial * initial - number) >= precision)
(dbx) print initial
4.13666
(dbx) cont
stopped in main at line 9
    9              while (abs(initial * initial - number) >= precision)
(dbx) print initial
4.00226
(dbx) cont
The square root is 4.00
execution completed, exit code is 0
(dbx) quit
```

In this *dbx* session, we first displayed the program by using the *list* command. This command can be used to see any range of lines from the source program. Here, we have listed the first 20 lines of the program, which in this case is the entire program. Next, we set a breakpoint at line 9. The *run* command started the execution as explained earlier and stopped at the breakpoint. We then gave a *step* command to execute the next statement. This command executed the next statement, which is the first statement of the function *abs*. *Step* executes one statement and halts after that. The *cont* command continued the execution until the next breakpoint, which was set at line 9. The value of the variable *initial* was examined here by displaying it with the *print* command.

The next statement is executed by the use of the *next* command. In this case, the entire function *abs* was executed and the program execution halted at line 10. *Step* and *next* both execute one source line at a time; *next* steps through an entire function invocation within a line, but *step* will step through only one source line of the invoked function. This is the only difference between the *step* and the *next* commands.

We continued the execution, each time halting at the breakpoint to examine the value of the variable *initial*. *Dbx* was used here to examine the various values that the variable *initial* took before it had a value that could be accepted as the square root with the given precision. Of course, we took recourse to this approach because the main purpose was to show the use of some additional *dbx* features. The values of the variable *initial* through the various iterations can be printed very easily with the *trace* command, as shown in the following example:

dbx a.out
```
dbx version of 9/26/83 10:42 (ucbmonet).
Type 'help' for help.
```

```
reading symbolic information ...
(dbx) trace initial
(1) trace initial in main
(dbx) run 16
initially (at line 6): initial = 0.0
after line 6:  initial = 1.0
after line 10: initial = 8.5
after line 10: initial = 5.19118
after line 10: initial = 4.13666
after line 10: initial = 4.00226
The square root is 4.00
execution completed, exit code is 0
(dbx) quit
```

2.1.3 Miscellaneous Dbx Commands

Dbx has some additional commands, so we will discuss some of the more commonly used ones. The *dump* command is used to print the names and values of all active variables. The *whatis* command is used to get the declaration of a variable. The *which* command provides us with the full qualification of the variable. The commands which print the source program can be made to print from a specified file by the use of the *file* command. This is particularly helpful when the program source resides in more than one file. The *use* command is useful if the source files reside in different directories. *Dbx* also provides an *alias* feature that can be used to provide abbreviations for command strings along with optional arguments; thus, the alias

```
alias br(l)  "stop at l"
```

will expand the *dbx* command

```
br(5)
```

to

```
stop at 5
```

Dbx provides a startup file called .dbxinit that is read by *dbx*, and any commands in the file are executed immediately upon invoking *dbx*. Normally *alias* commands should be stored in this startup file so that they do not have to be repeated by the user on each invocation. *Dbx* also provides some machine-level commands which are not discussed here. If you need on-line assistance, the *help* command provides a synopsis of *dbx* commands.

Here is a final example of a *dbx* session using the same square root example but with two files. The function *abs* is in the file /d1/d2/d3/file2.c; the other part of the program resides in the file /d1/d2/d3/file1.c.

```
dbx a.out
dbx version of 9/26/83 10:42 (ucbmonet).
Type 'help' for help.
reading symbolic information ...
(dbx) list 1,20
    1    #include <stdio.h>
    2    main (argc,argv)
    3    int argc;
    4    char *argv[];
    5    {
    6            float abs(),number,precision=.001,initial=1.0;
    7            number=atoi(argv[1]);
    8
    9            while (abs(initial * initial - number) >= precision)
   10                    initial = (number/initial + initial) / 2.0;
   11            printf("The square root is %.02f",initial);
   12    }
(dbx) file /d1/d2/d3/file2.c
(dbx) list 1,20
    1    float abs(number)
    2    float number;
    3    {
    4            if (number < 0)
    5                    return(-number);
    6            else
    7                    return(number);
    8    }
(dbx) file /d1/d2/d3/file1.c
(dbx) stop at 9
(3) stop at "file1.c":9
(dbx) run 25
stopped in main at line 9 in file "file1.c"
    9            while (abs(initial * initial - number) >= precision)
```

```
(dbx) dump
main(argc = 2, argv = 0x7fffeb1c, 0x7fffeb28), line 9 in "file1.c"
initial = 1.0
precision = 0.001
number = 25.0

in "a.out":
errno = 0
realloc_srchlen = 4
_sibuf = 0
_lastbuf = 4604
_sobuf = 0
_dbargs = 0
environ = 2147478312
_iob = ARRAY

(dbx) which initial
file1.main.initial
(dbx) whatis initial
float initial;
(dbx) status
(3) stop at "file1.c":9
(dbx) delete 3
(dbx) cont
The square root is 5.02
execution completed, exit code is 0
(dbx) quit
```

Dbx is normally available on the BSD version of UNIX. If you do not have access to *dbx*, then you probably have *adb* or *sdb* on your system. Let us now look at these debuggers.

2.2 Adb

Adb is another debugger; it is probably the lowest-level debugger in the UNIX world. It is an assembly-level debugger rather than a source-level debugger like *dbx* or *sdb*. This feature of *adb* enables debugging of programs which are compiled without the $-g$ option. *Adb* also serves other purposes. We will briefly discuss the use of *adb* for debugging and then show how *adb* can be used for other operations.

2.2.1 Use of Adb as a Debugger

Consider the following program:

```
#include <stdio.h>
int div_res,add_res;
main(argc,argv)
int argc;
char *argv[];
{
add_res=add(atoi(argv[1]),atoi(argv[2]));
div_res=div(atoi(argv[1]),atoi(argv[2]));
printf("Addition result is %d, division result is %d\n",
        add_res,div_res);
}
add(param1,param2)
int   param1,param2;
{
add_res = param1 + param2;
}
div(param1,param2)
int   param1,param2;
{
div_res = param1 / param2;
}
```

This program computes the result of addition and division of two numbers passed to it on the command line. Let us compile and run it:

```
a.out 21 0.9
Memory fault - core dumped
```

Core dump! Let us invoke *adb* to debug the program. *Adb*, like *dbx*, is invoked with two arguments. The first argument is the name of the executable object file. The second argument is the name of the core file dumped. The following is an *adb* session:[*]

```
adb a.out core
$c
_div(15,0) from       _main+59
_main(3,7fffe78c,7fffe79c) from       start+3d
```

---

[*]Executed on a VAX 11/785 running 4.3 BSD.

```
$r
pllr    1fffee
plbr    7fea8600
p0lr    400000c
p0br    806a8200
ksp     7ffffd5c
esp     ffffffff
ssp     ffffffff
psl     3c00002
pc      ee          _div+a
usp     7fffe744
fp      7fffe744
ap      7fffe758
r11     18a38
r10     7fffe788
r9      7fffe79c
r8      7fffe78c
r7      1729c
r6      80097908
r5      1541f
r4      ffff
r3      153f0
r2      0           start
r1      45          start+45
r0      15          start+15
_div+a:             movl    r0,_div_res
$e
_environ:   7fffe79c
_errno:     0
mcount:     5
_div_res:   0
_add_res:   15
__iob:      0
__smallbuf: 172c
_realloc_srchlen:       4
_end:       0
minbrk:     17c8
curbrk:     17c8
$q
```

From the above session we can see the obvious lack of user friendliness in *adb*. First, invocation of *adb* is followed by silence! The *$c* command gives the trace of execution. In the above session, the execution terminated in the

function *div*. This function was invoked in the function *main*. Thus the *$c*
command can be used to get a rough idea about the location of the problem.
The *$r* command is useful for those who are interested in the assembly-level
working of the program. It shows the contents of the various registers at the
time the program was terminated. The command *$e* displays the contents of
the various external variables that are associated with the program. The
variable *add_res* got the value of Hex 15, which is decimal 21. The variable
div_res has a value of 0. Finally, the *$q* command quits an *adb* session.

2.2.2 Running a Program under Adb Control

Adb has several features that can be used to run a program under its control.
Breakpoints, as explained earlier, are used for suspending the execution of a
program at a prespecified instruction. In *adb*, breakpoints can be easily set
relative to a function. An understanding of the assembly code generated by the
compiler is required to set breakpoints at other locations. Breakpoints at
function entries are set in a program with the following command:

> *function_name* **+ 4 :b**

A more general form of setting a breakpoint is

> *function_name* **+4,** *count* **:b** *command*

where *count* is the number of occurrences of the breakpoints to be skipped
and *command* is any *adb* command to be executed at that breakpoint.
   If you want to see the status of the various breakpoints that are active in
your routine, execute the *$b* command. After setting the breakpoints, the next
step is to actually run the program using the *:r* command. The program will
run until it reaches the first breakpoint. At this point, you may wish to
examine the values of some variables. This can be done by specifying the
address or name of the variable followed by a slash (/) followed by a letter
indicating the format in which you want the data to be displayed. The
following format letters are most frequently used:

b	one octal byte
c	one character
d	one word decimal integer

o   one octal word
f   double float
i   one instruction
s   null terminated character string

After examining the various data values, you may wish to continue the execution of the program. The execution of a program can be continued by the *:c* command. You can delete a breakpoint by issuing the command

```
function_name + 4:d
```

The following *adb* session demonstrates the use of some of the features of *adb* that were discussed above. Once again we are looking at the same program that was discussed in the previous section.

```
adb a.out
add+4:b
div+4:b
$b
breakpoints
count   bkpt            command
1       _div+4
1       _add+4
:r 21 0.9
a.out: running
breakpoint      _add+4:         addl3   8(ap),4(ap),r0
add_res/d
_add_res:
_add_res:       0
:c
a.out: running
breakpoint      _div+4:         divl3   8(ap),4(ap),r0
add_res/d
_add_res:
_add_res:       21
:c
a.out: running
floating exception (integer divide by zero trap)
stopped at      _div+a:         movl    r0,_div_res
$q
```

In the above *adb* session, we set breakpoints at the two functions, *add* and *div*. We examined the values of the variables *add_res* and *div_res* at these breakpoints. The program passed the first breakpoint set at the function *add* without aborting execution; however, it encountered a divide by zero condition in the *div* function. *Adb* was able to inform us about this error. Clearly, the second argument, 0.9, was converted to a zero by the *atoi* function. Our program can function correctly only for integer values greater than zero.

2.2.3 Miscellaneous Adb Commands

The *,n:r* command is useful for running a program by skipping the first breakpoint. The corresponding command for continuing the program is *,n:c*. The command *:s* is used for executing one instruction at a time. The command *:k* is used for killing a process that is being debugged. The *:c* command continues execution and lets *adb* catch the UNIX *quit* and *interrupt* signals and pass them on to the program being debugged. This can be used to test the interrupt-handling routines of a program. The *:c 0* command also continues execution but does not pass these signals to the program being debugged.

2.2.4 Other Uses of Adb

Adb can also be used for other purposes. We will look at two likely uses of *adb*. First, *adb* can be used for converting a number from one number system to another. We will see later that we can also use *sdb* for this purpose. The command *number=odx* instructs *adb* to convert the specified number into its octal, decimal, and hexadecimal equivalents. The default radix of the number to the left is hexadecimal. Here is an example of an *adb* session for number conversion:

```
adb - -
0t256=o
        0400
0o200=odx
        0200    128    80
12=odx
        022     18     12
$q
```

In the above *adb* session, we first get the octal equivalent of decimal 256. The

0t before the number is used to force the number on the left to be interpreted in decimal radix. In the second example, the *0o* is used to force the radix to be octal. It converts the octal number 200 to its octal (*o*), decimal (*d*), and hexadecimal (*x*) equivalents. The default radix is hexadecimal. In the last example, *adb* is used to convert the hexadecimal number 12 to its octal, decimal, and hexadecimal equivalents.

Adb can also be used for listing the i-node numbers and the names of the files in a directory. In the System V implementation of the file system, the directory itself is a file consisting of a 16-byte entry for each file in the directory. The first two bytes indicate the i-node number of the file. The next 14 bytes store the name of the file. Below is an *adb* session displaying the contents of the directory named *dir*. The first column indicates the i-node number; the second column indicates the name of the file.

```
adb dir -
0,-1?d8t14cn
0:              60985           .
                24886           ..
                39729           read
                48433           readfifo
                38169           readfifo.c
                48178           readmount.c
                27653           filesys
```

The *adb* command *0,-1?d8t14cn* is used to dump the contents of the file starting at address zero up to the end of the file. The *-1* address indicates end of file (EOF). The remaining characters of the *adb* command are used to specify the format in which the data is to be dumped. The *d* format dumps the first two bytes as an integer. The *8t* specifies spaces to be inserted before the next character is displayed. The *14c* dumps the next 14 characters, and, finally, the *n* format forces a newline. We have discussed *adb* very briefly because *sdb* and *dbx* are more powerful and user friendly for most debugging needs. We discussed *dbx* in the first section. Let us now proceed to see how *sdb* can be used as a debugging tool.

2.3 Sdb

Sdb is probably the most popular and definitely the most useful debugger available on System V. It can be used to debug C and FORTRAN 77 programs. In this chapter we will demonstrate the use of *sdb* to debug C programs.

2.3.1 Invoking Sdb

Sdb takes three arguments. The first argument is the name of the object file, the second argument is the name of the core file, and the third argument is a colon-separated list of directories where the source files are located. All the arguments are optional. By default, *sdb* takes a.out as the object file and core as the core file. When *sdb* is invoked, it checks for the status of the object files and their source files. It displays warning messages if the source files are not present or if the source files were modified after the object files were created. These warning messages can be disabled by the use of the −W flag when *sdb* is invoked.

Let us now look at some of the features of *sdb*. We will use the same program that was used in the discussion on *dbx*. This program performs addition, division, multiplication, and subtraction on two numbers. It has four functions to perform these operations and to print the result.

In the program, we have introduced one bug. This is the same bug that we had debugged using *dbx*. Let us compile the program. Remember to use the −g option. Now that we have compiled the program, let us run it:

```
a.out 22 -2
EMT trap - core dumped
```

The attentive reader will notice that this message is different from the one that was displayed for the same error in an earlier version of the program. Here, the program was run on a different machine with a different version of UNIX.

Let us now try to debug the program using the same strategy that we used earlier. The first task is to locate the bug. The closer we are to the bug, the more successful is the debugging. Let us run *sdb* as follows:

```
sdb a.out core
0x102 in div:24: printf("of division is %d ",*res);
*q
```

The above invocation of *sdb* gives us a lot of information about the bug. We know the statement which was responsible for the core dump. Notice that in the new environment the core was dumped while printing the result of division and not while computing it. As shown, *sdb* takes us to the problem statement without any explicit command. It waits for user input by displaying the prompt "*". The *q* command was given to quit the *sdb* session.

Now that we have located the statement which was responsible for the core dump, let us rerun the program to identify the bug:

```
sdb a.out -
No core image
*/div
6: int num[2],add_res,div_res,sub_res,mul_res;
*/
10: div(num,&result.div_res);
*/
20: div(num,res)
*20b
div:23 b
*r 22 -1
Breakpoint at
div:23: res = num[0] / num[1];
*res
0x2c0408
*0x2c0408/ld
0
*num[0]
22
*num[1]
-1
*s
div:24: printf("of division is %d ",*res);
*res
0xfffffffea
*0xfffffffea/ld
Data address not found
*q
```

The above session illustrates many important features of *sdb*. Let us examine each of the commands used. The first command, /div, was used to search for the occurrence of the word *div* in the source program. Because we know that the bug is in the function *div*, we had to locate appropriate statements to put breakpoints. The first occurrence of *div* is a declaration of the variable *div_res*. We therefore searched for the next occurrence. This we did by using the same pattern-searching command, /. *Sdb* remembered the last pattern searched and continued to search accordingly. This time the statement having the *div* function invocation was displayed. We would have preferred to have the breakpoint placed at the beginning of the first statement in the function itself. This prompted us to look for the next occurrence of *div*. This time we got to the function itself, so we set our breakpoint there. The breakpoint was set by using the command *20b*. This set a breakpoint at line 23 and not at line 20, as would have been expected! Notice that there is no executable statement at line 20; therefore, *sdb* set the breakpoint at the next executable statement, which is at line 23. Next we ran the program with two arguments, using the *r* command. The *r* command takes arguments, which in our case were *22* and *-2* . The program started executing and suspended execution when we reached the first breakpoint.

In this session there was only one breakpoint. At this point we started examining the contents of the variables that were passed to the *div* function. *Sdb* needs the name of a variable to be able to display its content. The variable *res* is an address. The contents of *res* were displayed when we gave the name of this variable as a command to *sdb*. Once we have the address, we can display the contents of the address by giving *sdb* the address followed by a / followed by the format in which we wish to have the contents displayed. The format *ld* means display the content as a four-byte integer. *Sdb* clearly indicated that the content of *res* is 0. Similarly, we examined the contents of the array *num*. So far there was no sign of a bug. We stepped through the first statement in this function by using the *s* command. This executed the first instruction, which was the breakpoint instruction. Having executed this instruction, we examined the values of all the variables again. We used the same set of commands to examine the new values of the variables. Two things should immediately strike the reader. First, the value of *res* itself has changed. Certainly, we had no intention of doing that. Also, the content of *res* can no longer be displayed because it is an illegal address. It is now a trivial task to come to the conclusion that we are manipulating the address of *res* rather than the contents of *res*. Hurray!! We have just finished debugging a program using *sdb*.

Let us study in more detail the commands that we used in the above session. The pattern-searching command */pattern* can be used to search for any regular expressions. The program searches for the specified pattern in a forward direction from the current position. A backward search is possible using the command *?pattern?*. The *b* command is used for setting breakpoints. The general syntax is *line-number b sdb-commands*. *Sdb-commands* is a series of semicolon-separated *sdb* commands. *Line-number* is the line in the source file where you wish to place the breakpoint. The *sdb-commands* are the commands that you want *sdb* to execute when it reaches the breakpoint. If there are no commands specified on the breakpoint command line, *sdb* suspends the execution at the breakpoint, waiting for the user to enter some command. If commands are specified along with the breakpoint, *sdb* executes these commands when the breakpoint is reached and continues execution of the program. The *B* command is used to list the currently active breakpoints.

A breakpoint set at any line can be deleted using the command *line-number d*. If *line-number* is omitted from the command, *sdb* will let you delete breakpoints interactively. *Sdb* will display each breakpoint and wait for the user to enter a *y* or *d*. An input line starting with these letters is also accepted and interpreted accordingly. Any other input entered will not affect the displayed breakpoint. The command *D* deletes all breakpoints.

The command *s* lets you single-step through a statement. A number can be specified to indicate the number of lines to be executed. This command is similar to the command *S*; however, *S* treats function calls as single statements. The difference between the *S* and the *s* commands in *sdb* is the same as the difference between the *next* and the *step* commands in *dbx*.

Let us look at another *sdb* session, so we can study some additional *sdb* features. This time we will look at the program which computes the square root of a number. We will examine the value of the variable *initial* as it goes through the iterations, until it finally gets a value that is accepted as a square root.

```
sdb a.out -
No core image
*1
1: #include <stdio.h>
*p
1: #include <stdio.h>
*Control D
2: int (*signal())();
3: main (argc,argv)
4: int argc;
5: char *argv[];
6: {
7:      float abs(),number,precision=.001,initial=1.0;
8:      number=atoi(argv[1]);
9:      while (abs(initial * initial - number) >= precision)
10:             initial = (number/initial + initial) / 2.0;
           11:     printf("The square root is %.02f",initial);
*w
6: {
7:      float abs(),number,precision=.001,initial=1.0;
8:      number=atoi(argv[1]);
9:      while (abs(initial * initial - number) >= precision)
10:             initial = (number/initial + initial) / 2.0;
11:      printf("The square root is %.02f",initial);
```

```
12: }
13: float abs(number)
14: float number;
15: {
*z
11:     printf("The square root is %.02f",initial);
12: }
13: float abs(number)
14: float number;
15: {
16:     if (number < 0)
17:             return(-number);
18:     else
19:             return(number);
20: }
*9b
main:9 b
*r 25
Breakpoint at
main:9:        while (abs(initial * initial - number) >= precision)
*initial
1
*c
Breakpoint at
main:9:        while (abs(initial * initial - number) >= precision)
*initial
13
*c
Breakpoint at
main:9:        while (abs(initial * initial - number) >= precision)
*initial
7.46154
*c
Breakpoint at
main:9:        while (abs(initial * initial - number) >= precision)
*initial
5.40603
*c
Breakpoint at
main:9:        while (abs(initial * initial - number) >= precision)
*initial
5.01525
*c
```

```
The square root is 5.02Process terminated
*D
All breakpoints deleted
*9b initial
main:9 b
*r 25
1
13
7.46154
5.40603
5.01525
The square root is 5.02Process terminated
*D
All breakpoints deleted
*9b
main:9 b
*r 25
Breakpoint at
main:9:        while (abs(initial * initial - number) >= precision)
*c 3
Breakpoint at
main:9:        while (abs(initial * initial - number) >= precision)
*initial
5.40603
*c
Breakpoint at
main:9:        while (abs(initial * initial - number) >= precision)
*initial
5.01525
*enter newline
0x2c0400/2.25
*c
The square root is 5.02Process terminated
*p
9:     while (abs(initial * initial - number) >= precision)
*enter newline
10:               initial = (number/initial + initial) / 2.0;
*q
```

Let us go through the above *sdb* session. The command *1* printed line 1. The command *p* printed the current line, which was set to 1 by the previous command. When you enter a ^D (control D) in response to an *sdb* prompt, it prints the next 10 lines. These could be either 10 lines of source code, data, or instructions, depending upon the previous command. In the above case, the last *print* command operated on the source code; hence the next 10 lines of the source code were printed changing the current line number to 11. The *w* command printed a window of 10 lines around the current line. The command *z* printed the current line followed by the next 9 lines. The command *9b* set a breakpoint at line 9 and the command *r 25* ran the program under the control of *sdb* with the specified argument, which was 25. The program started executing and stopped at the first breakpoint. At this point we started examining the value of the variable *initial*. *Sdb* recognizes the type of the variable specified and prints it accordingly. You can print the variable in a different format. The general form of examining the value of a variable is *variable-name/count length format*. *Count* specifies the number of items to be displayed. *Length* specifies whether it is a one-byte, two-byte, or four-byte item and can be specified as follows:

b	one byte
h	two bytes
l	four bytes

Format determines how the variable will be displayed. The most commonly used formats for displaying a variable are in the following list:

c	character
d	decimal
u	unsigned decimal
o	octal
x	hexadecimal
g	double float
f	float
s	null terminated character string
a	characters starting at the specified address

The command *c* continued the execution of the program. This command can be followed by a count which specifies the number of breakpoints to ignore. The command *D* was used to delete all breakpoints. In the example, we first set a breakpoint at line 9. Then each time the program suspended execution at the breakpoint, we examined the value of the variable *initial*. There is a shortcut approach to do this, which was followed in the second part of the *sdb* session. We asked *sdb* to display the value of the variable *initial* at line 9 each time that line was executed. This was possible with the breakpoint command *9b initial.·*

It is possible to set a breakpoint but activate it only after the breakpoint has been crossed a prespecified number of times by using the *c count* command as we did by specifying *c 3*. In the current session, we were interested in the value of the variable *initial* after the third iteration. The program continued execution but skipped the first three occurrences of the breakpoint.

Newline (hit return key) is itself a command. If the previous command was to print the contents of a variable, entering a newline prints the next location. If the previous command was to print the source code, entering a newline prints the next line of the source code. In the above session, the first *newline* command printed the contents of the location 0c2c0400, because the previous command was to display data. The next time it was used, the *newline* command displayed the next source code line, because the previous command was *p*, which displayed a source code line. Finally, we exited the *sdb* session with a *q* command.

2.3.2 Miscellaneous Sdb Commands

Some of the other commonly used *sdb* commands will now be examined. The command *variable!value* sets the variable to the specified value. Type conversion is done according to the conventions of the C programming language. Character constants are specified as '*character*, e.g. *anchar!'s* will set the character variable *anchar* to *s*. The command *k* kills the program that is being debugged. To print any number in the specified length & format, use the command *number=length format*. *Length* and *format* follow the same conventions indicated earlier for printing the value of a variable. This command is useful to convert numbers between various number systems. The command *variable=length format* prints the address of the variable in the specified format. If the specification for the length or format is missing, then the default length is 1 and the default format is x. The command *function:variable* is used to print the value of a variable in the specified function. *!command* executes the specified UNIX command. The *sdb* command < *filename* lets *sdb* read commands from the specified file. At EOF, input is accepted from the standard input. The " *string* command prints the specified string.

The following *sdb* session shows some of the possible usage of these commands. The previous program which computes the square root of a number is used again.

```
sdb a.out -
No core image
*9b
main:9 b
```

```
*r 100
Breakpoint at
main:9:         while (abs(initial * initial - number) >= precision)
*number=
0x2c03f4
*0x2c03f4/1fI
100
*main:number
100
*!ls
a.out
aggr.c
aggr2.c
bin
debug.c
dir
env.2896
inctemp
mbox
*"This is a string\n
This is a string
*k
1566: Killed
*q
```

Notice the use of the newline character \n at the end of the string to be displayed. This was used to generate the *sdb* prompt on a new line.

2.4 Strip: Stripping Debugging Information

The debugging information generated in the executable code by the use of the −g option causes the code file to be bulky and inefficient. Once a module is debugged and tested, the debugging information including the symbol table is no longer important. This segment of the code can be eliminated using the *strip* command on the executable file. Once stripped, source code level debugging commands of symbolic debuggers such as *dbx* and *sdb* cannot be used correctly on the file. The −l and the −x options control the amount of information to be stripped. If the −l option is used then only the line number information is stripped. The −x option suppresses the stripping of static and external symbol information.

2.5 Ctrace

The last debugger that we are going to study in this chapter is *ctrace*. It is different from the other debuggers that we studied earlier: it is easy to understand how it works, but it is not very powerful and is not very elegant. To understand *ctrace*, imagine the absence of the debuggers that we have studied so far. Try to remember when you wrote your first few programs in school and had never heard of debuggers. What did you do to find the bugs in your program? Most novice programmers follow the same strategy: they insert *printf* statements in their programs to print variables and messages where a bug is suspected. When the bug is too complicated, they end up with more *printf* statements than the original program statements! *Ctrace* does exactly what you did when you debugged your first few programs, but the difference is that *ctrace* inserts the statements for you. You also have more control over the tracing features when you use *ctrace*.

2.5.1 Invoking Ctrace

Let us look at the following program:

```
      cat stringcmp.c #Line numbers are not part of the program/file.
1     #include  <stdio.h>
2     main(argc,argv)
3     int argc;
4     char **argv;
5     {
6         int count,i;
7         while (argv[1][i] != '\0' && argv[2][i] != '\0')
8         {
9           if (argv[1][i]  == argv[2][i] )
10                ++count;
11         ++i;
12         }
13        printf("No. of matched chars. in same position is %d\n",count);
14    }
```

The above program checks two strings and outputs the number of characters that match in the same position of each string. It stops the comparison when it encounters a null character in one of the strings. Let us use *ctrace* to trace the execution of the above program. *Ctrace* is invoked as follows:

```
ctrace < stringcmp.c > ctraceprog.c
```

Ctrace reads from standard input a C program to be traced. It outputs a C program to standard output. The output file has to be saved and then compiled. The output C program is a modified version of the input C program. It performs the same functions as the input C program, but in addition, it also outputs values of variables and statements as desired by the user. It has several options that can be used to control its trace output. We will study some of the more useful options.

To understand the working of the program, let us compile the *ctrace* output program and run it. It is not neccessary to use the −*g* option unless you are planning to use the other debuggers, like *sdb* or *dbx*.

```
cc ctraceprog.c
a.out    1123456qwert123456     1123456zxcvbas3456
   2 main(argc,argv)
   7 while (argv[1][i] != '\0' && argv[2][i] != '\0')
     /* i == 0 */
     /* argv[1][i] == 49 or '1' */
     /* argv[2][i] == 49 or '1' */
   8    {
   9    if (argv[1][i]  == argv[2][i] )
        /* i == 0 */
        /* argv[1][i] == 49 or '1' */
        /* argv[2][i] == 49 or '1' */
  10          ++count;
            /* count == 1 */
  11    ++i;
        /* i == 1 */
  12    }
   7 while (argv[1][i] != '\0' && argv[2][i] != '\0')
     /* i == 1 */
     /* argv[1][i] == 49 or '1' */
     /* argv[2][i] == 49 or '1' */
   8    {
   9    if (argv[1][i]  == argv[2][i] )
        /* i == 1 */
        /* argv[1][i] == 49 or '1' */
        /* argv[2][i] == 49 or '1' */
  10          ++count;
            /* count == 2 */
  11    ++i;
```

```
           /* i == 2 */
12     }
    /* repeating */
    /* repeated 5 times */
 9      if (argv[1][i]  == argv[2][i] )
        /* i == 7 */
        /* argv[1][i] == 113 or 'q' */
        /* argv[2][i] == 122 or 'z' */
11      ++i;
        /* i == 8 or '\b' */
12     }
 7 while (argv[1][i] != '\0' && argv[2][i] != '\0')
    /* i == 8 or '\b' */
    /* argv[1][i] == 119 or 'w' */
    /* argv[2][i] == 120 or 'x' */
 8     {
 9      if (argv[1][i]  == argv[2][i] )
        /* i == 8 or '\b' */
        /* argv[1][i] == 119 or 'w' */
        /* argv[2][i] == 120 or 'x' */
11      ++i;
        /* i == 9 */
12     }
 7 while (argv[1][i] != '\0' && argv[2][i] != '\0')
    /* i == 9 */
    /* argv[1][i] == 101 or 'e' */
    /* argv[2][i] == 99 or 'c' */
 8     {
 9      if (argv[1][i]  == argv[2][i] )
        /* i == 9 */
        /* argv[1][i] == 101 or 'e' */
        /* argv[2][i] == 99 or 'c' */
11      ++i;
        /* i == 10 */
12     }
    /* repeating */
    /* repeated 4 times */
 9      if (argv[1][i]  == argv[2][i] )
        /* i == 14 */
        /* argv[1][i] == 51 or '3' */
        /* argv[2][i] == 51 or '3' */
10            ++count;
              /* count == 8 or '\b' */
```

```
11      ++i;
        /* i == 15 */
12      }
 7 while (argv[1][i] != '\0' && argv[2][i] != '\0')
   /* i == 15 */
   /* argv[1][i] == 52 or '4' */
   /* argv[2][i] == 52 or '4' */
 8     {
 9        if (argv[1][i]  == argv[2][i] )
          /* i == 15 */
          /* argv[1][i] == 52 or '4' */
          /* argv[2][i] == 52 or '4' */
10               ++count;
                 /* count == 9 */
11      ++i;
        /* i == 16 */
12      }
   /* repeating */
   /* repeated 2 times */
 7 while (argv[1][i] != '\0' && argv[2][i] != '\0')
   /* i == 18 */
   /* argv[1][i] == 0 */
13 printf("No. of matched chars. in same position is %d\n",count);
   /* count == 11 */No. of matched chars. in same position is 11

   /* return */
```

The above output shows the tracing features of *ctrace*. The number on the left-hand side indicates the line number in the original source program. After every statement, the values of the variables in that statement are printed. If the statement involves a condition testing, the values of the variables involved in the condition are printed. If the statement involves an assignment of a new value to a variable, that new value is printed.

In the above program, the first executable statement is the *while* statement. This statement involves three different variables, *argv[1][i]*, *argv[2][i]*, and *i*. *Ctrace* prints the values of these three variable using the C language convention for comments. Similarly, the values of the other variables involved in the execution of subsequent statements are printed along with the corresponding statements.

Ctrace is intelligent enough to detect loops in the program and to discontinue tracing when it detects them. It does so after tracing the statements twice. It restarts tracing in a loop only after it encounters a different execution sequence within the loop. When tracing of a loop is continued, it displays the number of times the loop was executed while the tracing was stopped. In the above program, the first seven characters in the two strings are the same; therefore, the *while* loop executes the same sequence of instructions during the comparison of the first seven characters. *Ctrace* traced the execution sequence during the first two cycles and then discontined the tracing until a different execution sequence was encountered. In our session, after the first two cycles, the next five cycles of the loop were not traced. *Ctrace* indicates the number of repetitions in the loop that were not traced. The lines

```
/*repeating */
/*repeated 5 times */
```

indicate that the tracing was stopped for the previous five repetitions of the loop. Tracing is continued again if a different sequence of instructions is executed within a loop. In our program, this occurred when the characters being compared were no longer the same.

The rest of the output traces the comparison of the characters in the two input strings inside the *while* loop until the program exits the loop. The remaining statements outside the loop are executed and their output is also traced. Finally, the program exits with the message /* *return* */.

2.5.2 Tracing Infinite Loops with Ctrace

How will *ctrace* detect infinite loops? It indicates the presence of an infinite loop by printing a warning message each time a statement sequence is executed 1000 times. Consider the following program, which is a modification of the earlier string-matching program. A semicolon has been inserted at the end of the *while* statement, forcing the statement to execute an infinite loop – a very common mistake!

```
     cat loopstrcmp.c #Line numbers are not part of the program/file.
1    #include <stdio.h>
2    main(argc,argv)
3    int argc;
4    char **argv;
5    {
6       int count,i;
7       while (argv[1][i]!='\0' && argv[2][i]!='\0');/*infinite loop*/
8          {
```

```
 9      if (argv[1][i]  == argv[2][i] )
10             ++count;
11     ++i;
12     }
13     printf("No. of matched chars. in same position: %d\n",count);
14  }
```

After the program generated by *ctrace* is compiled and run, we get the following trace:

```
ctrace < loopstrcmp.c > newprog.c
cc newprog.c

  2 main(argc,argv)
  7 while (argv[1][i]!='\0' && argv[2][i]!='\0')
    /* i == 0 */
    /* argv[1][i] == 49 or '1' */
    /* argv[2][i] == 49 or '1' */;
  7 while (argv[1][i]!='\0' && argv[2][i]!='\0')
    /* i == 0 */
    /* argv[1][i] == 49 or '1' */
    /* argv[2][i] == 49 or '1' */;
    /* repeating */
    /* still repeating after 1000 times */
    /* still repeating after 2000 times */
    /* still repeating after 3000 times */
    /* still repeating after 4000 times */
    /* still repeating after 5000 times */
    /* still repeating after 6000 times */
Hit DEL Key
```

This output shows the use of *ctrace* for detecting infinite loops.

The execution sequence of *ctrace* can be controlled at execution time. This is possible through the invocation of *ctron* and *ctroff* functions to turn tracing on and off respectively. Suppose that in the string-matching program, we wanted to trace the program only if the two strings to be compared are not the same. Here is how you would do it:

```
  1  #include <stdio.h>
  2  main(argc,argv)
  3  int argc;
  4  char **argv;
```

```
 5  {
 6    int count,i;
 7  #ifdef CTRACE
 8    if (strcmp(argv[1],argv[2])==0)
 9      ctroff();
10  #endif
11    while (argv[1][i]!='\0' && argv[2][i]!='\0')
12    {
13      if (argv[1][i]  == argv[2][i] )
14            ++count;
15      ++i;
16    }
17    printf("No. of matched chars. in same position: %d\n",count);
18  }
```

(As mentioned earlier, the line numbers shown here do not form part of the program.) The output of the *ctrace*-generated program run with the same two arguments looks like this:

a.out 1345 1345

```
 2 main(argc,argv)
 8     if (strcmp(argv[1],argv[2]) ==0)
       /* argv[1] == "1345" */
       /* argv[2] == "1345" */
       /* strcmp(argv[1],argv[2]) == 0 */
 9             ctroff();
    /* trace off */No. of matched chars. in same position: 4
```

The condition for tracing is enclosed in the sequence *ifdef CTRACE* and *endif* because you would not be interested in executing *ctroff* during the normal execution of the program. *Ctrace* defines the preprocessor variable *CTRACE*. The code enclosed in the sequence is compiled only if *CTRACE* is defined. During normal execution, the *CTRACE* preprocessor variable is not defined.

2.5.3 More Ctrace Options

Ctrace has many other options that can be used while generating the output C program. These options are provided to control the tracing of the program and to reset default settings.

The *−f* option allows you to trace only selected functions. This option must be followed by a blank-separated list of functions. The −*v* option is the complement of the −*f* option. It traces all functions except those specified in the list following the −*v* option. *Ctrace* traces a maximum of 20 variables in a statement. This default can be changed by the −*t* option. *Ctrace* can also be used to generate C programs to convert data from one number system to another. This is facilitated by the −*o*, −*x*, −*u*, and −*e* options, which print the data in octal, hexadecimal, unsigned, and floating-point format, in addition to the default formats. The default format is normally sufficient.

Here is a program generated by *ctrace* that converts any argument in decimal to its octal and hexadecimal equivalent:

```
main(arc,argv)
int argc;
char **argv;
{
   int i;
   i = atoi(argv[1]);
}
```

Let the name of the program file be conv.c. Let us run the *ctrace*-generated program as follows:

```
ctrace -o -x < conv.c > temp.c
cc temp.c
a.out 21

1 main(argc,argv)
6 i = atoi(argv[1]);
   /* argv[1] == 2147478482 or 017777765722 or 0x7fffebd2 or "21"*/
   /* i == 21 or 025 or 0x15 */
   /* return */
```

The trace indicates the change in the value of the variable i. This value is printed in the default decimal form as 21. It is also printed in its octal and hexadecimal equivalents as 025 and 0x15 respectively.

Another option that is useful is the −*p* option. It can be used to save the trace output in a different file. The default file is standard output. The −*p* option can be used as follows:

```
ctrace -p'fprintf(fp_trace,' < cprogram.c > output.c
```

The program will have to open a file explicitly for saving the traced output. This could be done by the following code:

```
/**** in the global declaration section ***/
#ifdef CTRACE
FILE *fp_trace,*fopen();
#endif
/***** in the execution section of the main program *****/
#ifdef CTRACE
fp_trace = fopen("TRACE.out","w");
#endif
```

The declaration of the *FILE* pointer has to be global, because the file will be used in all functions where tracing is turned on. While invoking *ctrace*, you must set the −*v* option appropriately to turn tracing off in the main function. This is required because if the *fprintf* statement inserted is executed prior to the opening of the file, it will give an execution-time error, as it will attempt to write to an unopened file. A much more simple technique is to redirect the trace output to the standard error file stderr. This avoids the complications of opening the file explicitly; thus, the command

```
ctrace -p'fprintf(stderr,' < cprogram.c > output.c
```

will generate a C program which will redirect the trace output to the stderr file.

Finally, you should realize that *ctrace* has a few bugs in it. Please read the UNIX reference manual for a note on the bugs in this utility.

3 Language Development Tools

UNIX provides a sophisticated environment for the development of language processors. This environment would not have been possible without the availability of *yacc* and *lex*. *Yacc*, or Yet Another Compiler Compiler, and *lex*, a LEXical analyzer, are utilities that can be used for a variety of tasks. Many programmers do not use these utilities because they are intimidated by compilers and parsing techniques. It is important to realize that these utilities can be used to develop user-friendly interfaces, to parse user input, to search for regular expressions, to develop filters, and other purposes.

M4 is another utility that could well have been classified as a filter. It is commonly used as a front end to language processors. It provides a more advanced form of macro processing than the macro substitution capability provided by preprocessors of languages like C and FORTRAN. The first two sections of this chapter discuss the theoretical foundations required to understand *yacc* and *lex*. The rest of the chapter discusses *yacc*, *lex*, and *M4* with numerous examples showing the use of these tools.

3.1 Theoretical Foundations

This section is primarily for readers who have never taken a course in compiler theory. What is a parser? What is a scanner? These words are often used by those who wish to sound advanced and sophisticated! After reading this section, you can also attempt to throw some jargon at your fellow programmer who has not yet read this book.

Parsing is the process of checking that the syntax of any input matches a given grammar. To simplify it further, consider the following set of rules:

```
Expression -----> integer * integer
           OR
Expression -----> integer + integer
           OR
Expression -----> integer - integer
           OR
Expression -----> integer / integer
```

These rules indicate that an expression can be either a product, sum, difference, or quotient of two integers. An input of the form

```
35 * 42
```

satisfies the above set of rules. An input of the form

```
23 - 42 + 23
```

does not satisfy the given set of rules. Parsing is the process of determining if the input satisfies the rules and a parser is the program which performs the function of parsing. There are various methods, know as parsing techniques, for determining the validity of the input string. The grammar rules are often known as production rules. The symbols in the production rules that appear on the left-hand side are known as nonterminal symbols. Symbols that never appear on the left-hand side of the production rules are known as terminal symbols. Scanning or lexical analysis is the process of reading the input and segregating it into logical pieces. These pieces are known as tokens. In the first example, the input *35 * 42* is segregated into three tokens: *35, *,* and *42.*

Figure 3.1 illustrates the working of the parser and the scanner. The input source is tokenized by the scanner, which is also called the lexical analyzer. These tokens are read by the parser. The parser gets the token itself and an

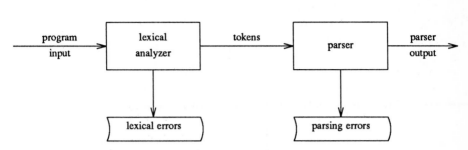

Figure 3.1 Interaction between Parser and Lexical Analyzer

attribute associated with the token. If the input cannot be tokenized, the scanner reports an error. If the input token is not appropriate, the parser reports an error. The parser should be intelligent enough to recover from an error. Simple parsers report the first error and collapse! Most situations require some kind of an error recovery. *Lex* is a utility that helps us in developing a scanner; *yacc* is a tool for building the parser. With complex production rules, we can develop complex languages. In the next section we will see how we can develop a simple parser and a scanner using the traditional method.

3.2 An Example of a Parser and a Scanner

Let us write a C program to parse the simple grammar discussed earlier. Remember that we need a scanner to tokenize the input. Let us write a function that can perform the task of the scanner and another function that will do the work of a parser.

```
#include <stdio.h>
#define OPR     3
#define INT     4
main()
{
   if    (yyparse()==0)
         printf("Input string correctly parsed\n");
   else
         printf("Syntax error encountered during parsing \n");
}
```

```
yyparse()
{
  if (yylex()==INT)
       if (yylex() == OPR )
              if (yylex()==INT)
              {
                     return(0);
              }
  return(-1);
}
yylex()
{
  static char achar=' ';

  while ((achar==' ' || achar=='\n' || achar=='\t') && achar !=EOF)
       achar=getchar();
  if (achar==EOF)
       return(-1);
  if (achar== '/' || achar == '*' || achar == '+' || achar == '-')
  {
       achar=getchar();
       return(OPR);
  }
  else
       if (achar >= '0' && achar <= '9')
       {
              while (achar >= '0' && achar <= '9' && achar!=EOF)
                     achar=getchar();
              return(INT);
       }
  return(-1);
}
```

In the above program, we have three functions. The function *main* calls
yyparse which in turn invokes *yylex*. *Yyparse* performs the task of the parser,
and *yylex* performs the task of the scanner, or lexical analyzer. *Yylex* informs
yyparse about the type of token it encountered in the input. For the sake of
simplicity, we have only two types of tokens in this example. They are *INT*
and *OPR*. *INT* indicates that the token encountered is a nonnegative integer;
OPR indicates that the type of the token is a binary operator. *Yylex* skips
white spaces like tabs, newline characters, and blanks. The above parser
checks to see if the first token is of type *INT*. It then checks for the second
token. If the second token is of type *OPR*, it looks for the third token. If the

third token is an *INT*, it stops parsing and displays a message to report successful parsing; however, if it fails to get the right token at any of the three checkpoints, it aborts parsing and reports an error.

The above example is an elementary parser in a nutshell. We have used the C programming language to do the parsing for a relatively simple grammar. The complexities involved in more powerful languages are often very intricate. Writing C programs is difficult for complex languages and results in inelegant code. In addition, if the language to be parsed changes, these changes can be more easily incorporated if the parser is written using *yacc*. In the following sections, we will see how this task can be accomplished very elegantly by writing *yacc* and *lex* specifications.

3.3 Yacc and Lex: An Introduction

Lex is a tool that reads a specifications file and generates the lexical analyzer. If the parser and scanner that we wrote earlier in C were instead written using *yacc* and *lex* specifications, *lex* would have generated the function *yylex* and *yacc* would have generated the function *yyparse*. If we compile the two outputs together using the appropriate libraries, we have an executable parser. The interaction between *yacc* and *lex* is indicated in Figure 3.2.

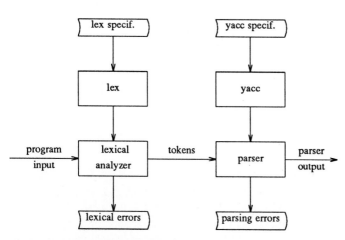

Figure 3.2 Parser Using Yacc and Lex

The function names, *yylex* and *yyparse*, are those which are actually used by *yacc* and *lex*. *Yacc* and *lex* also share other information. This will be explained as we proceed further in the chapter.

We will next attempt to write a parser and a scanner for the above grammar using *yacc* and *lex*. *Lex* takes as input a *lex* specifications file and outputs a C program. This specifications file has the general format as shown below:

> *definitions*
> %%
> *lex regular expressions and actions*
> %%
> *User functions*

Only the first %% is essential; the rest of the source is optional. The second part, involving regular expressions and actions, is very important. We will write the *lex* specifications file for the small scanner that we wrote earlier using the C language. The task is to recognize an integer or any of the operators +, -, *, and /. Any other characters in the input will result in an error message.

Following is the *lex* specifications file:

```
%%
[0-9]+          { return(INT); }
[-*+/]          { return(OPR); }
[\t ]   ;
    .                   { printf("Lexical analyzer error\n");
                          exit(-1);
                        }
%%
yywrap()
{
        return(1);
}
```

This specifications file uses two of the three sections that a *lex* specifications file can have. The section which has definitions in it is not used. The second section contains regular expressions on one side and actions on the other side. The actions are enclosed in parentheses and are executed when a string matching the regular expression is encountered. The regular expression *[0-9]+* matches one or more occurrences of digits. The expression *[-*+/]* matches any single occurrence of any of the enclosed operators. To ignore any blanks and tab characters in the input, the rule

```
[\t ] ;
```

is used. Finally, the regular expression . (dot) matches any character except newline.

The actions executed are very simple. The program returns a value whenever a desired token is encountered. The action associated with the last regular expression prints an error message whenever an unrecognized character is detected in the input. The function *yywrap* is invoked at EOF. A return value of 1 from *yywrap* indicates that no further input is available. The *lex* library also provides the *yywrap* function. There are a number of reserved functions and variables like *yywrap* which are supplied by the *lex* and the *yacc* libraries and these can be redefined by the user. The *lex* library can be accessed by using the −*ll* option on the *cc* command line.

Let us now look at the *yacc* specifications file, which has a structure that is very similar to the *lex* specifications file:

declarations
%%
yacc rules and actions
%%
User functions

Only the first %% is required; the rest of the input is optional. *Yacc* rules consist of production rules with associated actions. Actions are statements that are executed when the input matches the corresponding production rule. They are C statements which are grouped together in braces to form a block. Actions may be placed at the end of the production rule, or they may be sprinkled in between various symbols on the right side of the production rule. Declarations are of two types, C program declarations and *yacc* declarations. C program declarations have to be enclosed in %{ and %}. *Yacc* declarations are of various types. Some of the more common ones are *start* and *token* declarations. The *start* declaration specifies the starting nonterminal symbol for the production rules. The *token* declarations identify the terminal symbols that are used in the production rules. Any symbol that is not declared as a token must have a production rule with that symbol appearing on the left side of the rule.

Here is the *yacc* specifications program for the simple expression-recognizing parser:

```
%token INT OPR
%start expr
%%
expr    : INT OPR INT
          {
          printf("The input expression was syntactically correct\n");
          }
        | error
          {
          printf("The input expression was syntactically incorrect\n");
          }
%%
```

The simple grammar has production rules as explained earlier. The | mark indicates an alternative production rule. In the above specifications program the alternative production rule indicates a symbol called *error*. This is a reserved symbol which indicates that an error has occurred. It means that the input failed to match any of the production rules for the nonterminal symbol. The declaration section indicates that there are two tokens, *INT* and *OPR*. These tokens therefore appear only on the right-hand side of the production rules. The actions are fairly self-explanatory.

3.3.1 Tying It All Together

Now that we have the *yacc* and *lex* specifications file, let us see how we can run *yacc* and *lex* and actually create the executable parser. The command to run *yacc* is

yacc *file-name*

File-name is the name of the file which has the *yacc* specifications. The execution of this command creates a file called y.tab.c, which is a C program that has the function *yyparse*. The command to run *lex* is

lex *file-name*

File-name is the name of the file that contains the *lex* specifications. The execution of this command creates a file called lex.yy.c, which is a C program that has the function *yylex*.

Now we need a *main* function that can invoke *yyparse*. Here is a simple C program that can provide us with the *main* function:

```
#include <stdio.h>
main()
{
        yyparse();
}
#include "y.tab.c"
#include "lex.yy.c"
```

Now we are all set to compile the program and run it. Compiling the program is a trivial task. Use the standard *cc* command. You may occasionally have to use the *yacc* or *lex* libraries. The *yacc* library is invoked by using the −*ly* option and the *lex* library can be used by specifying the −*ll* option on the *cc* command line. It is not always neccessary to use the *yacc* and *lex* libraries; we can create the executable a.out parser by using the following *cc* command:

```
cc main.c -ly
```

Main.c is the program that has the *main* function in it. The *yacc* library was required because we use the *error* option, which invokes a function called *yyerror* which we have not provided explicitly. As an exercise, try running the parser with various inputs and check to see how some input strings result in acceptance messages, while other input strings result in error messages.

3.3.2 Lex Regular Expressions

Lex regular expressions are probably the closest to the regular expressions that are accepted in the academic world. These expressions are either made of text characters which match the input characters verbatim or operator characters which have special interpretations. Operator characters are

" [ ] ^ − ? . * + | ( ) $ / { } % < >

The special meanings associated with *lex* operator characters are explained in Table 3.1.

In the earlier example, we saw a couple of instances of *lex* regular expressions. The regular expression *John* matches the string *John* character for character. The regular expression *[0−9]+* that we used earlier matches one or

TABLE 3.1 Lex Operator Characters

Operator	Interpretation	Example
"	The quotation character " indicates that all characters between a pair of quotes are to be interpreted as text characters without any special meaning.	*string*"+*" will match the string *string+*" but not *string++*.
\	The backslash character is used to turn off the special meaning of any operator character. Several C language escapes are also recognized. This character is also used to escape into octal.	The regular expression in the preceding example can be rewritten as *string*\+*. Also \176 can be used to match the tilde (~) character.
[]	This pair of characters is used to group classes of characters. Within these square brackets, the only operator characters understood are \, −, and ^. The \ character is used to escape the special meaning of these characters. The − operator is used to specify a range of characters. The ^ character, which must appear as the first character after the left bracket, is used to indicate that the resulting string is to be complemented with respect to the computer character set.	[a−z] matches all lowercase letters. [^XYZ] matches all characters except X, Y, and Z. [A2O] matches the characters A, 2, and O.

more occurrences of a digit. The wide range of operator characters available in *lex* can be used for developing powerful filters.

3.3.3 Examples of Lex Usage

It is not necessary to use *lex* with *yacc*. *Lex* alone provides a powerful tool for generating C programs that can function as filters or translators. We will now proceed to write some *lex* specifications files to generate some useful programs. Consider the following *lex* specifications file:

```
%%
\40*        { printf(" "); }
[\t]        {printf(" ");  }
john        {printf("John"); }
```

```
#.*    { }
```

This specifications file
1. Compresses multiple adjacent blanks in the file to a single blank.
2. Eliminates all strings which start with a # character and end in a newline character.
3. Replaces the tab character by a single blank character.
4. Converts all occurrences of the word *john* to *John*.
5. Prints everything else verbatim.

TABLE 3.1 Lex Operator Characters (contd.)

Operator	Interpretation	Example
.	The dot character is used to match any character except the newline character.	The expression *.a* matches the character *a* anywhere in the text except after the newline character.
?	This character is used to indicate an optional element of an expression.	*XY?Z* matches strings *XZ* or *XYZ*; *Y* is the optional element.
*	This character is used to indicate zero or more occurrences of a character or a class of characters.	*a** matches zero or more occurrences of the letter *a*. *a[a–z]** matches a string of lowercase letters starting with *a*, including the string *a*.
+	This character is similar to the * character except that it needs at least one occurrence of the specified character or class of characters.	*a[a–z]+* matches any string of lowercase letters starting with *a* but the length of the string must be greater than 1.
() |	The () characters are used to indicate groupings. Groupings are particularly useful in conjunction with the | alternation character.	*(Unix)|(UNIX)* matches either *Unix* or *UNIX*.

The C program which invokes the *yylex* function generated by *lex* is

```
cat main.c
#include <stdio.h>
main()
{
        while (1)
                yylex();
}
```

```
yywrap()
{
        exit(0);
}
#include "lex.yy.c"
```

If the name of the *lex* specifications file is lex.ll and if the name of the file containing the *main* function is main.c, then the following commands will create the executable a.out to perform the required functions:

```
lex lex.ll
cc main.c
```

TABLE 3.1 Lex Operator Characters (contd.)

Operator	Interpretation	Example
^	When this character occurs outside the [] operators, the regular expression following this character is matched only at the beginning of a line.	*^(start)* matches the string *start* only at the beginning of a new line.
$	If the last character of an expression is a $, the regular expression is matched only at the end of a line.	*endofline$* matches the string endofline only if it occurs at the end of a line.
{ }	These operator characters are used to specify repetitions or definition expansion. *Lex* definitions are explained in a separate section.	*0{1,5}* looks for one to five occurrences of *0*.
< >	The < and > characters are used to specify start conditions. These are explained in detail later.	*<str1>start* matches the string *start* only if the start condition *str1* is on.
%	This operator character is used to separate *lex* specification segments as explained earlier.	

Let us look at another example of a *lex* specifications file. This time our aim is
1. To count all occurrences of the word *John.*
2. To truncate all real numbers with decimal points to their integer values.
3. To substitute all occurrences of a lowercase letter following a period with an uppercase letter. This will also be done if a blank separates the period and

the lowercase letter.

The program file containing the *main* function has been modified to declare some variables and to print the count of occurrences of the word *John* at end of input. Here is the modified program file:

```
#include <stdio.h>
int i,count_john;
main()
{
        while (1)
                yylex();
}
yywrap()
{
        printf("The word John occurred %d times\n", count_john);
        exit(0);
}
#include "lex.yy.c"
```

The *lex* specifications file is as follows:

```
%%
John    { ECHO;
          ++count_john; }
[0-9]+\.[0-9]* { i = 0;
          while (yytext[i]!='.')
          {
                printf("%c",yytext[i]);
                ++i;
          }
        }
\.\40*[a-z]    { i=0;
          while (yytext[i] < 'a' || yytext[i] > 'z')
          {
                printf("%c",yytext[i]);
                ++i;
          }
          printf("%c",yytext[i] -  32);
        }
```

In this example we have introduced more features of *lex*. First, *lex* provides us with a variable called *yytext* which supplies us with the token that was matched. *Yyleng* is another variable supplied by *lex*. This integer variable has the length of the last string matched. The *yywrap* function does something more than exiting: it provides us with a suitable function where all statistics about the input can be displayed at EOF. We have used this function to display the count of the occurrences of the word *John* in the input. Very often we have to examine the matched string and then print it. One way to do so is to use the *printf* statement to print the variable *yytext*. This statement is so often used that *lex* provides a brief form for doing the same: the *ECHO* word performs the function of printing the currently matched string.

3.3.4 Lex Definitions

Very often we come across regular expressions that form the elements of other regular expressions to be used in *lex*. Instead of repeating the regular expression elements each time, it is more convenient and often more readable to name the element and then use that name rather than the regular expression that makes up the element. *Lex* definitions provide this mechanism as a form of macro substitution. Here is an example of a *lex* specifications file that uses definitions:

```
INTEGER [0-9]+
%%
{INTEGER}        {
        printf("Integer encountered\n");
        }
{INTEGER}\.{INTEGER}   {
        printf("Real number encountered\n");
        }
```

In this example we print the message *Integer encountered* when there is an integer in the input. When a real number is encountered with a decimal point in it, the message *Real number encountered* is printed. *INTEGER* is used to define the regular expression element that consists of a series of consecutive digits.

3.3.5 Context Sensitivity

Sometimes the meaning of a string or a token depends on the tokens around it. This is often referred to as context sensitivity. Left context sensitivity implies that the meaning of the token depends on the token that preceded the present token. *Lex* provides a mechanism known as start conditions to support left context sensitivity. It is possible to write a lexical analyzer to perform left context sensitivity without the use of start conditions. However, the amount of C code required will increase substantially. The basic concept involved in the use of start conditions is to set and unset them when certain events occur. They function like flags. Start conditions must be declared in *lex* using the following format:

```
%start start1 start2 start3 ...
```

Start1, start2, and *start3* are the names of the start conditions that will be used in the lexical analyzer. To set a start condition, use the action statement

```
BEGIN start1
```

where *start1* is the name of a start condition. To unset all start conditions, use the action statement

```
BEGIN 0;
```

To match a string to a regular expression only when a start condition *start1* is active, use the following:

```
<start1>reg_expr    {actions}
```

where *start1* is the name of the start condition, *reg_expr* is any *lex* regular expression, and *actions* are C language statements. The *actions* are executed only when the input string matches the regular expression and the start condition is set.

The next *lex* specification file converts a two-digit integer amount into its alphabetic representation. It expects as its input a dollar sign followed by a digit followed by another digit. For example, if the input is *$23*, the output will be *Twenty three dollars.* The *lex* specifications file for this program is shown below:

```
%start  TT ZZ DD UU TN
%%
\$      {
        BEGIN TT;
        }
<TT>[0-9]       {
        tenth = yytext[0];
        BEGIN 0;
        switch (yytext[0])
        {
         case '0' : BEGIN ZZ;
                    break;
         case '1' : BEGIN TN;
                    break;
         default  : BEGIN DD;
                    break;
        }
        }
<ZZ>[0-9]       {
        BEGIN 0;
        switch(yytext[0])
        {
         case '0' : printf("Zero dollars");
                    break;
         case '1' : printf("One dollar");
                    break;
         case '2' : printf("Two dollars");
                    break;
         case '3' : printf("Three dollars");
                    break;
         case '4' : printf("Four dollars");
                    break;
         case '5' : printf("Five dollars");
                    break;
         case '6' : printf("Six dollars");
                    break;
         case '7' : printf("Seven dollars");
                    break;
         case '8' : printf("Eight dollars");
                    break;
         case '9' : printf("Nine dollars");
                    break;
        }
```

```
        }
<TN>[0-9]        {
        BEGIN 0;
        switch(yytext[0])
        {
         case '0' : printf("Ten dollars     ");
                   break;
         case '1' : printf("Eleven dollars");
                   break;
         case '2' : printf("Twelve dollars");
                   break;
         case '3' : printf("Thirteen dollars");
                   break;
         case '4' : printf("Fourteen dollars");
                   break;
         case '5' : printf("Fifteen dollars");
                   break;
         case '6' : printf("Sixteen dollars");
                   break;
         case '7' : printf("Seventeen dollars");
                   break;
         case '8' : printf("Eighteen dollars");
                   break;
         case '9' : printf("Nineteen dollars");
                   break;
        }
        }
<DD>[0-9]        {
        BEGIN 0;
        switch(tenth)
        {
         case '2' : printf("Twenty ");
                   break;
         case '3' : printf("Thirty ");
                   break;
         case '4' : printf("Forty ");
                   break;
         case '5' : printf("Fifty ");
                   break;
         case '6' : printf("Sixty ");
                   break;
         case '7' : printf("Seventy ");
                   break;
```

```
        case '8' : printf("Eighty ");
                   break;
        case '9' : printf("Ninety ");
                   break;
        }
        switch(yytext[0])
        {
        case '0' : printf("dollars");
                   break;
        case '1' : printf("One dollars");
                   break;
        case '2' : printf("Two dollars");
                   break;
        case '3' : printf("Three dollars");
                   break;
        case '4' : printf("Four dollars");
                   break;
        case '5' : printf("Five dollars");
                   break;
        case '6' : printf("Six dollars");
                   break;
        case '7' : printf("Seven dollars");
                   break;
        case '8' : printf("Eight dollars");
                   break;
        case '9' : printf("Nine dollars");
        }
        }
```

The C program with the *main* function is listed below:

```
#include <stdio.h>
char tenth;
main()
{
        while (1)
                yylex();
}
yywrap()
{
        exit(0);
}
```

```
#include "lex.yy.c"
```

In this *lex* program we have used four start conditions. They are *TT, DD, ZZ,* and *TN.* The lexical analyzer first checks the first character. If it is a *$* sign, it sets the *TT* condition. It then checks the next character, which is expected to be the tens position digit. Here, in the actions associated with *<TT>[0−9],* the tens position digit is stored in the variable *tenth.* The *TT* start condition is unset so that the next input digit will not match the regular expression associated with this start condition. It then examines the tens position digit. If it is a *0,* the *ZZ* start condition is set. If it is a *1,* the *TN* start condition is set. If it is neither *0* nor *1,* by default it sets the *DD* start condition, which implies that the character is a digit between *2* and *9* inclusive. When the next input character is read, actions associated with the active start condition are executed. At this point, only one of the three start conditions *TN, DD,* or *ZZ* is set. The actions associated with these conditions actually do the required conversion. Try to understand some of the drawbacks of the above lexical analyzer. Will it accept input of the form "$3asd5"? What will be the output for this input ?

3.3.6 More on Yacc Usage

Earlier we saw how *yacc* was used to parse a simple arithmetic expression consisting of two integers separated by a binary operator. We will now look at *yacc* more closely. The heart of *yacc* is the second section, which consists of *yacc* rules and actions. *Yacc* rules are productions that define the grammar. Some amount of practice is required to master the technique of writing production rules. Each rule is made up of tokens and/or nonterminal symbols. Each nonterminal symbol must appear on the left side of a production rule. There is a special nonterminal symbol, called the *start* symbol, which by default is the left-side nonterminal symbol of the first rule. It is possible to override this rule by using the line

```
%start symbol
```

where *symbol,* which must appear on the left side of some production rule, becomes the start symbol. All symbols that do not appear on the left side of any production rule are assumed to be terminal symbols, or tokens, and have to be declared accordingly by the line:

```
%token token-name
```

where *token-name* is the name of any token which is passed to *yacc* by the lexical analyzer.

3.3.7 Another Example of Yacc Usage

By now we know that *yacc* is used to parse a language, but it is important to finalize your understanding of the language before you start defining the production rules. Let us try to define a simple language that will provide a user-friendly interface to query a flat file. The basic idea will be to convert this user-friendly language into an *awk* statement and to translate field names into field positions. This will require an additional input file, during the translation phase, which can map field names into field positions. Let us now start our thinking process for defining the language. We know that most users find the word *select* very user friendly in query languages. Let us therefore make a decision that our query must start with the word *select*. Let us provide the language with some selection facility based on values in fields. Of course, we also have to provide some printing facilities as an output of our query. We will simplify our task by providing some basic print capabilities in the form of printing the fields of the selected records. We then scribble some possible queries:

```
Select from supplier_file if ((qty_supplied > 100) and
        (city        = "Detroit" ))
        then
        print supplier_no,supplier_name,supplier_addr

Select from part_file if (part_no = 2020)
        then print part_name
```

Now that we know what our language looks like, let us start writing the *yacc* specifications file for this language:

```
%start query
%token _select _from _fieldfile _if _open _close _then _and _lesseq
%token _field _value _greater _equal _less _greateq _print _comma _or
%%
query    : _select _from _fieldfile
            _if _open selection_clause _close
```

```
        _then _print print_clause
                {
                }
selection_clause : selection_clause conj selection
        |       selection
                {
                }
conj    : _and
        |       _or
                {
                }
selection : _open select_fact _close
        |       select_fact
                {
                }
select_fact : _fieldfile oper _value
                {
                }
oper        : _greater
        |       _equal
        |       _less
        |       _greateq
        |       _lesseq
                {
                }
print_clause : print_clause _comma _fieldfile
        |       _fieldfile
                {
                }
%%
yyerror(str)
char *str;
{
        fprintf(stderr,"There is a syntax error in the query\n ");
        exit(-2);
}
```

In the above production rules, all our terminal symbols start with an underscore; therefore, there is a production rule for all symbols that do not start with an underscore because these are nonterminal symbols. The production rules shown above indicate that our query starts with the words *select from*. We then indicate the name of the file on which the query should operate. This is followed by an *if*, a parenthesized selection criteria, and finally a *print* specification.

The second production rule indicates that the selection criteria consist of many elements separated by a conjunction. The third production rule defines a conjunction to be either an *or* or an *and*. The next production rule defines an element of the selection criteria to be optionally parenthesized. The fifth production rule specifies that each element consists of a field, followed by a relational operator, followed by a value to be used for selection. The next production rule defines an operator to be either a >, <, =, >= or <=. Finally, the last production rule indicates that the print specification consists of a list of field names separated by commas. There is a recursion involved in this production rule, since the nonterminal symbol *print_clause* appears on both sides of the production rule. Since this nonterminal symbol appears on the left side of the resultant production, such a recursion is known as left recursion. The same production rule could also have been written as

```
print_clause :  _fieldfile   _comma print_clause
         | _fieldfile
```

This production rule is right recursive. *Yacc* users are encouraged to use left recursive rules.

Having written the *yacc* specifications file, the next important task is to test it with some input data. We also have to provide a lexical analyzer to give these production rules the required tokens. Here is the *lex* specifications file for the query parser:

```
%%
[Ss][Ee][Ll][Ee][Cc][Tt]                    {
                        ECHO;
                        return(_select);
                        }
[Ff][Rr][Oo][Mm]                 {
                        ECHO;
                        return(_from);
                        }
[Ii][Ff]                         {
                        ECHO;
                        return(_if);
                        }
"("                              {
                        ECHO;
                        return(_open);
                        }
```

```
")"                              {
                        ECHO;
                        return(_close);
                        }
[Tt][Hh][Ee][Nn]        {
                        ECHO;
                        return(_then);
                        }
[Aa][Nn][Dd]            {
                        ECHO;
                        return(_and);
                        }
">"                     {
                        ECHO;
                        return(_greater);
                        }
"<"                     {
                        ECHO;
                        return(_less);
                        }
"="                     {
                        ECHO;
                        return(_equal);
                        }
">="                    {
                        ECHO;
                        return(_greateq);
                        }
"<="                    {
                        ECHO;
                        return(_lesseq);
                        }
"print"                 {
                        ECHO;
                        return(_print);
                        }
","                     {
                        ECHO;
                        return(_comma);
                        }
[Oo][Rr]                         {
                        ECHO;
                        return(_or);
```

```
                    }
[A-Za-z][A-Za-z0-9]*              {
                         ECHO;
                         return(_fieldfile);
                         }
([0-9][0-9]*\.[0-9][0-9]*)|([0-9]+)|(\".*\")  {
                         ECHO;
                         return(_value);
                         }
%%
yywrap()
{
        return(1);
}
```

We have set up the *lex* specifications file in a way that can accept reserved words like *select* in both lowercase and uppercase letters. We are using the same token designator _fieldfile for both file names and field names. The last regular expression accepts constants. Acceptable constants are integers, real numbers with decimal points, or strings enclosed in double quotes. We do not accept newline characters in our string constants. *ECHO* is used to print the matched token. We can now complete the query parser with a small C program, as listed below:

```
#include <stdio.h>
main()
{
        yyparse();
}
#include "y.tab.c"
#include "lex.yy.c"
```

Our query parser is now ready to check for syntax errors in user queries. Let us run some queries and see the results.

query:
```
select from data     if (name  = "John")
        then print name
```
output:
```
select from data     if (name  = "John")
        then print name
```
query:

```
select from data     if (( name  = "John")
        then print no
```
output:
```
select from data     if (( name  = "John")
There is a syntax error in the query
        then
```

We have intentionally introduced a syntax error in the second query. Our parser detects this error. The first query is syntactically correct and the parser does not complain about it.

3.3.8 Action from Yacc!

Now that we think our parser works, we need some action! Our goal is to translate a query into an *awk* statement. We need to do the translation in the *yacc* action statements. Our input consists of a data file, a description file which has the names of the fields in the data file, and the query itself. The field names used in a query must be present in the description file. We will open a file called query in write mode in which the *awk* statement will be written. In our *yywrap* function, we will close this file, make it executable, and run it. Here is the *yacc* specifications file with actions incorporated:

```
%{
char desc_file[35],err_message[40];
int field_no=0,eof=2,count,found;
extern char yytext[];
%}
%start query
%token _select _from _fieldfile _if _open _close _then _lesseq
%token _field _value _greater _equal _less
%token _greateq _print _comma _or _and
%%
query     : _select _from _fieldfile
                { /*  Access the description file which is   */
                  /*    suffixed .desc                       */
                  strcpy(desc_file,yytext);
                  strcat(desc_file,".desc");
                  fp_desc = fopen(desc_file,"r");
                  while(1) {
                      /*  Fill the field_name array with the names*/
                      /*  of the fields in the descriptin file.   */
```

```
        /*  The position in the array + 1 indicates */
            /*  field position in the file          */
            eof=fscanf(fp_desc,"%s",field_name[field_no++]);
            if (eof==EOF) break;
        }
    }
            _if _open
        {
        /*   Query file to write the awk statement  */
        /*   is opened in the main function.        */
        /*   Start completing the query here        */
        fprintf(fp_query,"(");
        }
                selection_clause _close
        {
        fprintf(fp_query,")");
        }
                _then _print
        {
        /*   translate into awk print statement    */
        fprintf(fp_query,"print");
        }
        print_clause
selection_clause: selection_clause conj selection
    | selection
conj         : _and
        {
        /* translate AND into awk && operator       */
        fprintf(fp_query,"&&",yytext);
        }
    | _or
        {
        /* translate OR into awk || operator        */
        fprintf(fp_query,"||",yytext);
        }
selection: _open
        {
        /* In selection condition                   */
        /* output the ( character verbatim          */
        fprintf(fp_query,"(");
        }
                select_fact _close
        {
```

```
        /* output the ) character verbatim        */
            fprintf(fp_query,")");
            }
    |              select_fact
            {
            }
select_fact: _fieldfile
            {
               /* Check if the field was defined in the     */
               /* description file and get its position     */
            found = -1;
            for (count=0;count < field_no; ++count)
                    if (strcmp(yytext,field_name[count])==0)
                    {
                            found = count;
                            break;
                    }
            if (found == -1)
            {
                    strcpy(err_message,"Field not found: ");
                    strcat(err_message,yytext);
                    yyerror(err_message);
            }
              /* array pos. 0 corresponds to field pos. 1.*/
              /* array pos. + 1 gets field pos.           */
            fprintf(fp_query,"$%d",found+1);
            }
                    oper
            {
            }
                    _value
            {
            fprintf(fp_query,"%s",yytext);
            }
oper       : _greater
            {
               /* translate relational operators           */
            fprintf(fp_query,">");
            }

        | _equal
            {
               /* translate = in input to ==, an awk oper. */
```

```
        fprintf(fp_query,"==");
                }
        | _less
                {
                fprintf(fp_query,"<");
                }
        | _greateq
                {
                fprintf(fp_query,">=");
                }
        | _lesseq
                {
                fprintf(fp_query,"<=");
                }
print_clause : print_clause _comma
                {
                fprintf(fp_query,",");
                }
                  _fieldfile
                {
                /* check if field to be printed was defined */
                /* in the description file and get its pos. */
                found = -1;
                for (count=0;count < field_no; ++count)
                        if (strcmp(yytext,field_name[count])==0)
                        {
                                found = count;
                                break;
                        }
                if (found == -1)
                {
                        strcpy(err_message,"Field not found : ");
                        strcat(err_message,yytext);
                        yyerror(err_message);
                }
                fprintf(fp_query,"$%d",found+1);
                }
        | _fieldfile
                {
                found = -1;
                for (count=0;count < field_no; ++count)
                        if (strcmp(yytext,field_name[count])==0)
                        {
```

```
                        found = count;
                                break;
                        }
                if (found == -1)
                {
                        strcpy(err_message,"Field not found : ");
                        strcat(err_message,yytext);
                        yyerror(err_message);
                }
                fprintf(fp_query,"$%d",found+1);
                }
%%
yyerror(str)
char *str;
{
fprintf(stderr,"There is a syntax error in the query\n %s\n",str);
exit(-2);
}
```

The *lex* specifications file is the same as before, only the function *yywrap* has been modified as follows:

```
%%
yywrap()
{
        /*   The description file was suffixed with   */
        /*   a .desc. Remove the suffix to get the    */
        /*   name of the data file.                   */
        desc_file[strlen(desc_file)-5] = NULL;
        fprintf(fp_query," }\' %s\n", desc_file);
        fclose(fp_query);
        system("chmod 700 query;query");
        return(1);
}
```

And finally, here is the C program with the *main* function which invokes the parser:

```
#include <stdio.h>
FILE *fopen(),*fp_desc,*fp_query;
#define MAXFIELDS 20
char field_name[MAXFIELDS][35];
```

```
main()
{
        /*   open the file to write the awk statement    */
        fp_query = fopen("query","w");
        fprintf(fp_query,"awk \'{ if ");
        yyparse();
}
#include "y.tab.c"
#include "lex.yy.c"
```

The main program consists of three statements. In the first statement, we open a file called query in write mode. The second statement outputs the initial words that comprise the *awk* statement to be generated. In the *yacc* specifications file we build up the *awk* statement. In the first production rule, we get the name of the data file on which the query is to be run. A file subscripted with .desc is opened. This file has the description of the data file; it has the names of the fields in the same order in which the data appears in the data file. A string array *field_name* is filled with this information. This array is searched whenever a field name is encountered in the query file. In the production rule for the nonterminal *select_fact*, we translate the field name in the query file into a field position for use by *awk*. This is done by searching the string array *field_name* in which the field names are stored. A similar approach is adopted in the production rule for *print_clause*. In this rule, we translate the print clause into an *awk* print statement by using field positions. The function *yywrap* which is invoked when the end of the query file is reached, has statements to close the query file, make it executable, and run it. Our query processor is all set to run! Let us try running a query:

```
cat data
12      12.32   John
13      14.12   Jim


cat data.desc
no
salary
name
cat q1
select from data    if (name  = "John")
                then print name,no,salary
a.out < q1 ## a.out is the executable query processor
select from data    if (name  = "John")
                then print name,no,salary
John 12 12.32
```

You can see that the query itself is also a part of the output. This can be suppressed by removing the *ECHO* statements from the *lex* specifications file.

Everything is fine so far, because our query was correct; however, there are many problems with our query processor. First, it has no error reporting or error recovery features. Error reporting is a trivial task. Error recovery is a nontrivial task that needs a good understanding of how the parser works. In the next section we will modify our query processor so that it will

1. Allow for more than one query in our input.
2. Provide error-reporting features.
3. Report error diagnostics on a new line.
4. Provide error recovery features so that if there is an error in one query, we will skip that query and continue to parse from the next query.

Here is our modified program with the *main* function:

```
#include <stdio.h>
#define MAXFIELDS 20
FILE *fopen(),*fp_desc,*fp_query;
char field_name[MAXFIELDS][35],last_token[25];
int error_ind=0;
main()
{
        fp_query = fopen("query","w");
        yyparse();
}
#include "y.tab.c"
#include "lex.yy.c"
```

The *main* function has changed slightly: we have added a string variable, *last_token*, which we will use for storing the last error token. Our aim is to report the error diagnostics after we encounter a newline character. Error messages should not be reported in the middle of input lines. We are also building up the initial segment of the *awk* statement in the *yacc* file rather than in the *main* function. This is necessary because we may have more than one query and therefore may require more than one *awk* statement. The flag *error_ind* will be used to execute the query only when the flag is not set to one. Thus the *awk* statement for a query is not executed if an error was detected during the parsing stage. The rewritten *yacc* specifications file, with the original comments removed, is as follows:

```
%{
char desc_file[35],err_message[40];
int field_no=0,eof=2,count,found;
extern char yytext[];
%}
%start query
%token _select _from _fieldfile _if _open _close _then _and
%token _lesseq _NEWLINE _comma _or _semi
%token _field _value _greater _equal _less _greateq _print
%%
query       :  query _select _from _fieldfile
                  {
                  strcpy(desc_file,yytext);
                  strcat(desc_file,".desc");
                  fp_desc = fopen(desc_file,"r");
                    while(1) {
                    eof=fscanf(fp_desc,"%s",field_name[field_no++]);
                    if (eof==EOF) break;
                    }
                  }
                       _if
                       _open
                  {
                    /* write the initial part of the awk stat.  */
                  fprintf(fp_query,"\n awk \'{ if (");
                  }
                       selection_clause
                       _close
                  {
                  fprintf(fp_query,")");
                  }
                       _then _print
                  {
                  fprintf(fp_query,"print");
                  }
                       print_clause _semi
                  {
                    /* Complete the awk statement and execute it*/
                  printf("\n***** Output of Query *****\n");
                  desc_file[strlen(desc_file)-5] = NULL;
                  fprintf(fp_query," }\' %s\n", desc_file);
                  fclose(fp_query);
                  system("chmod 700 query;query");
```

```
fopen("query","w");
        printf("\n");
        }
| _select _from _fieldfile
        {
        strcpy(desc_file,yytext);
        strcat(desc_file,".desc");
        fp_desc = fopen(desc_file,"r");
        while(1)
                {
                eof=fscanf(fp_desc,"%s",field_name[field_no++]);
                if (eof==EOF) break;
                }
        }
                _if
                _open
        {
        fprintf(fp_query,"\nawk \'{ if (");
        }
                selection_clause
                _close
        {
        fprintf(fp_query,")");
        }
                _then _print
        {
        fprintf(fp_query,"print");
        }
                print_clause _semi
        {
        printf("\n***** Output of Query *****\n");
        desc_file[strlen(desc_file)-5] = NULL;
        fprintf(fp_query," }\' %s\n", desc_file);
        fclose(fp_query);
        system("chmod 700 query;query");
        fopen("query","w");
        }
| error
        {
            /* process the error in the query         */
        strcpy(err_message,
            "**** Syntax error in the query");
            /* Skip up to the next semicolon or EOF   */
```

```
            throw_away();
                    yyerrok;
                    yyclearin;
                    } query
    selection_clause : selection_clause conj selection
            |               selection
    conj            : _and
                    {
                    fprintf(fp_query,"&&",yytext);
                    }
            | _or
                    {
                    fprintf(fp_query,"||",yytext);
                    }
            | error
                    {
                    strcpy(err_message,
                      "**** Syntax error : AND or OR expected");
                    throw_away();
                    yyerrok;
                    yyclearin;
                    } query
    selection : _open
                    {
                    fprintf(fp_query,"(");
                    }
                    select_fact
                    _close
                    {
                    fprintf(fp_query,")");
                    }
            | select_fact
            | error
                    {
                    strcpy(err_message,
                      "**** Syntax error : Invalid select clause");
                    throw_away();
                    yyerrok;
                    yyclearin;
                    } query
    select_fact : _fieldfile
                    {
                    found = -1;
```

```
        för (count=0;count < field_no; ++count)
                    if (strcmp(yytext,field_name[count])==0)
                    {
                            found = count;
                            break;
                    }
            if (found == -1)
            {
                    strcpy(err_message,"**** Field not found : ");
                    strcat(err_message,yytext);
                    yyerror(err_message);
            }
            fprintf(fp_query,"$%d",found+1);
            } oper _value
            {
            fprintf(fp_query,"%s",yytext);
            }
oper        : _greater
                {
                fprintf(fp_query,">");
                }

        | _equal
                {
                fprintf(fp_query,"==");
                }
        | _less
                {
                fprintf(fp_query,"<");
                }
        | _greateq
                {
                fprintf(fp_query,">=");
                }
        | _lesseq
                {
                fprintf(fp_query,"<=");
                }
        | error
                {
                strcpy(err_message,
                  "**** Syntax error : <, >, >=, = or <= expected");
                throw_away();
```

```
            yyerrok;
                  yyclearin;
                  } query
  print_clause : print_clause _comma
                  {
                  fprintf(fp_query,",");
                  }
                       _fieldfile
                  {
                  found = -1;
                  for (count=0;count < field_no; ++count)
                        if (strcmp(yytext,field_name[count])==0) {
                                found = count;
                                break;
                        }
                  if (found == -1) {
                        strcpy(err_message,"Field not found : ");
                        strcat(err_message,yytext);
                        yyerror(err_message);
                  }
                  fprintf(fp_query,"$%d",found+1);
                  }
          | _fieldfile
                  {
                  found = -1;
                  for (count=0;count < field_no; ++count)
                        if (strcmp(yytext,field_name[count])==0) {
                                found = count;
                                break;
                        }
                  if (found == -1) {
                        strcpy(err_message,"Field not found : ");
                        strcat(err_message,yytext);
                        yyerror(err_message);
                  }
                  fprintf(fp_query,"$%d",found+1);
                  }
          | error
                  {
                  strcpy(err_message,
                        "**** Syntax error : error in print clause");
                  throw_away();
                  yyerrok;
```

```
        yyclearin;
                } query
%%
yyerror(str)
char *str;
{
        strcpy(last_token,yytext);
        error_ind =1;
}

throw_away()
{
        while (yytext[0] != ';' )
                yylex();
}
```

There are many things worth noting in this *yacc* specifications file. First, we have extended our grammar to accommodate more than one query. We have also introduced a semicolon as a query delimiter. This delimiter will be used for error recovery. The first production rule is left recursive to enable multiple queries. It would have been possible to achieve the same using right recursion; however, as stated earlier, *yacc* does not encourage the use of right recursion. We close the query file whenever we encounter a semicolon and then execute the file. A semicolon at the end of an error query is taken care of in the *lex* specifications file. The next section discusses the error recovery features that were incorporated in the query processor.

3.3.9 Error-Handling Techniques

Yacc provides some features for error handling. These features are not very powerful, but if used properly they can provide easy and elegant recovery from a parsing error. We will not make an attempt to study the implementation of *yacc* in order to understand how it provides error recovery, but we will concentrate on a simple technique that will suffice for most applications.

Yacc provides a token named *error* that is used exclusively for error handling. It is used to indicate the occurrence of an error token. For example, in the query processor the production rule for conjunction indicates that the nonterminal *conj* could either be an _*and*, an _*or*, or an error token. It is here that appropriate code to recover from a syntax error is introduced. The first step is to decide upon a token up to which we can skip after encountering an error. The second step is to find a symbol from which we can start. In our query processor, we decide to skip up to a semicolon and start looking for a new query; therefore our error production rules have an error token followed by a query symbol. In between these, we have the error recovery code in which we execute three statements. The first statement is an invocation of the function *throw_away*, which skips all tokens up to a semicolon. The next two statements merely indicate to the parser that we have recovered from the error and that the present look-ahead token should be cleared.

If we do not perform any actions upon encountering an error token, the default action is to call the function *yyerror* and to terminate parsing after this function is executed. This function can be provided by the user. The argument to this function is a string which is typically an error message to be displayed. Since this function is invoked every time an error occurs, it is an appropriate place to store the error token in a string, so that we can report it when we encounter a newline character. When a query is parsed correctly, we close the query file and execute it. The modified segment of the *lex* specifications file is as follows:

```
;                       {
                        ECHO;
                        /*   If no error was encountered in the query   */
                        /*   execute the awk file of the query          */
                        if (error_ind != 0)
                        {
                                fclose(fp_query);
                                fopen("query","w");
                                printf("\n");
                                error_ind =0;
                        }
                        return(_semi);
                        }
        [\n]            {
                        ECHO;
                        /* Check if an error is pending to be reported */
                        if (strlen(err_message) > 0)
                        {
                                fprintf(stderr,"%s\n",err_message);
                                fprintf(stderr,
                                  "** Last token parsed was %s\n",last_token);
                        }
                        err_message[0] = NULL;
                        }
```

The rest of the lex specifications file requires no change.

3.3.10 More on Error Handling

The modified *lex* specifications file shows how error reporting can be done elegantly and without many complications. We report an error message only when we encounter a newline character in the input. This keeps error messages on separate lines. The error message itself is stored in a string upon the occurrence of an error token, which may have occurred several tokens before the occurrence of the newline character. When an error token occurs, we skip up to a semicolon. This indicates that a semicolon may be passed as a token to the *throw_away* function rather than to the main parser. This would occur only during an occurrence of an error. The *lex* specifications file handles this situation by checking for the *error_ind* flag when a semicolon is encountered. If we are presently reading an error query, we close the query file and reopen it. This eliminates the execution of an incomplete *awk* statement as a result of the error query. A fresh query file is opened for a new *awk* statement which will correspond to the next input query.

While there are other methods of handling errors in *yacc*, the method used for the query parser is sufficient for most applications. This example illustrates a strategy to recover from an error token. It does not make any attempt to explain how *yacc* actually implements this recovery feature. A knowledge of parsing techniques and an understanding of the implementation details of *yacc* are necessary to understand further details about the complicated world of error recovery in parser generators like *yacc*.

3.3.11 Predefined Pseudovariables

The value returned by the lexical analyzer for each token can be accessed and manipulated within a *yacc* rule. Predefined pseudovariables are used to access these values. These variables begin with a dollar sign ($) and are followed by an integer. The integer refers to the position of the terminal symbol within the rule. The special pseudovariable $0 refers to the left-hand nonterminal symbol. In the rule:

```
result: VAR1 + VAR2 + VAR3
        { $0 = $1 + $3 +$5; };
```

$1 would be assigned the value of *VAR1*, *$2* would be assigned the value returned by the terminal symbol +, and so on until *$5* is assigned the value returned by *VAR3*. The result of the computation is assigned to the nonterminal *result*. Predefined pseudovariables are particularly helpful during

the parsing and evaluation of arithmetic expressions.

3.3.12 Handling Ambiguous Grammars

Ambiguous grammars are grammars which may generate a conflict during the process of parsing. Consider the following grammar, designed to generate a parser which will parse a very small subset of arithmetic expressions:

```
%token _integer
%%
expression : expression '+' expression
           | expression '*' expression
           | _integer
%%
```

This grammar is ambiguous because when the parser encounters an expression like *32 + 43 * 23*, it does not know whether to interpret it as *(32 + 43) * 23* or *32 + (43 * 23)*. The first interpretation involves a reduction upon encountering the first three tokens. The alternative interpretation involves a shift upon encountering the same tokens. Reduction implies evaluation of the parsed tokens. Shift implies looking forward for another token and postponing the evaluation of the tokens encountered. These conflicts are reported by *yacc* as warning messages; however, *yacc* will use its own disambiguating rules to resolve such conflicts. It is advisable to detect the productions that are responsible for these conflicts. *Yacc* provides a −*v* option that creates a file called y.output that lets you have an insight into the working of the parser. The y.output for the ambiguous grammar under consideration is as follows:

```
state 0
        $accept : _expression $end
        _integer   shift 2
        .  error
        expression   goto 1

state 1
        $accept :  expression_$end
        expression :   expression_+ expression
        expression :   expression_* expression
        $end   accept
        +   shift 3
```

```
     *   shift 4
     .   error


state 2
        expression :  _integer_      (3)
        .  reduce 3
state 3
        expression :  expression +_expression
        _integer  shift 2
        .  error
        expression  goto 5
state 4
        expression :  expression *_expression
        _integer  shift 2
        .  error
        expression  goto 6
5: shift/reduce conflict (shift 3, red'n 1) on +
5: shift/reduce conflict (shift 4, red'n 1) on *
state 5
        expression :  expression_+ expression
        expression :  expression + expression_      (1)
        expression :  expression_* expression
        +   shift 3
        *   shift 4
        .  reduce 1


6: shift/reduce conflict (shift 3, red'n 2) on +
6: shift/reduce conflict (shift 4, red'n 2) on *
state 6
        expression :  expression_+ expression
        expression :  expression_* expression
        expression :  expression * expression_      (2)
        +   shift 3
        *   shift 4
        .  reduce 2
5/127 terminals, 1/300 nonterminals
4/600 grammar rules, 7/750 states
4 shift/reduce, 0 reduce/reduce conflicts reported
4/350 working sets used
memory: states,etc. 45/12000, parser 2/12000
3/600 distinct lookahead sets
0 extra closures
9 shift entries, 1 exceptions
```

```
3 goto entries
0 entries saved by goto default
Optimizer space used: input 25/12000, output 9/12000
9 table entries, 3 zero
maximum spread: 257, maximum offset: 257
```

The above output gives a lot of information about the parser. We will look at a section that gives us information about the various conflicts that could arise during parsing:

```
5: shift/reduce conflict (shift 3, red'n 1) on +
5: shift/reduce conflict (shift 4, red'n 1) on *
state 5
        expression :  expression_+ expression
        expression :  expression + expression_     (1)
        expression :  expression_* expression
        +  shift 3
        *  shift 4
        .  reduce 1
```

The underscore character tells us that the parser has seen the input to the right of it. Now, the parser has three possible alternatives: it could reduce the expression that it has just seen; or, if the input symbol is a +, it could shift into state 3; or, if the input symbol is a *, it could shift into state 4. In *yacc* specifications files, with many production rules, the y.output file can be used in locating ambiguous production rules; *yacc* by itself will only report the number of occurrences of ambiguous production rules and not the rules themselves. For most practical purposes, this is the main use of the y.output file. It is almost always possible to rewrite an ambiguous grammar into a nonambiguous grammar. This can be a tedious task and at times even unnecessary; however, at times when the parser starts behaving strangely, it may be worthwhile going through the y.output file.

3.3.13 A Final Note on Yacc

We have seen some of the major features of *yacc*. *Yacc* provides some more features which are mostly helpful for resolving ambiguities. Once you have understood the features of *yacc* presented in this section, you will find it easy to grasp more advanced features. Finally, now that you know *yacc*, you will no longer have to deal with cryptic languages as you can start writing your own translators!

3.4   M4: A Macro Processor

M4 is a macro processor that can be used for a variety of purposes. Its primary use is as a front end to language compilers like C, FORTRAN, and Pascal. It can also be used as a simple filter to translate nonprogramming input text. It has capabilities to handle arguments, to perform arithmetic computations, to include external files, and to divert processed files for later inclusion. It provides conditional operations reminiscent of the *if-else* statement of programming languages, and it also supports a range of string manipulating functions.

3.4.1   Getting Started

Like most UNIX filters, *m4* reads from the standard input or from the specified file(s). The processed output is written to the standard output. Macros can be either user-defined or built-in. Users can define their own macros by using the built-in macro *define*.

Some programmers like the use of *begin* and *end* to enclose program blocks and compound statements. C provides the use of { and } to perform the same function. Here is a sample input to *m4* which can be used by those who write programs using *begin* and *end*. The output of *m4* is an equivalent C program which uses { and }.

```
cat inp.m
define(begin,{)
define(end,})
main()
begin
        printf("%s is the first argument\n",argv[1]);
        func(argv[1]);
end
func(str)
char str[];
begin
        for (i=0;i<strlen(str);++i)
                    printf("%c\n",str[i]);
end
m4 inp.m


main()
```

```
{
        printf("%s is the first argument\n",argv[1]);
        func(argv[1]);
}
func(str)
char str[];
{
        for (i=0;i<strlen(str);++i)
                printf("%c\n",str[i]);
}
```

M4 has replaced the character string *begin* with { and the character string *end* with }. This was specified as input to the *m4* processor by the use of the *define* statements. Note that the input text has changed so that only the macro names have been expanded. All other characters, including newline characters, have been copied out verbatim. This is probably the simplest possible use of the *m4* macro processor. The following sections discuss more useful and interesting features of *m4*.

3.4.2 Suppressing Macro Expansion

Sometimes there are situations in which a macro expansion is to be suppressed. Consider the following input text:

```
define(begin,{)
define(end,})
main()
begin
        printf("begin : %s is the first argument\n",argv[1]);
        func(argv[1]);
end
```

Clearly, the *begin* in the *printf* statement is not to be expanded. This calls for a mechanism to suppress the macro expansion. The left and right single quotes are used for suppressing macro expansion. Thus the *begin* in the *printf* statement can be protected from *m4* expansion as follows:

```
define(begin,{)
define(end,})
main()
begin
        printf("'begin' : %s is the first argument\n",argv[1]);
        func(argv[1]);
end
```

M4 always strips one level of single quotes; the input text

```
define(str,4)
This is an input text to m4.
Here is a string to be processed by m4: str
Here is a double quoted string ''str''
and here is a single quoted string 'str'
and watch this: ''''
define(str2,str)
Here is another string to be processed by m4: str2
```

will be evaluated by *m4* as

```
This is an input text to m4.
Here is a string to be processed by m4: 4
Here is a double quoted string 'str'
and here is a single quoted string str
and watch this: ''

Here is another string to be processed by m4: 4
```

Note that a macro can be defined using another macro. Macro *str2* has been defined using macro *str*. Also, note the blank line in the output text. Can you explain why it is there?

The right and left quote characters for suppressing macro expansions can be changed by using the built-in macro *changequote*. Thus the % character can be made the new quote character by using the *changequote* macro:

```
changequote(%,%)
```

The quote characters can be restored by the use of the *changequote* function without any arguments.

3.4.3 More on Macro Definitions

Macros can be removed by the use of the built-in macro *undefine*; thus, *undefine('str2')* will remove the definition of the macro *str2*. It is possible to check whether a macro has been defined by the use of the *ifdef* function. The syntax of ifdef is

```
ifdef(ifmac,arg1,arg2)
```

where *ifmac* is any quoted macro string. If this macro is defined, the value of *ifdef* is the second argument, *arg1*, otherwise the value of *ifdef* is the third argument, *arg2*. The following example illustrates the use of *ifdef*:

```
cat example.m
define(newmac,100)
ifdef('newmac',defined,not_defined)
ifdef('notdef',DEFINED,not_DEFINED)
m4 example.m

defined
not_DEFINED
```

3.4.4 Processing Arguments

M4 macros can also handle arguments. Arguments in macros are syntactically similar to arguments in shell scripts. Thus *$1* refers to the first argument, *$2* refers to the second argument and *$n* refers to the *n*th argument. Thus the macro

```
define(somemac,$1*$3+$2)
```

when invoked as

```
somemac(12,32,43)
```

will generate

```
12*43+32
```

Only arguments *$1* to *$9* are accessible. *$0* gives the name of the macro itself. Arguments can be very skillfully used to create powerful macro substitution facility. In the following example, the function *strcmp3* outputs C code to check that the three strings passed to this macro as arguments are the same. It returns a value of zero if the three strings are the same and a nonzero value otherwise.

```
define(st,strcmp)
define(strcmp3,'if (st($1,$2)==0) return(st($2,$3));else return(-1)')
```

It is a good practice to quote the substitution text while defining macros.

3.4.5 Arithmetic Manipulation

M4 also provides a simple mechanism, the built-in macro *eval*, which can perform arbitrary arithmetic on integers. Here is a simple example:

```
cat some_input
define(M, 'eval($1*$2)')
M(10,5)
m4 some_input

50
```

The macro arguments have not only been expanded but they have also been evaluated.

3.4.6 Diversions and Inclusions

M4 provides a capability to divert the output of processing into temporary files. These diversions can be reinstalled at a later time. Output can be diverted into nine possible diversions. The built-in macro *divert* sends the output to the specified diversion. This diversion continues until the macro *divert* is encountered without any argument. The diversion can be reinstalled by the use of the macro *undivert*. Here is an example:

```
cat example.m
This example illustrates the use of the diversion
mechanism in macro processing. Let us 'divert' the
next two lines of text into diversion number 1. divert(1)
This is a line to be diverted
This is another line to be diverted
divert()End of diversion.
This line  follows the diversion.
Let us invoke the diversion here. undivert(1)
The invocation of the diversion ends here.
m4 example.m
This example illustrates the use of the diversion
mechanism in macro processing. Let us divert the
next two lines of text into diversion number 1. End of diversion.
This line  follows the diversion.
Let us invoke the diversion here.
This is a line to be diverted
This is another line to be diverted

The invocation of the diversion ends here.
```

It is possible to include external files by the use of the built-in macro *include*. Thus *include(incl_file)* will include the file incl_file at the point where the invocation is made.

3.4.7 Other Features

M4 also provides many other built-in macros which can be used for various purposes. The *ifelse* built-in macro can be used to evaluate conditionals. The general syntax is

```
ifelse(str1,str2,str3,str4,str5,str6,str7.....);
```

where *str1*, *str2*, *str3*..... are different strings. First string *str1* is compared to *str2*. If they are equal, the result is *str3*, otherwise *str4* is compared to *str5* and if they are the same strings, the result is *str6*, otherwise the result is *str7*. This evaluation process continues until a value is found or until the arguments are exhausted. If the required argument is missing the result is the null string. The following examples show various forms of the *ifelse* macro evaluation process:

```
cat example.m
***** Example 1 ********
ifelse(abcd,abcd,defg)
***** Example 2 ********
ifelse(abcd,bccd,defg,pqrs,pqrs,rstu)
***** Example 3 ********
ifelse(abcd,abcd)
***** Example 4 ********
ifelse(abcd,bacd,defg,pqrs)
m4 example.m
***** Example 1 ********
defg
***** Example 2 ********
rstu
***** Example 3 ********

***** Example 4 ********
pqrs
```

In example 3, the third string was missing. The *ifelse* was therefore evaluated as a null string.

M4 also provides many built-in macros for string manipulation. The most commonly used string-manipulating macros are explained in Table 3.2. Let us use some of these macros:

```
***** Example 1 ********
substr(abcd,1,2)
***** Example 2 ********
index(abcd,bc)  index(abcd,ad)
***** Example 3 ********
define(CONST,100)dnl
***** Example 4 ********
len(abcd','abcd)
***** Example 5 ********
translit(abcdef,ade,145)
```

When these examples are given as input, *m4* will produce the following output:

```
***** Example 1 ********
bc
***** Example 2 ********
1 -1
***** Example 3 ********
***** Example 4 ********
9
***** Example 5 ********
1bc45f
```

The comma in the last example has to be quoted to protect it from being interpreted as an argument separator. Without these quotes, *m4* would have returned a string length of 4.

TABLE 3.2 String-Manipulating Macros

Macro	Use
substr(str,s,l)	Returns the substring of string *str* starting at position *s* and of length *l*. If *l* is omitted, the rest of the string starting at position *s* is returned.
len(str)	Returns the length of the string *str*.
index(str1,str2)	Returns the position in string *str1* where string *str2* starts. If *str2* is not found in *str1* a value of -1 is returned.
translit(str1,str2,str3)	Translates characters in string *str1* which are also found in string *str2*. The resulting characters in *str1* are the characters in *str3* which correspond to characters in *str2*.
dnl	Deletes all characters following it up to and including the newline character

3.4.8 A Bit of Advice

M4 will expand all macros known to it. Users cannot be expected to know all the available macros, and therefore some words in the input text may be erroneously interpreted as macros. One of the possible solutions is to redefine each macro as follows:

```
define(_LEN_,defn('len')) undefine('len')
```

This command, for example, will rename the macro *len* to *_LEN_*. The macro *defn* returns the quoted definition of its arguments. Another precaution is to change the quote characters as explained earlier using the built-in macro *changequote*.

4 System Development Tools

The UNIX operating system is very rich in utilities that help the programmer and the system analyst in developing programs and systems. We saw the use of debuggers in Chapter 2. While the purpose of a debugger is to help a programmer find bugs, it is often necessary to optimize the execution efficiency of these programs. *Lint* is a UNIX utility that helps in writing C programs which are free from bugs and which are space efficient, clean, and portable. It also detects syntax errors in C programs.

Systems are normally developed as a group of programs rather than as a single program. These programs are often developed by a team of programmers. It is necessary to coordinate the interrelationship of the various programs. *Make* is the UNIX utility that is helpful for maintaining the interrelationship. Once the system is developed, or during the various phases of the development of the system, various versions have to be maintained. UNIX provides its own Source Code Control System (SCCS) to maintain the different versions. *Prof* and *gprof* are tools that can be used to improve the execution efficiency of any program. These are the utilities that we will study in this chapter. The use of these utilities can greatly reduce the development time of any project. Software products which make use of these utilities are also easy to maintain.

4.1 Lint: A C Program Checker

C is a not a strongly typed language. This characteristic of the C programming language allows many programs to pass error free through the compiler. Equivalent programs written in a language like Pascal would not enjoy such a relatively easy passage through the compiler. Apart from weak type checking, the C compiler also does not provide for any compile-time checking of array subscripts or argument types. *Lint* is a program that reports the various inconsistencies that can exist in a program. Portability aspects are also reported by *lint*.

4.1.1 Lint: Getting Started

Here is a simple C program that computes the square root of a number:*

```
    cat lint1.c
 1  #include <stdio.h>
 2  main(argc,argv)
 3  int argc;
 4  char **argv;
 5  {
 6      int i,number;
 7      double sqrt();
 8      number = atoi(argv[1]);
 9      printf("%.02f is the square root of %d\n",
10              sqrt((float)number),number);
11  }
```

This program computes the square root of an integer that is passed to it as its first argument. Let us pass it through *lint* and see what it has to report about the program:

```
lint lint1.c
lint1.c
==============
(6)  warning: i unused in function main
(11)  warning: main() returns random value to invocation environment
warning: argument unused in function:
    (3)  argc in main
==============
```

---

*Line numbers shown in the examples are not part of the program or file.

```
name used but not defined
    sqrt        lint1.c(10)
function returns value which is always ignored
    printf
```

(The numbers in parentheses indicate line numbers in the program.) The first warning reported by *lint* informs us that the variable *i* was declared but never used in the program. The second warning informs us that the function *main* does not return any value while exiting. The argument *argc* in the function *main* is also unused and this is reported by *lint*. In addition, the function *sqrt* was not defined in this program file. It is a math library function; *lint* does not know about this and hence complains.

Lint expects the programmer to use the value returned by every function. While this is a good practice, it is not always necessary to do so. In the program lint1.c, the value returned by the *printf* function is not used and *lint* does not miss reporting it. In this example, *lint* was used to find unused variables, undefined functions, and functions which returned a value that was never used. Unused variables are often a source of storage inefficiency.

Programs are usually developed in modules and each module is tested separately. *Lint* will continue to report warnings about functions that are not defined in the same program module. The −*u* option can be used to suppress such complaints. This option can also be used to suppress complaints about external variables which are defined and not used or used and not defined. *Lint* will report the following warnings on the file lint1.c when used with the −*u* option:[*]

```
lint -u lint1.c
lint1.c
==============
(6)   warning: i unused in function main
(11)   warning: main() returns random value to invocation environment
warning: argument unused in function:
    (3)   argc in main
==============
function returns value which is always ignored
    printf
```

Clearly the complaint about the function *sqrt* has been suppressed.

Lint also reports problems in which a function may be defined but not used. Let us look at one such program and see how *lint* helps us in detecting such unused functions. This program simply reads an input number and checks to see if that number is a positive integer. It reports an error message if the input

---

[*]Output shown in the examples corresponds to lint version 1.5 on UNIX System V.

number is not a positive integer. The function *perror* is wrongly invoked instead of the function *merror*.

```
    cat lint2.c
1   #include <stdio.h>
2   main()
3   {
4       int number,eof;
5       printf("Input any positive number ");
6       eof=scanf("%d",&number);
7       if ((eof != 1) || ( number < 0 ))
8               perror();
9   }
10  merror()
11  {
12  fprintf(stderr,"The input number is not a positive integer\n");
13  }
```

Let us pass this program through *lint*:

```
lint lint2.c
lint2.c
===============
(9)  warning: main() returns random value to invocation environment
===============
name defined but never used
    merror      lint2.c(11)
value type declared inconsistently
    perror      llib-lc(357) :: lint2.c(8)
function called with variable number of arguments
    perror      llib-lc(357) :: lint2.c(8)
function returns value which is always ignored
    printf          fprintf
```

Lint reports that the function *merror* has been defined but not used. The function *perror* is actually a system function that has been wrongly invoked with the wrong number and type of arguments. *Lint* also reports this error. Note that none of these errors would be detected by the C compiler.

4.1.2 Using a Variable before Setting It

In C, automatic and register variables are uninitialized. It is always a good
practice to initialize these variables before they are used. If a variable is used
before it is initialized, the results are unpredictable; *lint* reports such
situations. *Lint* uses an algorithm for detecting such cases. This algorithm
excludes situations in which *goto* statements are used extensively.

Here is a C program that is used to check to see if an input number exists
in a given list of integers. The list is read from a file called list. An
appropriate message is printed to indicate if the match was successful.

```
        cat lint3.c
    1   #include <stdio.h>
    2   main()
    3   {
    4       int i,list[10],input,eof;
    5       FILE *fp,*fopen();
    6
    7   /* Open the file having the list of numbers */
    8       fp = fopen("list","r");
    9
   10   /* read the list of numbers into the required array */
   11       while(1)
   12       {
   13               eof=fscanf(fp,"%d",&list[i++]);
   14               if ((eof==EOF)||(i==10)) break;
   15       }
   16
   17   /* Read the required input number */
   18       printf("Input the number to be searched :");
   19       eof=scanf("%d",&input);
   20       if (eof != 1)
   21       {
   22       fprintf(stderr,"Error in reading the input number\n");
   23       exit(-1);
   24       }
   25
   26   /* Check if the input number exists in the list */
   27       for (i=0;i<10;++i)
   28               if (list[i]==input)
   29               {
   30               printf("Matched\n");
```

```
31                 break;
32              }
33
34   /* If the number does not exist print the error message */
35      if (i==10)
36              printf("No match\n");
37   }
```

Let us pass this program through *lint*:

```
lint lint3.c
lint3.c
==============
(13)  warning: i may be used before set
(37)  warning: main() returns random value to invocation environment
==============
value type declared inconsistently
    exit        llib-lc(45) :: lint3.c(23)
function returns value which is always ignored
    printf          fprintf
```

Lint reports that the variable *i* was used before it was initialized. Indeed, we presumed that the value of *i* was zero in line 13 when we first used it. This is not necessarily true, and *lint* is a good tool to report such cases. In addition, *lint* flags a warning message about the exit function. The exit function returns a value of type *void*! This is not explicitly declared in the program and a return value of type *int* is assumed. This inconsistency is reported by *lint*. Other warnings reported by *lint* were explained in the previous example.

4.1.3 Infinite Loops and Unreachable Statements

Lint attempts to detect infinite loops and unreachable statements. Specifically, possibilities of infinite loops caused by *while* or *for* statements are detected. Unreachable statements are normally unlabeled statements following a *return*, *goto*, *break*, or *continue* statement. Here is an example in which *lint* reports unreachable statements:

```
cat lint4.c
1   somefunction(i,j)
2   int i,j;
3   {
4       int p;
5       p=i+j;
6       if (p>10)
7               return(p);
8       else
9               return(12.52);
10      p=i*j;
11  }
```

Lint reports the unreachable statement as follows:

```
lint lint4.c
lint4.c
===============
(11)  warning: function somefunction has return(e); and return;
warning: statement not reached
    (10)
===============
name defined but never used
    somefunction        lint4.c(3)
```

Lint reports here that the statement in line 10 will never be executed. Most C compilers would also report this problem. The inconsistency in the return value of the function is also reported. In addition, *lint* also reported that the function *somefunction* is defined but not used.

Some programmers use the *break* statement in a switch statement for the sake of consistency, as in the following:

```
cat lint5.c
1   extern ERROR;
2   simple_func(i,j)
3   int i,j;
4   {
5       switch(i)
6       {
7       case 1: return(1);
8               break;
9       case 2: return(32);
```

```
10              break;
11      default: return(ERROR);
12              break;
13      }
14  }
```

Lint will report all the *break* statements as unreachable, as indeed they are!

```
lint -u lint5.c
lint5.c

==============
(14)  warning: function simple_func has return(e); and return;
warning: argument unused in function:
    (3)   j in simple_func
warning: statement not reached
    (8)             (10)            (12)
```

Programs generated by *yacc* and *lex* have many such switch statements. Statements about unreachable *breaks* can be suppressed by the −*b* option. In addition the −*v* argument can be used to suppress complaints about arguments not used in a function; thus the following *lint* report suppresses most complaints reported earlier:

```
lint -ubv lint5.c
lint5.c

==============
(14)  warning: function simple_func has return(e); and return;
```

4.1.4 Type-Checking Features

Lint offers type-checking features that are not offered by the C compiler. When operands of various types appear in an expression, these operands are converted to a common type. While the free use of operands of various types is one of the powerful features of the C language, it is often a source of bugs. *Lint* provides type-checking features which include

1. Checking the data types of function arguments.
2. Checking the data types of the values returned by functions.

3. Checking the data types of the operands of the -> and . operators.
4. Assigning integers to pointers.
5. Checking assignments of pointers to various data types.

Here is a program to illustrate the type checking features of *lint*:

```
cat lint6.c
1  #include <stdio.h>
2  main()
3  {
4    int eof,number;
5    while(1)
6    {
7      eof = scanf("%d",&number);
8      if (eof == EOF) break;
9      printf("The square root of %d is %f\n",number,sqrt(number));
10   }
11 }
```

The program prints the square root of any integer that is read from the standard input. The library function *sqrt* actually returns a value of type *double*. It also takes an argument which is of type *double*. We have not indicated this in our program. As a result, the program is very likely to give wrong results. The C compiler will not flag any warnings to indicate the possibility of a bug. Let us see what *lint* has to say about this program:

```
lint lint6.c -lm
lint6.c
===============
(11)  warning: main() returns random value to invocation environment
===============
value type used inconsistently
    sqrt        llib-lm(20) :: lint6.c(9)
value type declared inconsistently
    sqrt        llib-lm(20) :: lint6.c(9)
function argument ( number ) used inconsistently
    sqrt( arg 1 )       llib-lm(20) :: lint6.c(9)
function returns value which is always ignored
    printf
```

The −*lm* option directs lint to the math library for linking functions not defined in the program file. *Lint* reports that the argument to *sqrt* and the value returned by *sqrt* have been declared and used inconsistently. This example illustrates how *lint* can be used to detect bugs. Clearly, the program would not run correctly without some changes in the declarations. *Lint* will also complain about assignment of integers to pointers. When a *long* is assigned to an *int*, there is a likelihood of some truncation in the value. Such cases are also reported by *lint*.

4.1.5 Miscellaneous Features of Lint

Lint also reports on statements that include other forms of redundancy and inconsistency. Consider the following program, which does virtually nothing:

```
     cat lint7.c
 1   main()
 2   {
 3       int i,*j;
 4       i = 35.0;
 5       j = &i;
 6       if (i==i)
 7           {
 8               *j--;
 9               i=j;
10           }
11   }
```

If we pass it through *lint*, it will report the following messages:

```
lint lint7.c
lint7.c
==============
(11)  warning: main() returns random value to invocation environment
warning: illegal combination of pointer and integer:
    (9)  operator =
warning: null effect
    (8)
```

Lint has cleverly reported all the inconsistencies and redundancies in the program.

4.1.6 Other Options in Lint

Lint can be invoked with several options. Some of the options in *lint* are not consistent across various versions of *lint*. While most of the *lint* options discussed in this chapter are generally available, it would be advisable to consult your local manual for more precise options. Some of the other options that can be used while invoking *lint* are explained in Table 4.1. The −*l* and the −*o* options are discussed in section 4.1.8.

4.1.7 Controlling Lint in C Programs

Lint recognizes certain comments in C programs which it uses to decide about the severity of error messages to report. Table 4.2 describes the various comments and their effect on *lint*. Programs lint8.c and lint9.c illustrate the use of *lint* directives in C programs. These programs compute the sum of two numbers. The function *add* returns the sum of two numbers. The third argument, *result*, is unused in the function.

TABLE 4.1 Other Options in Lint

Option	Effect
−a	Suppresses warnings for assignments of *long* ints to *ints*.
−p	Enables warning messages that detect portability problems.
−x	Suppresses warning messages about unused variables referred to by external declarations.
−h	Used to to make *lint* less strict about the errors that it reports. This option suppresses heuristic tests that attempt to intuit bugs, improve style, and reduce waste.
−o	Creates a *lint* library.
−l	Refers to a *lint*-created library.

```
    cat lint8.c
 1  #include <stdio.h>
 2  main()
 3  {
 4      int    int1,int2,eof;
 5      eof=scanf("%d%d",&int1,&int2);
 6      if (eof != 2)
 7              exit(-1);
 8      printf("Add. result is %d\n",add(int1,int2));
 9  }
10  add(x,y,result)
11  int x,y,*result;
12  {
13      return(x+y);
14  }
```

Let us run *lint* on program lint8.c

```
lint lint8.c
lint8.c
===============
(9)  warning: main() returns random value to invocation environment
warning: argument unused in function:
    (11)   result in add
===============
value type declared inconsistently
    exit        llib-lc(45) :: lint8.c(7)
function called with variable number of arguments
    add         lint8.c(12) :: lint8.c(8)
function returns value which is always ignored
    printf
```

If the −*v* option is used, *lint* reports the following:

```
lint -v lint8.c
lint8.c
===============
(9)  warning: main() returns random value to invocation environment
===============
value type declared inconsistently
    exit        llib-lc(45) :: lint8.c(7)
```

```
function called with variable number of arguments
     add          lint8.c(12) :: lint8.c(8)
function returns value which is always ignored
     printf
```

TABLE 4.2 Lint Directives

Comment	Meaning
/* NOT REACHED */	Suppresses warning messages about statements that *lint* thinks are unreachable.
/* NOSTRICT */	Suppresses strict type checking for the next expression.
/* ARGSUSED */	Temporarily enables the -*v* option for the present function.
/* VARARGS*n* */	If a function definition is preceded by this comment, *lint* will check for the first *n* arguments of this function in all function calls.

Lint complains about inconsistencies in the number of arguments in the function *add*. It also complains about the unused argument *result* in the same function. The −*v* option was used to suppress warnings about unused arguments. Now let us use *lint* directives in the above program to suppress these warnings:

```
    cat lint9.c
1   #include <stdio.h>
2   main()
3   {
4       int    int1,int2,eof;
5       eof=scanf("%d%d",&int1,&int2);
6       if (eof != 2)
7               exit(-1);
8       printf("Add. result is %d\n",add(int1,int2));
9   }
10  /* VARARGS */
11  /* ARGSUSED */
12  add(x,y,result)
13  int x,y,*result;
14  {
15      return(x+y);
16  }
```

With the directives inserted, *lint* reports as follows:

```
lint lint9.c
lint9.c
==============
(9)  warning: main() returns random value to invocation environment
==============
value type declared inconsistently
    exit         llib-lc(45) :: lint9.c(7)
function returns value which is always ignored
    printf
```

In the modified version of the program with *lint* directives, *lint* did not complain about a variable number of arguments in the function *add* because of the directive /* VARARGS */. It did not complain about unused arguments because of the use of the *lint* directive /* ARGSUSED */.

4.1.8 Lint Libraries

In projects involving multiple files, *lint* will need the definition of functions declared in other files to suppress spurious warning messages. These *lint* libraries can be created by using the −*o* option on the *lint* command line. These libraries can be subsequently referenced by the use of the −*l* option or by specifying the full names of the library files. If c1.c is the program file with the function *func1* and if c2.c is the program file that uses the function *func2*, then a *lint* library can be created and used, as shown below:

```
    cat c1.c
1   func1(i,j)
2   int *i,j;
3   {
4       j= *i +j;
5   }

    cat c2.c
1   func2()
2   {
3       func1();
4   }
```

```
lint -o nlib cl.c
===============
name defined but never used
    func1        cl.c(3)
lint c2.c llib-lnlib.ln
===============
name defined but never used
    func2        c2.c(2)
function called with variable number of arguments
    func1        cl.c(3) :: c2.c(3)
```

In the second invocation of *lint*, we did not use the −*l* option to use the newly created *lint* library but instead used the name of the *lint*-created library file. This was necessary because the library file was not moved to the *lint* library directory where *lint* stores its libraries.

4.2 Make: A Program to Maintain Programs

Most programming projects involve a large number of programs or modules. Each module has a role in the system and these modules are linked to each other to produce the final system. Each module has a corresponding set of source programs, some of which are shared by the various modules. The source programs undergo various changes as the system is enhanced or modified. In large projects it is very difficult to keep track of all the files which have undergone changes. Subsequently, in the absence of *make*, when a new version is to be installed, all the source files are compiled and linked because it may be a tedious process to find only those files which need to be recompiled and linked. It is much more efficient to have only the affected modules recompiled.

Make is a utility that helps us to maintain projects involving many programs. It stores the dependencies between the various files and creates object modules only if they have not been updated since the files on which they depend were updated. It also reports about missing files. It has some built-in knowledge about target file creation based on file suffixes.

4.2.1 Getting Started with Make

The most important file required when *make* is used is the Makefile. Actually, this file can have any of the names makefile, Makefile, s.makefile, or s.Makefile. This file stores the description of the various dependencies between the files involved in the system. The *make* command reads this file and decides on the action to be taken to create the required target files. Consider a program called final which can be obtained by linking the three object modules mod1.o, mod2.o, and mod3.o. This dependency can be made known to *make* by the line

```
final : mod1.o mod2.o mod3.o
```

To get the file final from the three separate object modules, it is necessary to run the following command:

```
cc -o final mod1.o mod2.o mod3.o
```

The three modules mod1.o, mod2.o and mod3.o depend on the C source files mod1.c, mod2.c, and mod3.c respectively. Figure 4.1 illustrates the dependencies between the various files in the system.

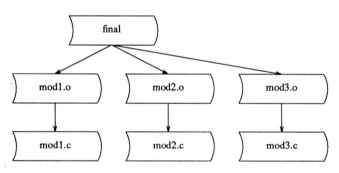

Figure 4.1 Dependencies for Make

These dependencies can be expressed in the Makefile as follows:

```
mod1.o : mod1.c
mod2.o : mod2.c
mod3.o : mod3.c
```

The three object modules can be created from their source files by running the commands

```
cc -c mod1.c
cc -c mod2.c
cc -c mod3.c
```

Now that we know the dependencies and also the commands to be run to get the required object modules from the source files, let us tie this information together in the Makefile:

```
cat Makefile
final : mod1.o mod2.o mod3.o
        cc -o final mod1.o mod2.o mod3.o
mod1.o : mod1.c
        cc -c mod1.c
mod2.o : mod2.c
        cc -c mod2.c
mod3.o : mod3.c
        cc -c mod3.c
```

The Makefile listed above has two kinds of lines. Lines with colons in them describe the dependencies. The files to the left of the colons are the target files; the files to the right of the colons are the dependencies or the prerequisite files. All lines following these lines, beginning with a tab character and continuing up to the next line describing a dependency, are UNIX commands which specify how to get the target file from the dependencies. When we run the *make* command, it will try to create the target files only if the dependents are newer than the targets.

Let us look at various modification times for the dependents and see how the target files are updated. The creation/modification times are as follows:

Filename	Creation/Modification time
final	Dec 17 10:00:00 EDT 1986
mod1.o	Dec 14 9:00:00 EDT 1986
mod2.o	Dec 16 9:00:00 EDT 1986
mod3.o	Dec 15 11:00:00 EDT 1986
mod1.c	Dec 14 12:00:00 EDT 1986
mod2.c	Dec 14 11:00:00 EDT 1986
mod3.c	Dec 12 12:00:00 EDT 1986

Let us run *make*:

```
make
       cc -c mod1.c
       cc -o final mod1.o mod2.o mod3.o
```

Make understands that mod3.c is older than mod3.o and that therefore mod3.o is up to date. Similarly, *make* also understands that mod2.o is up to date; however, mod1.c was modified after the creation of mod1.o, and therefore mod1.o needs to be recreated, so *Make* runs the *cc −c mod1.c* command to create the mod1.o file. Finally, as a result of the recreation of the file mod1.o, the file final has also to be recreated. The command *cc −o final mod1.o mod2.o mod3.o* is run to create the final executable file final.

4.2.2 Internal Rules of Make

Make has a set of internal rules that it uses to create target files from the dependencies. These rules are used by *make* to create the target files in the absence of explicit specifications of these rules in the *make* description file. These rules are tabulated in Table 4.3. The *Target* column of the table refers to the file to be created, if necessary. The *Dependent* column refers to the file on which the target file depends, and the *Rule/commands* column shows how the target files are created.

These rules are sufficient for most applications. Later, we will see the use of some more inference rules. Since *yacc* and *lex* both generate C programs, *make* uses the *yacc/lex* file to generate the C source if it is necessary to do so. The resulting file is compiled to produce the .o file. If a .y or a .l file is not found in the directory, the .c file is compiled directly. It is important to understand that the inference rules may often encounter multiple paths they could follow in order to transform a file with one suffix to a file with another suffix. This problem is resolved by the use of the dependency list for *.SUFFIXES*. The default list for *.SUFFIXES* is

```
.SUFFIXES: .o .c .y .l .s
```

The order of the suffixes in the list is important. *Make* searches for files with any of the suffixes from the list. If multiple files are found, the order in the *.SUFFIXES* list is used to derive the target file. The significance of this list is demonstrated below by the use of *yacc*, *lex*, and C program files. The *.SUFFIXES* list has first to be cleared before setting it.

```
ls
try.y try.l try.c
cat makel
try.o :
touch try.y try.l
make -f makel
        yacc  try.y
        mv y.tab.c try.c
        cc -O -c try.c
cat make2
 .SUFFIXES :
 .SUFFIXES : .o .c .l .y .s
f2    : try.o
        cc -o f2  try.o
touch try.y try.l
make -f make2
        lex try.l
        mv lex.yy.c try.c
        cc -O -c try.c
```

TABLE 4.3 Internal Make Rules

Target	Dependent	Rule/commands
x.o	x.c	cc −c x.c
x.o	x.s	as −o x.s
x.o	x.y	yacc x.y
		cc −c y.tab.c
		rm y.tab.c
		mv y.tab.o x.o
x.o	x.l	lex x.l
		cc −c lex.yy.c
		rm -f lex.yy.c
		mv lex.yy.o x.o
x.c	x.y	yacc x.y
		mv y.tab.c x.c
x.c	x.l	lex x.l
		mv lex.yy.c x.c
x.a	x.c	cc −c x.c
		ar rv x.a x.o
		rm −f x.o

The *touch* command is used to update the modification times of the files. The *make* description file make1 uses the default *.SUFFIXES* list. It uses the try.y file to generate try.c. In the second example, the *.SUFFIXES* list has been changed so that the .1 appears before the .y. *Make* therefore gives try.1 a priority over the try.y file. In the second case, the try.c file is generated from the try.1 file. The *−f* option is used to specify the name of the *make* description file.

4.2.3 Macros and Comments in Make

Make has a very elementary macro substitution facility. Macro definitions have the general format

```
string1 = string2
```

All leading blanks and tabs from *string1* and all trailing blanks and tabs from *string2* are stripped. Subsequent occurrences of *$(string1)* are replaced by *string2*. Some examples of macro definitions are

```
LIBRARIES = /usr/local/lib1 /usr/local/lib2 /usr/local/lib3
2wert   =
cdebug = -g
```

The first example shows the use of macros to set the *LIBRARIES* string to a set of three blank-separated libraries. This form of macros is most useful for referring to multiple library files by a single name. The second example sets the macro *2wert* to the null string. In the final example, the macro *cdebug* is assigned the string *−g*.

Comments in the *make* description files are all characters starting from the sharp (#) sign up to the end of the line.

4.2.4 A More Advanced Example

As explained earlier, *make* is particularly useful when the number of files involved in a project is very high. Figure 4.2 illustrates the dependencies involved in the development of a query processor for a DBMS. The emphasis is on the dependencies of the various modules and not on the actual functions performed by each module. The hierarchy indicates that all the parent modules are dependent on the children modules. Thus module query depends on the modules qp.o, qex.o, and libs.a. Libs.a is a library file with two members, lib1.o and lib2.o. Lib1.o depends on the source files lib1.c, com.h, and lim.h. Other dependencies in the figure can be interpreted similarly.

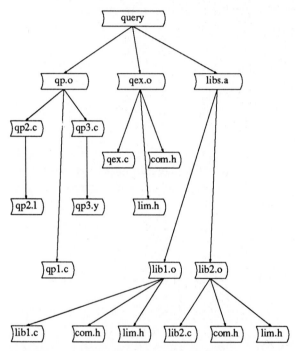

Figure 4.2 Dependencies for a Query Processor

The makefile to maintain the query processor is shown below:

```
query : qp.o qex.o libs.a
        # first level of dependency
        # query depends on qp.o qex.o and libs.a
        cc -o query qp.o qex.o libs.a
qp.o  : qp1.c qp2.c qp3.c
        # dependencies of module qp.o
        cc -o qp.o qp1.c qp2.c qp3.c
```

```
qp2.c : qp2.l
        lex qp2.l
        mv lex.yy.c qp2.c
qp3.c : qp3.y
        yacc qp3.y
        mv y.tab.c qp3.c
qex.o : qex.c lim.h com.h
        # dependency of the module qex.o
        cc -c qex.c
libs.a : lib1.o lib2.o
        #dependency of module libs.a
        ar rv libs.a lib1.o lib2.o
lib1.o : lib1.c com.h lim.h
        cc -c lib1.c
lib2.o : lib2.c com.h lim.h
        cc -c lib2.c
```

This is the most elementary form of the Makefile for the query processor project; it does not make use of macros or the inference rules of *make*. Let us use macros and inference rules to compress the *make* description file. The rewritten Makefile is shown below:

```
QSRC = qp1.c qp2.c qp3.c
INCLUDES = lim.h com.h
OBJECTF = qp.o qex.o libs.a
query : $(OBJECTF)
        cc -o query $(OBJECTF)
qp.o  : $(QSRC)
        cc -o qp.o $(QSRC)
libs : libs(lib1.o) libs(lib2.o)
qex.o lib1.o lib2.o : $(INCLUDES)
```

The inference rules of *make* and the macro facilities are very often useful for making terse and elegant *make* description files. The use of parentheses for maintaining archive libraries is illustrated in the dependency line

```
libs : libs(lib1.o) libs(lib2.o)
```

This line updates the library archive libs.a for the two members lib1.o and lib2.o. The rules for updating the library .o files have already been discussed.

4.2.5 Internal Macros

Make uses five different forms of macros which are internally maintained. They are *$*, $@, $<, $?*, and *$%*. These macros are extremely useful for writing rules for building target files. We saw the inference rules that are used by *make* to create target files. These rules were explained using specific file names. It is possible to change the default inference rules by providing a dependency line with the two suffixes to the left side and a null string to the right. This line is followed by a set of commands to be executed in order to create the target from it dependencies. Here is a rule to change the default rules for creating .o files from .c files:

```
.c.o :
        cc -g -c $<
```

The macro *$<* expands to the name of the file that is out of date with the target. In the above example, it expands to the .c file. The *$** macro expands to the file name of the dependent with the suffix deleted. The above inference rule can be rewritten as

```
.c.o :
        cc -g -c $*.c
```

The macro *$@* expands to the name of the target file. The default rule to get a .c file from a .y file can be changed to produce a detailed output of the parsing action in a file suffixed as .y.output by using the *$@* macro, as follows:

```
.y.c :
        yacc -v $<
        mv y.tab.c $@
        mv y.output $*.y.output
```

The macro *$?* is expanded when rules for the creation of the target file are explicitly specified. It is the list of files that are out of date with respect to the target file. The makefile, which will print the names of the end nodes of the dependency tree which were updated after the query file was created, can be rewritten as follows:

```
INCLUDES = lim.h com.h
SOURCEF = qp1.c qp2.1 qp3.y qex.c lim.h com.h lib1.c lib2.c
OBJECTF  = qp.o qex.o libs.a
dummy : $(SOURCEF)
        ls $?
        touch dummy
query : $(OBJECTF)
        cc -o query $(OBJECTF)
        touch dummy
qp.o  : qp1.c qp2.c qp3.c
        cc -o qp.o qp1.c qp2.c qp3.c
libs : libs(lib1.o) libs(lib2.o)
qex.o lib1.o lib2.o : $(INCLUDES)
```

A file called dummy is used to have the same modification time as the file query. It is *touch*ed every time the *query* file is updated. The command *touch* sets the modification time of the specified file to the current time.

The macro *$%* is evaluated only when the target file is an archive library member. If the archive library member has the form *lib(file1.o)*, then *$%* expands to the library member file1.o and the macro *$@* expands to lib.

4.2.6 Include Capability of Make

Make has an *include* capability which makes it possible to include other files in the *make* description file. If a line starts from the first column with the word *include* and is followed by a file name, then that file name is read by the *make* program. The *make* description file for the query processor can be rewritten as follows:

cat macros.mk
```
INCLUDES = lim.h com.h
SOURCEF = qp1.c qp2.1 qp3.y qex.c lim.h com.h lib1.c lib2.c
OBJECTF  = qp.o qex.o libs.a
```

cat makefile
```
include macros.mk
dummy : $(SOURCEF)
        ls $?
        touch dummy
query : $(OBJECTF)
        cc -o query $(OBJECTF)
```

```
      touch dummy
qp.o    : qp1.c qp2.c qp3.c
        cc -o qp.o qp1.c qp2.c qp3.c
libs  : libs(lib1.o) libs(lib2.o)
qex.o lib1.o lib2.o : $(INCLUDES)
```

4.2.7 Preset Make Macros

Make has a set of macros which are preset. These macros are used primarily in the inference rules of *make*. Some of the important preset macros are listed in Table 4.4. A − (minus) in the *Preset value* column of the table indicates that the macro is set to blank.

TABLE 4.4 Preset Make Macros

Macro	Preset value	Description
MAKE	*make*	*Make* program to be used
YACC	*yacc*	*Yacc* program to be used
YFLAGS	−	Flags used in *yacc* invocation
LEX	−	*Lex* program to be used
LFLAGS	−	Flags used in *lex* invocation
CFLAGS	−o	Flags used by the C compiler
CC	*cc*	C compiler
AS	*as*	The assembler program

These macros can be reset in the *make* description file like any other user-defined macros. For example, to make *newcc* the default C compiler instead of *cc*, redefine the macro CC as

```
CC = newcc
```

This will invoke *newcc* as the C compiler instead of *cc*.

4.2.8 Command Line Options

The *make* program takes a number of command line flags. It is also possible to set macros on the command line and to specify the targets to be updated.

This is very useful for intentionally creating pieces of the system instead of the whole system. Some of the commonly used flags are explained in Table 4.5. If a target is not specified on the command line, the default target is the first one specified in the file. Let us look at some examples of the use of command line options:

```
cat make1
final.o : incl.h

touch final.c
make -f make1
        cc -O -c final.c

touch final.c
make -s -f make1

touch final.c
make -n -f make1 #the displayed command is not actually executed
        cc -O -c final.c
```

It is possible to reset macros on the command line. Once these macros are set on the command line, they remain unchanged by any further assignments. Here is an example of using the debug option $-g$ in the cc command by resetting the macro *CFLAGS*:

```
cat make1
final.o : incl.h

touch make1
make -f make1 "CFLAGS=-g"
        cc -g -c final.c
```

4.2.9 Interaction with Environment Variables

Make uses shell, or environment, variables. All environment variables are treated as macro definitions. In case of conflicts, the macro assignments override environment variables. This default action can be reversed by the use of the $-e$ command line option. Of special interest is the *MAKEFLAGS*

TABLE **4.5** Commonly Used Make Flags

Option	Description
−s	Do not print the command lines before executing them.
−n	Do not execute the commands, only print them.
−r	Do not use the built-in rules.
−t	*Touch* the target files. Do not run any commands to update them.
−p	Print the set of macro definitions and target descriptions.
−f	Use the specified file as the *make* description file.
−d	Debug the *make* description file. Print the detail information on files and times examined.
−i	Ignore the error codes returned by the executed commands.
−e	Give priority to environment variables over macro assignments.

variable. This variable is always set by *make* and has the value corresponding to the command line options. The −*f*, −*p*, and −*d* options are not included when this variable is set.

4.2.10 Other Uses of Make

Make can also be used for maintaining projects involving files that do not have any programs involved. A typical application would be to maintain a set of user manuals. User manuals normally have a certain amount of dependencies involved. *Make* rules concerning appropriate dependencies can be built among the various sections. Rules can be simple *echo* statements to display warnings that a change in one section may warrant changes in some other sections. The section number of the other affected sections can also be displayed. This book was written using *make* to maintain the dependency between the index and the chapters. Each chapter was maintained in a separate file. A new index was generated whenever any of the files containing the individual chapters were *touch*ed.

4.3 SCCS: Source Code Control System

Most programmers often find it necessary to maintain multiple copies of a program. For example, when a version of the program may is already in use, they find it safe to create a backup copy of the program before actually tampering with it. This is particularly important when reverting back to the old version of a program becomes necessary. This simple method of maintaining different versions works well for two or three versions; however, it becomes extremely unwieldy and inefficient when one needs to handle multiple versions and a large number of program files are involved. SCCS is a collection of programs that help the programmer in controlling various versions of a program. It does not store multiple copies of a program, but instead it stores the incremental changes that the program undergoes. It also allows the programmer to store comments associated with each new version. It has an elegant mechanism to identify and number different versions and each version has a time associated with it which indicates the time when changes were incorporated in the version, along with an associated comment. There is always only one physical file stored for all the different versions of a program.

4.3.1 Getting Started with SCCS

Let us look at a simple C program to add two numbers. After the program is tested, it is installed in an appropriate directory. The simple C program is listed below:

```
cat temp.c
#include <stdio.h>
/* %E% */
main(argc,argv)
int argc;
char **argv;
{
int num1,num2;
printf("Add. result is %d\n",atoi(argv[1])+atoi(argv[2]));
}
```

The significance of the commented line is explained in Section 4.3.7. We can ignore it for the present discussion. An SCCS file for the program is created by using the *admin* command, as follows:

```
admin -itemp.c s.temp.c
rm temp.c
```

The $-i$ option specifies the raw file from which an SCCS file is to be created. The name of the target SCCS file, which must have the prefix s., is the second argument to the *admin* command. Once *admin* has created the required SCCS file, the original file is no longer required and can be removed.

There are various situations that may arise after the original program is created. After the program has been operational for some time, a user may request an enhancement. For example, in the simple program that we have, a user may request that the program provide a capability to print the result of subtraction of the two numbers. The first task of the programmer is to look at the original program. Remember that the program itself is stored in an SCCS file. The SCCS file is not a C program file, and therefore it is not practical to edit this file; however, the *get* command enables the programmer to retrieve the original version of the file, as follows:

```
get s.temp.c
1.1
9 lines
ls -l temp.c
-r--r--r--  1 rst       grpr          163 Jun 11 20:56 temp.c
cat temp.c
#include <stdio.h>
/* 86/06/11 */
main(argc,argv)
int argc;
char **argv;
{
int num1,num2;
printf("Add. result is %d\n",atoi(argv[1])+atoi(argv[2]));
}
```

The *get* command retrieves the original version of the file, displays the number of lines in the file, and displays the version that was retrieved. In the example, version 1.1 was retrieved, and the retrieved file has nine lines. You may have noticed that the second line has changed in the retrieved file! The *%E%* in the original file has been expanded to *86/06/11*. *%E%* is an SCCS identification keyword which is expanded to the date on which the version was created. There are many more keywords that are available for use in SCCS which will be explained later in Section 4.3.7. The newly retrieved file cannot be edited. Of course, it is possible to circumvent this problem by changing the permissions of the file and edit it; however, SCCS will not store the edited version of the file unless it is specifically informed that the file is to be retrieved for editing.

4.3.2 Getting a SCCS File for Editing

An SCCS file can be retrieved for editing using the $-e$ option. This option informs SCCS that a new version will eventually be created. The retrieved file has the appropriate modes to enable editing. The program is retrieved for editing as follows:

```
get -e s.temp.c
1.1
new delta 1.2
9 lines
ls -l temp.c
-rw-r--r--  1 rst      grpr          158 Jun 11 21:15 temp.c
```

The $-e$ option displays the number of the version that was retrieved and also the number of the new version that will eventually be installed. The last line displays the number of lines in the retrieved program.

After the required changes are incorporated, the program is tested and a new version of the program is ready to be installed. The new version, edited to include the subtraction feature, looks as follows.

```
#include <stdio.h>
/* %E% */
main(argc,argv)
int argc;
char **argv;
{
int num1,num2;
printf("Add. result is %d\n",atoi(argv[1])+atoi(argv[2]));
printf("Sub. result is %d\n",atoi(argv[1]) - atoi(argv[2]));
}
```

The new version of the program is installed using the *delta* command:

```
delta s.temp.c
comments ? This version has the capability to add and subtract
1.2
1 inserted
0 deleted
9 unchanged
```

The *delta* command first prompts for comments. These comments are terminated by a newline character. The purpose of these comments is to keep track of the changes that were incorporated in the system. The new version number is also displayed. *Delta* also displays a brief description of the number of lines that were affected by the new changes. In the above program, we inserted one line and deleted none, and the remaining lines were not edited.

4.3.3 More on Version Numbering

In the previous sections, we started with version 1.1 of the program, and a subsequent change in the program resulted in version 1.2. If we continue to change the program, we will create version 1.3, 1.4, 1.5, etc. SCCS allows us to have a control on the version number of the new version created by using the *-r* option of the *get* command, which also allows us to retrieve any version we have saved. In general, an SCCS version number has the general form

```
release.level.branch.sequence
```

The SCCS version number is also referred to as an *SID* or a *delta* number. An SCCS version number has the general form of a tree structure, as indicated by the example in Figure 4.3.

Branching is necessary when a change is required in a version, if that change is not dependent on the versions already present. A new release number is used to indicate a major change in the file. Let us modify version 1.2 of our program to incorporate multiplication and division of two numbers. We must first get the file for editing:

```
get -e s.temp.c
1.2
new delta 1.3
10 lines
```

Once the file is available for editing, the required changes are made. The new

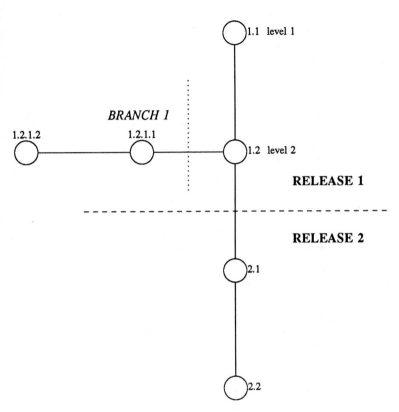

Figure 4.3 Example of an SCCS Tree

version is installed using the *delta* command, as follows:

```
delta s.temp.c
comments ?  Changes were made to print the product and quotient
1.3
2 inserted
0 deleted
10 unchanged
```

Our SCCS version tree at this point looks as shown in Figure 4.4. So far, we have not made any major changes in the program. We have merely

Figure 4.4 SCCS Tree after Two Deltas

enhanced the program to incorporate the result of the four basic operations. Suppose we get a request to compute the mean of the four resulting numbers? This would involve a major digression from the functions performed by the program so far. It is at such a juncture that we would decide to change the *release* number of the new version. This is done as follows:

```
get -e -r2 s.temp.c
1.3
new delta 2.1
12 lines
```

The $-r$ option is used along with the $-e$ option to get a version for editing, with the intention of creating a new release, whose number is specified with the $-r$ option. The program is edited to incorporate the required changes and is listed below:

```c
#include <stdio.h>
/* %E% */
main(argc,argv)
int argc;
char **argv;
{
int num1,num2,add_res,sub_res,div_res,mul_res;
add_res = atoi(argv[1])+atoi(argv[2]);
printf("Add. result is %d\n",add_res);
sub_res = atoi(argv[1]) - atoi(argv[2]);
printf("Sub. result is %d\n",sub_res);
mul_res = atoi(argv[1])*atoi(argv[2]);
printf("Mul. result is %d\n",mul_res);
div_res = atoi(argv[1])/atoi(argv[2]);
printf("Div. result is %d\n",div_res );
printf("The mean is %d\n",(add_res+div_res+mul_res+sub_res)/4);
}
```

This program does not handle all possible situations during its computation, because the sole purpose of this program is to illustrate the features of SCCS. The new release is installed as follows:

```
delta s.temp.c
comments ? This version prints the mean of the four results
2.1
10 inserted
 5 deleted
 7 unchanged
```

The evolution of our program can be indicated by the SCCS tree structure shown in Figure 4.5. The version with the new release is 2.1.

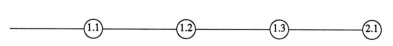

Figure 4.5 SCCS Tree with a New Release

4.3.4 Creating a New Branch

As explained earlier, the different versions of the program are actually stored in one physical file. Normally, only one version of the program is actually in production use. Consider a situation in which version 1.2 is in production use. Remember that version 1.2 computes the sum and difference of two numbers. If a user requests that the program print the sum of three numbers given to it as input on the command line, and then compute the difference of the first two numbers, a new version is required. If we do a *get* on the SCCS file s.temp.c, we will get version 2.1 for editing. Clearly, that is not the version we wish to alter; we therefore do a *get* on version 1.2. Since the changes that are to be incorporated in the new version are not to be applied to version 1.3 or version 2.1, SCCS forks a new branch at version 1.2, as shown here:

```
get -e -r1.2 s.temp.c
1.2
new delta 1.2.1.1
10 lines
```

```
delta s.temp.c
comments ? This version also prints the sum of three numbers
1.2.1.1
1 inserted
1 deleted
9 unchanged
```

The new SCCS tree for the program is shown in Figure 4.6. Any version of the program can now be retrieved for editing or listing by using the *get* command and by specifying the required version number. We have been using the −*r* option of SCCS to retrieve the required version. The −*t* option can be used to retrieve the last version in any specified release.

4.3.5 Unget: Undoing the Wrong!

Sometimes, after getting a file for editing using the *get* command with the −*e* option, we may realize that we have retrieved the wrong version for editing. Another possibility is that due to changes in requirements, there is no need to create a new version. These circumstances require the use of the *unget* command, which is used to inform SCCS that the file retrieved for editing is no longer in use. The situation after the *unget* is applied is exactly the same as the situation before the corresponding *get* with the −*e* option was run.

4.3.6 Simplifying an SCCS Structure

The SCCS tree should not be allowed to develop into a complex structure. Maintaining an SCCS file with a complex structure can be difficult, so if the SCCS structure becomes complex out of the evolution process, it should be simplified. Two commands that are useful for the purpose of simplifying the SCCS structure are *comb* and *rmdel*. *Comb* is used for combining two or more consecutive versions into a single version and to remove redundant versions. *Rmdel* is used to remove a version (or delta). Various restrictions exist for the removal of a version. Only the most recent version in a branch can be removed. In addition, this version must not have had a *get* −*e* applied to it currently for the purpose of creating a new version. Versions are removed or

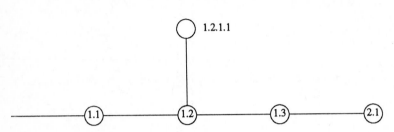

Figure 4.6 SCCS Tree with a Branch

combined only when their existence has only evolutionary significance. The simplified SCCS tree after running *comb* is shown in Figure 4.7. *Comb* is run as follows:

```
comb -cl.2.1.1,1.2,2.1 s.temp.c > temp.sh
chmod 700 temp.sh # make temp.sh executable
temp.sh # run temp.sh
```

The −*c* option is used to specify the list of versions to be preserved after the SCCS file is compressed. *Comb* does not perform the combination of versions but generates a shell script that can be executed to perform the actual combination of the various versions. We have redirected the output of *comb* into the file temp.sh. The modes of this file are changed to make it executable. Finally, the file is run to actually create the simplified SCCS structure after the combination of the deltas.

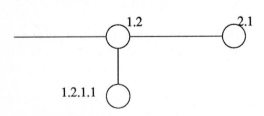

Figure 4.7 SCCS Tree after Applying Comb

The *prs* command is used for printing information about each version. The output of the *prs* command can be controlled by the −*d* option. By default, *prs* prints the information shown in Table 4.6. The status of the SCCS structure before combining the various deltas can be displayed using the *prs* command, as shown below:

```
prs s.temp.c
s.temp.c:

D 1.2.1.1 86/06/21 10:37:04 rst 9 2   00001/00001/00009
MRs:
COMMENTS: This version also prints the sum of three numbers


D 2.1 86/06/21 08:53:55 rst 7 6       00010/00005/00007
MRs:
COMMENTS:
This version prints the mean of the four results


D 1.3 86/06/21 08:16:20 rst  6 2          00002/00000/00010
MRs:
COMMENTS:
Changes were made to print the product and quotient


D 1.2 86/06/21 00:28:51 rst 2 1       00001/00000/00009
MRs:
COMMENTS:
This version has the capability to add and subtract

D 1.1 86/06/11 20:55:29 rst 1 0       00009/00000/00000
MRs:
COMMENTS:
date and time created 86/06/11 20:55:29 by rst
```

It would be also possible to run *prs* on the SCCS file after all the deltas were combined. This would display information about only three versions.

TABLE 4.6 Information Printed by Prs

Sequence *left to right* *top to bottom*	Information
1	Type of *delta*: R indicates that the delta was removed; D indicates that the delta still exists.
2	SCCS version number.
3	Date the version was created.
4	Time the version was created.
5	Login id of the creator of the version.
6	Sequence number of the version.
7	Sequence number of the predecessor version.
8	New lines inserted in this version.
9	Lines deleted in this version.
10	Lines unchanged in this version.
11	MRs: modification request numbers. Use of MRs is similar to the use of comments.
12	Comment string.

4.3.7 Id Keywords

Once we have a version which can be compiled and installed, there will be various information that we will want to store along with the file to be installed. Consider the following program:

```
cat idkey.c
#include <stdio.h>
main(argc,argv)
int argc;
char **argv;
{
        printf("The first argument is %s\n",argv[1])
}
```

If we had used SCCS to maintain the various versions of this program during its development (however ridiculous that may appear), we would have had several versions of this program source. Let us say that we installed version 1.4. Installing version 1.4 actually implies that we compiled version 1.4 and moved the executable to the appropriate directory. If at a later time we wish to know from which source version the object code was generated, there is no information stored in the object code that can tell us this. Identification keywords, or Id keywords, are used to include this and other such information in a file. They have the form *%k%*, where *k* is an uppercase letter. For example, *%R%* corresponds to the release number. These Id keywords can be inserted into the above program as follows:

```
cat idkey.c
#include <stdio.h>
main(argc,argv)
int argc;
char **argv;
{
        static char *SCCSID= " %Z% %R% %L% ";
        printf("The first argument is %s\n",argv[1]);
}
```

The name SCCSID was chosen arbitrarily. If there are several files to be compiled and linked together, then care must be taken to select different names and declare them appropriately to avoid compilation errors. When you get the file for installing, the Id keywords are expanded inline by SCCS.

The compiled object code will therefore have the expanded form of the Id keywords. Of course, SCCS will not expand the Id keywords when you get the file for editing, as it would store the expanded form when a *delta* is applied, and a subsequent *get* will not recognize the Id keyword! The *%Z%* is an important Id keyword that SCCS expands to a four character string @(#); *%R%* is expanded to give the release number and *%L%* is expanded to give the level number. Other commonly used Id keywords are shown in Table 4.7.

Let us try to install version 1.4 of this program with the Id keywords as follows:

```
get -r1.4 s.idkey.c
1.4
8 lines
cat idkey.c
#include <stdio.h>
main(argc,argv)
int argc;
char **argv;
{
        static char *SCCSID= " @(#) 1 4 ";
        printf("The first argument is %s0,argv[1]);
}
```

In this example SCCS expanded the Id keywords because the file was not retrieved for editing. We can now compile the program and install it as:

```
cc -o idks idkey.c
```

If at a later time we wish to identify the version number of the source file from which the object code was derived, we can use the *what* command, as explained in the next section.

4.3.8 What: Identify SCCS Files

What can be used to search for all occurrences of the pattern that *get* substitutes for the SCCS identification keyword %Z%. It displays everything up to a ", >, newline, \, or null character. Consider the object file idks which was installed in the previous section. The version number of the source file corresponding to this object file can be listed by the *what* command, as shown here:

```
what idks
idks
        1 4
```

This output of *what* can be changed by adding Id keywords from Table 4.7 to the variable SCCSID. If the definition of SCCSID is changed to

```
static char *SCCSID= " %Z% SCCS ID. INFO: **   %M% %E% %R% %L% ** ";
```

then the output of *what* would be as follows:

```
what idks
idks
        SCCS ID. INFO: **   idks.c 87/04/13 1 4 **
```

If the pattern @(#) that is substituted by *get* also happens to occur in the input file, *what* will not be able to distinguish it from the one substituted by *get*. It is also important to have the Id keywords compiled into the object module. Id keywords inserted in comment lines may not be useful because a good compiler will *strip* them from the object module.

TABLE 4.7 SCCS Identification Keywords

Id Keyword	Value after Expansion
%M%	The name of the SCCS file without the s. prefix.
%R%	Release number.
%L%	Level number.
%B%	Branch.
%S%	Sequence.
%E%	Date newest applied delta was created (yy/mm/dd).
%P%	SCCS file name.
%W%	Shorthand notation for *%Z%%M%tab character%R%%L%%B%%S%*.

4.3.9 More on Prs, Comb, and Rmdel

In the earlier example, when we used the command *comb*, we explicitly specified the versions to be preserved by using the −*c* option. If this option is not used, *comb* will create a shell script to preserve only the end nodes of the tree structure of the SCCS file along with those versions required to create the end node versions. Contrary to expectations, *comb* may not reduce the size of the SCCS file. Let us run *comb* on the SCCS file s.temp.c before some of the deltas were combined and see the versions which are preserved by SCCS. The −*d* option on the *prs* command will print only selected information for each version. The string *":I:"* associated with the −*d* option prints only the SCCS version number and is one of the many SCCS identification keywords. A complete list of keywords is available in the manual page for the *prs* command. The option −*e* is used to print information about all the versions. The list of versions present, followed by the list of versions present after *comb* is applied to the SCCS file s.temp.c, is shown by the use of the *prs* command:

```
prs -d":I:" -e  s.temp.c # display the versions present
1.2.1.1
2.1
1.3
1.2
1.1
comb s.temp.c > temp.sh # combine the versions to restructure the tree
chmod 700 temp.sh # make the shell script executable
temp.sh # run the shell script
prs -d":I:" -e s.temp.c # display the versions present after applying
comb
1.2.1.1
2.1
1.2
```

Figure 4.7 shows the SCCS structure after running *comb*. Now let us remove version 1.2.1.1 and use the *prs* command to display the list of the remaining version:

```
rmdel -r1.2.1.1 s.temp.c
prs -d":I:" -e s.temp.c
2.1
1.2
```

The final structure is shown in Figure 4.8. It contains only two versions.

4.3.10 Sccsdiff: Displaying the Difference in Versions

Sccsdiff displays the difference in two versions of the same SCCS file. Let us display the difference in versions 1.2 and 2.1 of the SCCS file s.temp.c:

```
sccsdiff -r1.2 -r2.1 s.temp.c
7,9c7,16
< int num1,num2;
< printf("Add. result is %d\n",atoi(argv[1])+atoi(argv[2]));
< printf("Sub. result is %d\n",atoi(argv[1]) - atoi(argv[2]));
---
> int num1,num2,add_res,sub_res,div_res,mul_res;
> add_res = atoi(argv[1])+atoi(argv[2]);
> printf("Add. result is %d\n",add_res);
> sub_res = atoi(argv[1]) - atoi(argv[2]);
> printf("Sub. result is %d\n",sub_res);
> mul_res = atoi(argv[1])*atoi(argv[2]);
> printf("Mul. result is %d\n",mul_res);
> div_res = atoi(argv[1])/atoi(argv[2]);
> printf("Div. result is %d\n",div_res );
> printf("The mean is %d\n",(add_res+div_res+mul_res+sub_res)/4);
```

SCCS retrieves the two versions from the SCCS file and passes the two files to *bdiff*. The output is therefore the difference in the two versions. The output of *bdiff* is similar to the output of *diff* and is explained in section 1.10. In this example, *sccsdiff* reports that version 2.1 can be created from version 1.2 by replacing lines 7 to 9 by the lines following the dashed line.

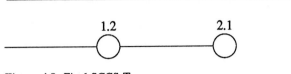

Figure 4.8 Final SCCS Tree

4.3.11 Cdc: Change Comments

The *cdc* command is used to change the comments associated with any version. This command prompts for the comment in exactly the same way as the *delta* command does. The new comment string is inserted before any existing comment strings. Another line, indicating the date, time, and the login id. of the user who changed the comment line, is also inserted. Let us change the comment line associated with version 2.1 of the SCCS file s.temp.c:

```
prs s.temp.c
s.temp.c:

D 2.1 86/06/21 15:45:03 rst 2 1        00010/00003/00007
MRs:
COMMENTS:
This version prints the mean of the four results

cdc -r2.1 s.temp.c
comments ?  This line illustrates the use of the cdc command

prs s.temp.c
s.temp.c:

D 2.1 86/06/21 15:45:03 rst 2 1        00010/00003/00007
MRs:
COMMENTS:
This line illustrates the use of the cdc command
*** CHANGED *** 86/06/21 16:21:45 rst
This version prints the mean of the four results
```

4.4 Make and SCCS

Earlier in the chapter we studied the use of *make* for maintaining projects involving many programs. *Make* uses the suffixes of files to determine their type. Unfortunately, SCCS files are determined by the prefix *"s."*. To overcome this problem, the tilde operator (~) is used to specify an SCCS file in the *make* description file. The internal rule to transform an SCCS C file to an object file is expressed as

```
.c~.o :
        get $(GFLAGS) -p $< > $*.c
        cc  $(CFLAGS) -c $*.c
        -rm -f $*.c
```

Make recognizes the *.c~* as a file prefixed with *"s."* and suffixed with *".c"*. Consider the following makefile:

```
cat makefile
final : mod1.o mod2.o
        cc -o final mod1.o mod2.o
```

The prerequisite files are mod1.o and mod2.o. Let us look at the files in the directory:

```
ls | paste - - - #list the files in the directory
makefile        s.mod1.c        s.mod2.c
```

Only the makefile and the two SCCS files are present. *Make* will use the *get* command to create mod1.c from s.mod1.c and mod2.c from s.mod2.c. These files are then compiled using the built-in rules to get the target file final. Let us look at the various steps that *make* executes to create the target file:

```
make
        get  -p s.mod1.c > mod1.c
1.1
7 lines
        cc -O -c mod1.c
        rm -f mod1.c
        get  -p s.mod2.c > mod2.c
```

```
1.1
4 lines
        cc -O -c mod2.c
        rm -f mod2.c
        cc -o final mod1.o mod2.o
```

The $-p$ option to *get* causes the text retrieved from the SCCS file to be written to the standard output. In addition, all output which normally goes to the standard output is redirected to file descriptor 2. It is worth noting that in the built-in rule for converting a C program stored in an SCCS format to a regular C file, the *get* command is used without any reference to a particular version. This defaults to the end node version with the highest release number and the highest level number. In order to retrieve a specific version, the rule to retrieve the file must be explicitly specified using the *get* command with the version number specified with the $-r$ option.

Make and SCCS together make an excellent set of tools for managing a project involving a large number of modules and/or many programmers. The writers of most of the utilities and commercially available software packages on the UNIX system used SCCS and *make* during the development phase.

4.5 Gprof and Prof: Profiling Tools

Profiling tools are helpful for the purpose of debugging and improving efficiency. UNIX provides *prof* and *gprof* to generate the profile of a program. *Gprof* is usually available on the BSD version. Generating a profile requires that the program be compiled with the $-p$ option; if using *gprof*, the $-g$ option is also required. After the program is compiled, it is executed like any normal program. During the execution of the program, a file called mon.out is created; the file may be named gmon.out if the $-g$ option was used to create the executable for use with *gprof*. *Prof* reads from the file mon.out and *gprof* reads from the file gmon.out to generate the execution profile. The example shown below shows how a profile can be generated with *prof*:

```
cc -p sqrt.c
a.out < inpfile
prof a.out
  %time  cumsecs  #call  ms/call  name
   41.7    0.08    118     0.71    _new
   33.3    0.15      1    66.68    _main
```

8.3	0.17	1	16.67	__doprnt
8.3	0.18	2	8.34	_read
8.3	0.20			mcount
0.0	0.20	29	0.00	__doscan
0.0	0.20	2	0.00	__filbuf
0.0	0.20	1	0.00	__flsbuf
0.0	0.20	29	0.00	__innum
0.0	0.20	146	0.00	_abs
0.0	0.20	2	0.00	_fstat
0.0	0.20	118	0.00	_func_sum
0.0	0.20	1	0.00	_gtty
0.0	0.20	1	0.00	_ioctl
0.0	0.20	1	0.00	_isatty
0.0	0.20	1	0.00	_printf
0.0	0.20	1	0.00	_profil
0.0	0.20	29	0.00	_scanf
0.0	0.20	28	0.00	_ungetc

The profile is generated in five columns. The first column shows the percentage time of the total execution time that was spent in executing the function shown in the last column. The second column indicates the running sum of the time accounted for by the function. The third column reports the total number of times the function was invoked. The fourth column is a display of the average number of microseconds required to execute the function once.

4.5.1 Use of the Profile

The profile generated can be used to find out the functions which consume the most time. Once these functions are identified, the code for these functions can be improved. Information about the number of times a function is invoked can also be used to identify possible bugs. In the above program, the function *main* was called only once but consumed a whopping 33.3 percent of the total execution time. The function *new* was invoked 118 times but consumed only 0.71 ms each time it was called. The other functions are mostly C language library functions. The task of the programmer is therefore to take a closer look at the *main* and *new* functions and modify the code to make these functions more efficient.

4.5.2 Using Gprof

Gprof is similar to *prof* in many respects but also provides many additional features. The program must be compiled with the *−pg* option. Once compiled and run, a file called gmon.out is generated. This file is then interpreted by running *gprof*. The following session shows the generation of a profile for a program that does virtually nothing, but which suffices to explain the profile generated by *gprof*:

```
cat demo_gprof.c
#include <stdio.h>
main()
{
        int i;
        for (i=0;i<100;++i)
                func1();
        for (i=0;i<100;++i)
                func2();
        for (i=0;i<100;++i)
                func3();
}
func1()
{
        int i;
        for (i=0;i<100;++i)
                func3();
}
func2()
{
        int i;
        for (i=0;i<100;++i)
                func3();
}
func3()
{
        int i,j;
        for (i=0;i<100;++i)
                ++j;
}

cc -pg demo_gprof.c
a.out
```

```
gprof a.out
```

The output generated by the last command is verbose, so only the relevant
sections are listed below:

```
%time  cumsecs  seconds    calls  name
 91.2     9.34     9.34    20100  _func3
  7.2    10.08     0.74           mcount
  1.0    10.18     0.10      100  _func1
  0.6    10.24     0.06      100  _func2
  0.0    10.24     0.00        1  _main
  0.0    10.24     0.00        1  _profil
```

The output shown above is similar to the profile generated by *prof*. *Cumsecs*
is the running sum of the time accounted for by the function and those listed
above it. *Seconds* is the total time consumed by the function. *%time*, *calls*,
and *name* display the percentage time of the total time consumed by the
function, the number of times the function was invoked, and the name of the
function, respectively.

In addition to the output shown above, *gprof* also generates a call graph
profile along with the relevant explanation, as shown below:

```
index  %time    self descendents  called+self   name     index
                                   called/total          children

                                                <spontaneous>
 [1]   100.0    0.00      9.50                  start [1]
                0.00      9.50         1/1        _main [2]
-----------------------------------------------------------------
                0.00      9.50         1/1        start [1]
 [2]   100.0    0.00      9.50         1        _main [2]
                0.10      4.65     100/100         _func1 [4]
                0.06      4.65     100/100         _func2 [5]
                0.05      0.00   100/20100         _func3 [3]
-----------------------------------------------------------------
                0.05      0.00   100/20100         _main [2]
                4.65      0.00 10000/20100         _func1 [4]
                4.65      0.00 10000/20100         _func2 [5]
 [3]    98.3    9.34      0.00       20100      _func3 [3]
-----------------------------------------------------------------
                0.10      4.65     100/100         _main [2]
 [4]    50.0    0.10      4.65         100      _func1 [4]
```

```
               4.65        0.00     10000/20100      _func3 [3]
       --------------------------------------------------
               0.06        4.65     100/100          _main [2]
 [5]     49.5  0.06        4.65     100              _func2 [5]
               4.65        0.00     10000/20100      _func3 [3]
       --------------------------------------------------
               0.00        0.00     1/1              _moncontrol [27]
 [9]     0.0   0.00        0.00     1                _profil [9]
       --------------------------------------------------
```

The explanation of the profile generated is also reported by *gprof*, as follows:

```
            The sum of self and descendents is the major sort
            for this listing.

            function entries:
index       the index of the function in the call graph
            listing, as an aid to locating it (see below).
%time       the percentage of the total time of the program
            accounted for by this function and its
            descendents.
self        the number of seconds spent in this function
            itself.

descendents
            the number of seconds spent in the descendents of
            this function on behalf of this function.
called      the number of times this function is called (other
            than recursive calls).
self        the number of times this function calls itself
            recursively.
name        the name of the function, with an indication of
            its membership in a cycle, if any.

index       the index of the function in the call graph
            listing, as an aid to locating it.

parent listings:
self*       the number of seconds of this function's self time
            which is due to calls from this parent.
descendents*
            the number of seconds of this function's
```

descendent time which is due to calls from this
parent.

called** the number of times this function is called by
this parent. This is the numerator of the
fraction which divides up the function's time to
its parents.

total* the number of times this function was called by
all of its parents. This is the denominator of
the propagation fraction.

parents the name of this parent, with an indication of the
parent's membership in a cycle, if any.

index the index of this parent in the call graph
listing, as an aid in locating it.

children listings:

self* the number of seconds of this child's self time
which is due to being called by this function.

descendent*
the number of seconds of this child's descendent's
time which is due to being called by this
function.

called** the number of times this child is called by this
function. This is the numerator of the
propagation fraction for this child.

total* the number of times this child is called by all
functions. This is the denominator of the
propagation fraction.

children the name of this child, and an indication of its
membership in a cycle, if any.

index the index of this child in the call graph listing,
as an aid to locating it.

Now that you have the program and the explanation of the call graph profile
listed before you, try to understand some of the numbers listed for the various
functions and for functions *func3* and *func2* in particular. These functions are
identified by index *[3]* and *[4]* respectively.

4.5.3 A Final Thought on Profiling

Profiling a program can be helpful in identifying functions which hog
execution time. Once a program is optimized, it must be recompiled without

the $-p$ or $-g$ options, because these options cause additional profiling code to be added to the original program code. In addition, the times reported in different runs of the same program with the same input data can be different. This is primarily due to other processes which may be running at the same time under different conditions. Various options are provided with both *prof* and *gprof*. Programs involving many functions may generate very long profile listings. The $-f$ option is useful when the call graph profile for only selected functions and their descendants is to be generated.

5 Database Management Systems

UNIX is becoming increasingly popular in the area of data management. During the earlier days of UNIX, the only tools available for data processing needs were the filters that we discussed in Chapter 1. While these filters are powerful for medium-sized applications, their limitations become very obvious when dealing with large applications. Applications involving multiple files of large sizes also demand more powerful tools than filters or conventional high-level language programming. In the past few years, many DBMS have been developed specifically for the UNIX system. These systems do not come as a part of the standard utilities and have to be purchased separately. In this chapter, we will study some of the terms and concepts involved in DBMS. We will also discuss some of the standard features that most of the commercially available systems provide. A very simple version of Ingres is available on most BSD UNIX systems, so we will take a close look at Ingres, since it is more readily available. Finally, some of the features of commercially available DBMS will be compared.

5.1 Theoretical Foundations

The subject of DBMS has evolved considerably in the last decade and continues to do so at an increasing rate. Presently, the term DBMS is loosely used. Software packages that do simple record-keeping functions are sometimes erroneously termed as DBMS. There is also a distinct difference between a DBMS and a database. The latter is actually a repository for stored data, while a DBMS is a collection of software routines that allows a user to manage the various aspects of this data. Some of the advantages of using a DBMS are as follows:

1. Data can be stored with minimal redundancy.
2. Data integrity can be maintained.
3. Data can be shared by many users.
4. Applications can become independent of the way in which the data is stored.
5. Security and standards can be enforced more easily.

There has been a considerable amount of research into deciding the best possible way of storing data for any application. This research has given birth to a term that is widely used in database jargon, *data model*. There are three important and commonly accepted data models: *hierarchical*, *network*, and *relational*. The relational model is considered state-of-the-art, and most of the DBMS available today on the UNIX system support this model. In this book, we will discuss the relational model only. The approach in discussing this model will be to look at the practical aspects of the terms involved rather than adhering to theoretical definitions.

A relational database is a collection of relations. Without aggravating the theoreticians too much, one can think of a relation as a table. Each record in the table is called a *tuple*. Fields in the record are called *attributes*. Some of these fields describe *key* fields, which are used to select records. The field that is selected to be the main key is referred to as a *primary key*; if two or more fields are required to make the record unique, these fields are grouped together to form a *composite key*. A *query language* is a language that is used to manipulate the contents of a database. This may involve retrieving the data, changing the existing data, or even changing the structure in which the data is stored.

5.2 Designing a Database System

One of the most important aspects of a database is its design. This involves designing records and deciding which fields are to be grouped together to form a record. While some designers design databases solely on intuition, such ad hoc designs often suffer from inefficiencies and redundancies in data storage. Relational databases can be designed systematically, using a set of rules which are commonly referred to as *normal forms*. There are five such normal forms. Normal forms have undergone some criticism, because they tend to degrade the performance of retrieval operations; however, performance is enhanced if there are frequent updates on nonkey fields. It is not always necessary to subject database designs to all the normal forms. The five normal forms are explained briefly in the next section.

5.2.1 Normal Forms

The explanation of the five normal forms given below is simplified and may deviate slightly from theoretically pure definitions.

The first normal form defines a given relation in a database as having a fixed number of fields. This means that all record occurrences for the same record type must have the same number of fields.

The second normal form states that a nonkey field must describe the whole key and not just a subset of the key. Consider the following relation:

supplier no.	city code	part supplied	city name

In the above relation, if *supplier no.* and *city code* form a composite key, and *city name* relates only to *city code* and not to *supplier no.*, then this relation has to be decomposed to form the following two relations:

supplier no.	city code	part supplied

and

city code	city name

The third normal form states that a nonkey field must not describe another nonkey field. The following relation violates third normal form:

part no.	description	storage loc. no.	storage location

The third normal form is violated here because *storage location* describes *storage loc. no.*. The relation has to be decomposed into two separate relations to satisfy the third normal form. These new relations are shown below:

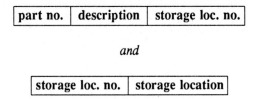

part no.	description	storage loc. no.

and

storage loc. no.	storage location

The fourth normal form is violated when a relation contains two or more independent multivalued facts about an entity. The following example should help to make this form clear. Consider a relation consisting of the following three fields:

student no.	course	friend

This relation violates the fourth normal form because we have a many-to-many relationship between students and courses and another many-to-many relationship between students and friends. In addition, these two relationships are independent of each other. The above relation must therefore be decomposed into two relations in order to satisfy fourth normal form:

student no.	course

and

student no.	friend

The fifth normal form states that a record type must not be structured in such a way that its contents can be reconstructed from smaller record types. Of course, it is always possible to restructure a record into smaller records with the same key field. This case is excluded from the above restriction.

Normal forms are applied sequentially. A database design must first be subjected to the first normal form, followed by the second, followed by the third, and so on.

5.3 QUEL: A Query Language

Once a database is designed, it is actually created using some DBMS, and data is loaded into the system. This data can be manipulated using a query language. A DBMS can have its own query language; however, thanks to certain standards being developed in the DBMS industry, there are two commonly used query languages, QUEL and SQL. SQL is more popular than QUEL and is supported by most of the commercially available DBMS packages. Ingres supports QUEL.[*] We will use QUEL to create a database consisting of two relations, suppliers and parts. These relations are described in Tables 5.1 and 5.2 respectively.

TABLE 5.1 Suppliers Relation

fields	type	length
supplier no.	integer	6
supplier name	string	25
part supplied	integer	7

TABLE 5.2 Parts Relation

fields	type	length
part no.	integer	6
part name	string	25
color	string	25
qty in stock	integer	9

The Ingres DBMS will be used to demonstrate most of the features of UNIX-based DBMS. In Ingres, it is necessary to explicitly name the database; therefore, let us create a database with the name partspdb. The command *creatdb* is used to create the database. In this chapter, we will assume that Ingres is installed in the directory */usr*. Of course the shell variable *PATH* has to be set properly to */usr/ingres/bin*, otherwise the full path name will be required for running any command.

A new database is created, as follows:

```
creatdb partspdb
database partspdb created
```

The database is created in the directory */usr/ingres/data/base/partspdb*. Once

---

[*]New commercial versions of Ingres also support SQL.

the new database is created, it is necessary to create the relations that form the database by using QUEL commands. An Ingres session can be started with a simple command as shown below:

```
ingres partspdb # partspdb is the name of the database
INGRES version 7.10 (10/27/81) login
Sat Jun 28 17:12:35 1986
go
*
```

Ingres displays a startup message along with the date and time. The asterisk (*) is the Ingres prompt. Now that we have initiated an Ingres session, let us create the required relations:

```
* create suppliers(supp_no=i4,supp_name=c25,part_supp=i4)
* create parts(part_no=i4,part_name=c25,color=c25,qty_stk=i4)
* \g
* * Executing . . .

continue
* \q
INGRES version 7.10 (10/27/81) logout
Sat Jun 28 23:32:24 1986
goodbye rst -- come again
```

Any command executed in the Ingres environment is a QUEL statement. In the above Ingres session, we have created two empty relations by using the QUEL statement *create*. Note the data types of each field. We have used the most basic data types that Ingres supports. These are the string data type, which is specified by a *c*, and the integer data type, which is specified by an *i*. The length associated with a string data type is the maximum length the field can have. The length associated with the integer data type specifies the number of bytes to be used to store the integer, with valid numbers being 1, 2, and 4. The *f* character can be used to specify a float data type. The query buffer is filled until the \g command actually executes the query. The \q command ends the Ingres session.

The relations created do not have any data; the database is empty and has to be loaded. There are two methods for doing this. One method is to load data directly from a flat file into the relation, which is referred to as bulk loading. Most DBMS provide this feature. Another method is to use the query language to load one relation at a time. In Ingres, bulk loading can be executed by using the QUEL statement *copy*. A single record can be added by the use of the *append* command. Let us copy five records from the flat file suppliers.d into the relation suppliers by using the *copy* statement:

```
cat suppliers.d
```

```
1231    John and Wills, Inc      3122
2121    Wilcox and Trass, Inc    1211
2131    IBMS Computers, Inc       2111
1214    Wills and Willey, Inc    3122
1218    Peter and Wiley, Inc      2111
```

```
ingres partspdb
INGRES version 7.10 (10/27/81) login
Sat Jun 28 23:57:45 1986
go
* copy suppliers(supp_no=c0tab,supp_name=c0tab,part_supp=c0nl)
* from "/a5/rst/cprogs/docs/suppliers.d"
* \g
* * Executing . . .

continue
* \q
INGRES version 7.10 (10/27/81) logout
Sat Jun 28 23:59:02 1986
goodbye rst -- come again
```

The suppliers relation is now loaded with five records. Let us now use the *append* command to add three records to the parts relation:

```
ingres partspdb
INGRES version 7.10 (10/27/81) login
Sun Jun 29 10:50:28 1986
go
* append parts(part_no = 3122,part_name="Partno3122",color="blue",
* qty_stk=200)
* append parts(part_no = 1211,part_name="Partno1211",color="green",
* qty_stk=250)
* append parts(part_no = 2111,part_name="Partno2111",color="red",
* qty_stk=20)
* \g
* \q
```

```
INGRES version 7.10 (10/27/81) logout
Sun Jun 29 10:50:30 1986
goodbye rst -- come again
```

The syntax of the *append* command is simple and easy to understand. The field names can be specified in any sequence. If a value is not specified for a field name, the default is a zero for numeric fields and a blank for string fields.

We now have a database with two relations. Each relation has some data in it. Let us run some queries to retrieve information from the database. A comment in QUEL is an arbitrary sequence of characters bounded on the left by ''/*'' and on the right by ''*/''. In Ingres, the concept of a range variable is important to understand. A range variable is associated with a relation. This variable is then used to refer to the fields of that relation in most QUEL statements. The range variable has to be specified only once in an Ingres session. Here are some sample queries:

```
* /* First query retrieves the part number of all green color  */
* /* parts. Second query retrieves the supplier number of all  */
* /* suppliers who supply green color parts. The second query  */
* /* is termed a join operation in relational DBMS jargon. See */
* /* Section 1.7 for a discussion on the UNIX join command.    */
* range of p is parts
* range of s is suppliers
* retrieve (p.part_no) where p.color = "green"
* \g
|part_no      |
|-------------|
|         1211|
|-------------|
(1 tuple)
continue
* retrieve (s.supp_no) where  p.part_no = s.part_supp and
* p.color="green"
* \g
|supp_n|
|------|
|  2121|
|------|
(1 tuple)
continue
*
```

Notice that the *retrieve* command also displays the total number of tuples retrieved. This count can be very helpful.

5.3.1 Aggregate Functions

Most query languages provide aggregate functions. Aggregate functions are used to provide operations like averaging, determining the maximum, determining the minimum, etc. QUEL supports aggregate functions. Here is a query to display the average of the quantity in stock for all parts:

```
* range of p is parts
* retrieve (avg_qty=avg(p.qty_stk))
* \g
|avg_qty   |
|----------|
|   156.667|
|----------|
(1 tuple)
continue
* \q
```

5.3.2 Modifying and Displaying Tables

Query languages also provide statements to add, delete, or modify records in a table. QUEL provides the *append* statement to add new records to a table. This command was used earlier to add records to the parts relation. The *replace* command is used to change the contents of an existing record. The *delete* statement is used to delete a record from a table. The *print* command can be used to display the contents of the entire table. Some QUEL queries that update the database are shown here:

```
* /* The contents of the two tables are displayed first    */
* /* The first query changes the color of part number 1211 */
* /* to black. The second query deletes the supplier record for */
* /* supplier number 1231                                   */
* /* print suppliers                                        */
* /* print parts                                            */
```

```
*  \g
*  * Executing . . .
suppliers relation
|supp_n|supp_name                    |part_supp   |
|------------------------------------------------|
|  1231|John and Wills, Inc      |        3122|
|  2121|Wilcox and Trass, Inc    |        1211|
|  2131|IBMS Computers, Inc       |        2111|
|  1214|Wills and Willey, Inc     |        3122|
|  1218|Peter and Wiley, Inc      |        2111|
|------------------------------------------------|
parts relation
|part_no       |part_name          |color     |qty_stk   |
|-----------------------------------------------------------|
|         3122|Partno3122          |blue      |        200|
|         1211|Partno1211          |green     |        250|
|         2111|Partno2111          |red       |         20|
|-----------------------------------------------------------|

continue
*  range of p is parts
*  replace p(color="black") where p.part_no = 1211
*  \g
*  * Executing . . .

(1 tuple)
continue
*  range of s is suppliers
*  delete s where s.supp_no = 1231
*  \g
(1 tuple)
continue
*  \q
```

5.3.3 Enforcing Security in QUEL

Relations in Ingres databases are owned by the user who creates them. The owner can restrict access to the relation by the use of the QUEL command *define permit*. This command enforces several levels of security on a relation. These levels include the following:

Operations	The user can restrict the operations that any given user can perform on the specified relation.
Attributes	The attributes of the relation which can be accessed by any given user can be restricted.
Time	The time when the relation can be accessed can be specified.
Days	The days on which the relation can be accessed can be specified by the use of three-character abbreviations for days of the week.
Users	Only specified users can be given access by specifying their login names.
Qualifications	Additional qualifications can be added to a user query accessing the relation, thus restricting access further.

The use of the *define permit* command can significantly slow any operation on a relation. Here is an example of the use of this command:

```
* /* Allow the user whose login is sst to retrieve only     */
* /* information on suppliers whose supp_no < 200. In        */
* /* addition, allow access only on Mondays between 7:00     */
* /* and 15:00.                                              */
* range of s is suppliers
* define permit retrieve of s
* to sst from 7:00 to 15:00
* on Mon
* where s.supp_no < 200
* \g
* * Executing . . .
```

Similarly, access to the same relation can be restricted to other users by additional *define permit* commands.

5.3.4 Enforcing Integrity in QUEL

In Section 5.1, it was mentioned that one of the advantages of using a DBMS is the ability to enforce data integrity. QUEL provides the *define integrity* command to enforce data integrity. The following command ensures that all updates to the suppliers relation will be completed only if the attribute *supp_no* is greater than 0:

```
* range of s is suppliers
* define integrity on s is s.supp_no > 0
* \g
* * Executing . . .
```

5.4 SQL: Another Query Language

SQL is a query language that is now considered an industry standard for querying relational databases. Some of the more popular DBMS packages, like Unify, Informix, and Oracle, support SQL. These vendors differ, however, in the versions of SQL that they support. Fortunately, the differences are minor. In the next few sections, we will see how one writes SQL queries. We will use the same database, consisting of the parts and suppliers relations, that was used to write QUEL queries.

5.4.1 Simple SQL Queries

Here are simple SQL queries which operate on a single relation:

```
# Retrieve the names of all parts
select part_name from parts

# Print the contents of the parts relation
select *
from parts

# Print the part number of all green color parts
select part_no
from parts where color="green'
```

In the first query, the *part_name* of all the parts in the parts relation is retrieved. In the next query, all the information stored in the parts relation is retrieved. Finally, a selection is made in the third query. The part number of green color parts only is retrieved.

5.4.2 SQL Queries on Multiple Relations

Here are some sample queries that operate on multiple relations:

```
# Retrieve the names of suppliers who supply green color parts
# This involves a join on two tables
select supp_name
from suppliers,parts
where color = "green" and part_supp=part_no
```

```
# Retrieve supplier names of suppliers who supply the
# at least one green part
# This is an example of a nested query.
select supp_name
from supplier
where part_supp in
        (select part_no
         from parts where color="green")
```

In the second example, the innermost query is evaluated first. This results in a temporary relation with a single column. A tuple (or record) in the outer query is selected only if the *part_supp* value for the tuple is found in the newly created temporary relation.

5.4.3 Retrieval Using Union

The *union* operator in SQL is used to retrieve the union of two separate retrievals. The following query retrieves the part number of those parts supplied by supplier number 1212 or the part numbers of parts that are green:

```
select part_supp from suppliers
        where  suppliers.supp_no = 1212
union
select part_no from parts
        where parts.color = "green"
```

Duplicates are removed from the output. Some implementations of SQL do not support the *union* operator.

5.4.4 Aggregate Functions

SQL provides a series of built-in aggregate functions. These functions can be used mostly with *select* statements and with the *having* clause. The use of this clause will be examined in a later section. The most commonly supported aggregate functions are shown in Table 5.3. These functions enhance the retrieval capabilities of SQL substantially.

TABLE 5.3 Aggregate Functions

Function name	Returned value
Count	Count of values
Sum	The addition of values
Avg	The average of values
Max	The maximum value
Min	The minimum value

Here are some examples of the use of aggregate functions:

```
# Display the part number and the quantity in stock of the part
# with the maximum number of parts in stock
select   part_no,max(qty_stk) from parts

# Display the average of the quantity in stock of all parts
select avg(qty_stk) from parts
```

5.4.5 Use of the Group by Clause

SQL provides the group by clause which can be used to group data in a relation based on some common value. This clause is particularly useful in cases where aggregate functions have to be used on subsets of the table rather than on the whole table. Let's look at an example:

```
# Display the total quantity in stock of all parts grouped by color
select color,sum(qty_stk)
from parts group by color
```

The *having* clause is used to select some groups that are created by the use of the *group by* clause. It is similar to the *where* clause that is used to select a record from a table. The only difference is that the *having* clause is used to select groups. The following example displays the color of those parts whose average quantity in stock is greater than 200:

```
select color,avg(qty_stk) from parts group by color
having avg(qty_stk) > 200
```

5.4.6 Using the Existential Quantifier

The existential quantifier is a powerful feature supported by SQL. The *select* clause that follows it determines the result of the operation. The quantifier evaluates to *true* if the select is nonempty. The following query selects supplier names of suppliers who supply at least one green-colored part:

```
select supp_name from suppliers
        where exists
                ( select * from parts
                where parts.part_no = suppliers.part_supp
                and parts.color= "green")
```

For each record in the suppliers file, the embedded *select* is evaluated. If at least one record is found that satisfies the embedded *select*, the required fields from the outer *select* are displayed.

5.4.7 Creating a Table Using SQL

Some implementations of SQL provide a capability to create tables in the query language. The *create* statement in the Informix implementation of SQL can be used as follows:

```
create table newtable(field1  integer,
                field2 integer,
                field3 float)
```

This statement creates a new table with the name *newtable*, which has three fields. The first two fields are of data type integer, and the third field is of data type float.

5.4.8 Update Operations in SQL

Updating a database can involve:

1. Adding a new record to a table
2. Deleting an existing record
3. Modifying an existing record

SQL provides *insert, delete,* and *update* statements to accomplish these tasks. These statements are used in the following examples:

```
# Add a new record to the parts relation
Insert into parts:
<2121,'Partno2121','green',300>

# Delete the record with part number 1121 from the parts relation
delete parts where part_no = 1121

# Change the color of part number 1132 to yellow
update parts
set color = 'yellow'
where part_no = 1132
```

In the *insert* statement, the sequence of values specified is the same as the sequence of columns from left to right in the table. If the sequence in the table is different, then it may be necessary to specify the sequence in the *insert* statement as

```
insert into parts(part_name,part_no,color,qty_stk)
<'Partno2121',2121,'green',300>
```

Some SQL implementations support *insert* statements to add multiple records in a single statement. There are also versions of SQL that provide an *insert* capability to add records to a table from a flat file.

5.5 Host Language Interface

Many DBMS provide a capability to embed queries in a high-level language. This capability is often called the host language interface. In most systems, this capability is supported by a library which has a set of functions that provide access to the database. The functions can then be called from a higher-level language program to perform the required task. Host language interfaces are very useful because most query languages are nonprocedural and therefore limited in their power. It is also not possible to assume that all end users will have a knowledge of the query language that the DBMS supports. Custom interfaces can therefore be provided by programming in a high-level language and using the host language interface. Interactions between flat files and databases are also better handled by using the host language interface feature of the DBMS.

5.5.1 EQUEL: Embedded QUEL

Ingres provides a more user-friendly interface than most DBMS available commercially. This is possible because the QUEL statements can be directly inserted in C programs with very minor changes. The resulting language consisting of C language and QUEL statements is called EQUEL. EQUEL statements start with a double pound sign (##) in the first column of each line.

Let us write a program in EQUEL to retrieve the part names of part numbers which are stored in a file named parts_file. We will be using the partspdb database with the two relations that we created earlier. Here is the required program with the host language interface, with comments inserted to explain the working of the program:

```
#include <stdio.h>
main()
{
/* declare the C variable to the EQUEL preprocessor */
##      char c_part_name[35];
##      int part_number,eof;
        FILE *fp_parts,*fopen();

        /* open the parts_file containing part numbers */
        fp_parts = fopen("parts_file","r");

/* specify the database to be used  */
/* declare the range variable */
```

```
##      ingres partspdb
##      range of p is parts
        while(1)
        {
                /* read the input part number */
                eof = fscanf(fp_parts,"%d",&part_number);
                /* check for end of file */
                if (eof == EOF) break;

/* retrieve the part name into the C variable c_part_name   */
/* only if the part no. matches the part no. in the file */
##              retrieve (c_part_name=p.part_name)
##              where p.part_no = part_number
##{
        /* output the part name */
        printf("The part name for part number %d \
                is %s\n",part_number,c_part_name);
##}
        }
}
```

This program has to be compiled and linked with the Ingres library routines to create the required executable program, as follows:

```
equel tryequel.q # Pass the program through the EQUEL processor
cc tryequel.c /usr/ingres/lib/libq.a # Compile the program
a.out
The part name for part number 2111 is Partno2111
The part name for part number 1211 is Partno1211
```

The EQUEL preprocessor translates the embedded EQUEL statements to C function calls. The resulting C program is then compiled with the Ingres library to create the final executable code. The output of the EQUEL preprocessor is shown below:

```
#include <stdio.h>
main()
{
        /* declare the C variable to the EQUEL preprocessor */
        char c_part_name[35];
        int part_number,eof;
```

```
FILE *fp_parts,*fopen();

/* open the parts_file containing part numbers */
fp_parts = fopen("parts_file","r");

/* specify the database to be used  */
/* declare the range variable */
{
        IIingres("partspdb",0);
}
{
        IIwrite("range of p=parts");
        IIsync(0);
}
while(1)
{
/* read the input part number */
eof = fscanf(fp_parts,"%d",&part_number);
/* check for end of file */
if (eof == EOF) break;

  /*retrieve the part name into the C variable c_part_name*/
/*only if the part number matches the part number in the file*/
    {
    IIwrite("retrieve(c_part_name=p.part_name)where p.part_no=");
    IIcvar(&part_number,6,4);
    IIwrite("");
    IIsetup();
    while(IIn_get(0))
            {
            IIn_ret(c_part_name,3);
            if(IIerrtest())continue;

            /* output the part name */
            printf("The part name for part number %d \
                    is %s\n",part_number,c_part_name);
            }
            IIflushtup(0);
    }
}
}
```

Another approach to having a host language interface is to invoke C functions directly rather than having a preprocessor do the job for you. This approach is taken by some of the commercially popular DBMS. An example of a C program to perform the same task as the EQUEL program above, using the Unify host language interface, is shown below:

```
#include <stdio.h>
$include "parts.h"
$include "file.h"
main()
{
    char c_part_name[35];
    int part_number,eof;
    FILE *fp_parts,*fopen();

    /* Open the parts file containing the part numbers */
    fp_parts = fopen("parts_file","r");

    /* Open the database */
    opendb("file.db",0);

    while (1)
    {

        /* read the input part number */
        eof = fscanf(fp_parts,"%d",&part_number);
        /* check for end of file */
        if (eof == EOF) break;
        /* Access the parts record with the part_number key */
        if (acckey(parts,&part_number)== 0)
        {
            /* Retrieve and store part name in the variable c_part_name */
            gfield(part_nam,c_part_name);
            printf("The part name for part number %d is\
                %s \n",part_number,c_part_name);
        }
    }
}
```

In the above program, we have used three functions which are provided by the Unify library, *opendb, acckey,* and *gfield. Opendb* is used to open the Unify database, which is stored in the file *file.db*. The second argument to *opendb* specifies any additional dictionary information to be read in. The function *acckey* makes a record current by retrieving it based on the key value supplied. It returns a value of *0* if a record with the specified key is found. The function *gfield* takes two arguments, a field name and a C variable. It retrieves the information for the specified field and places it into the specified C variable. The field must belong to a record that was made current with *acckey*. Unify provides two commands to compile and load the program, which embeds Unify library routines. Those commands are as follows:

```
ucc -c src.c  # to compile src.c
uld obj src.o  #to load the object
```

While the exact names of the functions used by the different packages vary, the functions performed and the concepts involved in embedding the calls are very similar. Familiarity with any one host language interface can be very helpful in understanding the interface provided by other systems.

5.6 Interaction with UNIX Files

Once a database is created, it has to be loaded with data. One method of loading a database is by using the query statement to add one record at a time, which can be grossly inefficient when one is dealing with large databases. Normally, the data to be loaded is available in the form of UNIX flat files. DBMS provide utilities to load the database directly into tables from flat files. In Ingres, the QUEL statement *copy* can be used to load data from flat files into the database internal structure. In Section 5.3, we used this statement to load the parts database. This facility is available in some DBMS as a separate shell-level utility. In Unify, this facility is available through the *DBLOAD* utility. The *DBLOAD* utility is invoked as shown here:

```
DBLOAD file.db parts parts.d  parts.sp
```

File.db is the file in which the database resides. The name of the relation to be loaded is parts. Parts.d is the name of the UNIX flat file from which data is to be loaded. Finally, parts.sp is the name of the file in which the file layout specifications are stored. The layout description consists of field names separated by the same character which separates the fields in the flat file.

5.7 DBMS and the UNIX File System

Designers of UNIX-based DBMS are quick to point out the drawbacks of the UNIX file system. A discussion of the UNIX file system is beyond the scope of this book; however, it is worth mentioning that one of the major problems with the UNIX file system is the limitation on the number of opened files allowed per process.* There are also other problems at the lower level of I/O management. Some vendors, most notably Unify, have circumvented this problem by bypassing the UNIX file system and using raw I/O. They claim to achieve several major advantages in their implementation.

5.8 Creating Forms for Data Entry

In the previous section, we saw the use of UNIX utilities to load a database from a UNIX flat file. This feature of loading a database is only possible when a flat file is available. Unfortunately, there are many occasions when the data is not available in flat files but instead exists on paper. This data must be loaded into the database by the use of forms which can be displayed on the screen for ease of data entry. The data entry person can then key the data into the system, using the form with minimal instructions. These forms can be created by programmers using a high-level language without any help from the DBMS; however, many DBMS designers recognize this need and provide a forms creating package to ease the job of creating forms. Informix provides *perform*, and Unify has the *paint* option in its menu driven environment to design forms; Ingres has *vifred*. The easiest way to create a form is to let the DBMS create a default form for each table; however, these forms are often too simple for actual usage (i.e., they don't contain sufficient information to assist the data entry person) and some customizing is normally required. Most of the forms packages are powerful enough to provide data validation, error messages, and help features.

5.9 Query by Forms

Query languages are very useful for end users who have some technical knowledge about computers, but most end users would find it very difficult to learn query languages. DBMS provide a capability to let naive users interact with databases through a friendlier interface. This interface is sometimes called Query by Forms. Traditionally, forms were used for entering information. Query by Forms is a feature that extends this idea further: it

---

*4.3 BSD UNIX is better than UNIX System V in this respect.

allows the user to enter data into fields in forms that are familiar to him or her. The DBMS software fills in the other information on the form by doing appropriate retrievals. Sometimes there are several rows which satisfy the retrieval criteria. Query by Forms allows the user to scroll through these rows. It is also possible to specify relational operators in the known fields and to search on regular expressions. Some DBMS allow the user to redirect the output to a printer or a flat file.

5.10 Report Writers

Most DBMS are used not only to store and retrieve data, but also to report the retrieved data in a presentable format. The function of report writers is to report data retrieved from the database based on some query, compute summaries if necessary, and then format the data in a familiar report-like fashion. Unfortunately, report writers are highly nonstandardized. Unlike SQL, which is now accepted as a standard query language, report writers do not have any standardized specifications language.

Let us use the parts-suppliers database to report the names, part numbers, supplier names, supplier numbers, and quantity in stock for each part. Most report specifications consist of the following basic segments:

Input Data
FUNCTION: Specify the data to be used for generating the report. Typically, this is a query that is supported by the DBMS. Some DBMS packages like Unify allow data from a flat file to be piped into the report. This makes the report writer available for use with data that may not necessarily be a part of the data base. The input may optionally be sorted.
Report Heading
FUNCTION: Print items at the beginning of a report. These items may include the name of the report, the date the report was printed, the report script that created the report, etc.
Report Footing
FUNCTION: Print information at the end of a report. The report footing is used to specify the summaries for the entire data set used in the report. It could also be used to print a banner specifying the end of the report.
Page Heading
FUNCTION: Print the heading of each page. Normally each page of a report has a page number, report name, column heading, and other miscellaneous information that may concern the data printed on the page.

Page Footing

FUNCTION: Print the footing on each page. Most reports have a common set of lines to be printed on each page. These lines could be warnings that the report has classified information, or a distribution list indicating the departments or people who would be receiving the report.

Control Field Heading

FUNCTION: Specify print action before a new sort field. This section is used to print summaries before a sort field changes its value.

Control Field Footing

FUNCTION: Specify print action after a new sort field. This section is used to print summaries after a sort field changes its value.

Detail Line

FUNCTION: Print information after each input record. This section is used to actually print the data in each row. Values computed based on data in each field are also printed.

Informix provides *Ace*, a report writer package that will be used to demonstrate the functions performed by a report writer. Here is an Ace report writer specification to print the part number, part name, supplier number, supplier name, and quantity in stock for each part:

```
database
partspdb
end

output
page length 20
report to "rep.out"
top margin 2
bottom margin 2
left margin 4
end

select part_no,part_name,supp_no,supp_name,stk_qty
from parts,suppliers
where part_no = part_supp
order by part_no
end

format
page header
        print column 25, "PAGE : ",
```

```
            column 33, pageno using "page <<<<",
            column 50, "DATE : ",
            column 59, today using "mm/dd/yy"
      skip 2 line
      print column 32, "SUPPLIER NO.",
            column 47, "SUPPLIER NAME"
      print column 32, "============",
            column 47, "============="
      skip 1 line

before group of part_no
      skip 1 lines
      print column 5, "Part no : ",
            column 15, part_no using "<<<<<",
            column 24, "Part name : ",
            column 37, part_name,
            column 52, "Qty in stock : ",
            column 67, stk_qty using "<<<<<"
on every row
      print column 35, supp_no using "<<<<<",
            column 47, supp_name
end
```

The report specifications listed above use some of the basic segments
discussed earlier. The *order by* clause in the selection query sorts the input
data by part number. The *before group of part_no* section signals a new part
number in the input. It is used to print the name and the quantity in stock of
the new part. The *on every row* segment is used to print each row of the data.
The *page header* section prints the specified heading on every page. The
heading consists of a page number and the date. The other sections are fairly
easy to understand. An optional format can be associated with a field or an
item to be printed, for example, the "<<<<<" format is used to print numeric
items left-justified. The *report to* clause outputs the report to the specified file.
A sample output of the Ace report specification is shown below:

```
       PAGE :   page 1            DATE :    07/10/86



           SUPPLIER NO.    SUPPLIER NAME
           ============    =============
```

```
Part no : 1211      Part name :  Partno1211      Qty in stock : 250
                                 2121             Wilcox Trass, Inc

Part no : 2111      Part name :  Partno2111      Qty in stock : 20
                                 1218             Peter and Wiley, Inc
                                 2131             IBMS Computers, Inc

Part no : 3122      Part name :  Partno3122      Qty in stock : 200
                                 1214             Rip Van Winkle, Inc



                    PAGE :  page 2              DATE :    07/10/86



                    SUPPLIER NO.   SUPPLIER NAME
                    =============  =============

                    1231           John and Wills Inc
                    1214           Rip Van Winkle, Inc
                    1231           John and Wills Inc

Part no : 4005      Part name :  Partno4005      Qty in stock : 1020
                                 200              Rolex Inc.

Part no : 4020      Part name :  Partno4020      Qty in stock : 1220
                                 303              Malax Freezers
```

5.10.1 Other Features of Report Writers

Some report writers provide the use of additional variables which are different from the ones used in the selection query. These variables can be used to store results of intermediate computations during the report generation phase. Math functions are also available in some report writers. Explicit features to compute averages and totals enhance the features of a report writer. It is also possible to redirect the output of a report to a printer and/or to a file. Some reserved data items are also available for commonly used report features, such as page numbers and date, which were used in the Ace report specification. Different types of formats are available for reporting numeric and nonnumeric items. Features to print items left-justified or right-justified, or to print numeric items with leading zeros, leading blanks, or a leading dollar sign are very common.

Default reports are provided by most DBMS packages to print tables in a format found suitable by the report writer.

5.11 Access Methods

During the query execution phase, the DBMS selects the best possible method of retrieving the data. This depends largely on the way the data is stored. Sequential access is the most simple form of accessing data. Most UNIX file management utilities use this access method and subsequently suffer in retrieval speed. Some of the popular access methods supported by UNIX-based DBMS packages are:

Hashing
Explicit Relationships
B-trees
ISAM

Hashing is good for searching on exact values, such as policy number or social security number. Its retrieval speed is not dependent on the size of the table to be searched. B-trees or ISAM structures are good if the user queries are based on ranges of values. Explicit relationships are, strictly speaking, not a feature of a relational DBMS; however, Unify provides this feature to maintain physical links between two or more relations. These links are maintained by the DBMS. In addition to improving retrieval time, it also enforces integrity checks on the relationship. There are some disadvantages associated with explicit relationships: pointers occupy storage space; updates are slow; and most serious drawback is perhaps the necessity to reconfigure the database when an explicit relationship is to be added or dropped.

5.12 Miscellaneous Features

The currently available DBMS packages provide a host of other features in their quest for a larger piece of the UNIX DBMS market. Security features include the capability to restrict access rights to only some users. Security features can be provided at field level, record level or file level.

In relational DBMS jargon, the term views refers to providing a window to the database. This window can be defined while creating the view. By letting a user have access to only that view, security can be enforced. Views are like any other tables; however, there is no physical data stored corresponding exactly with any view. Views can also be used to simplify complex queries.

Recovery features are provided by DBMS to maintain the integrity of a database after an abnormal termination of a job involving updates to the database. This often involves maintaining transaction logs as the database is updated.

Some DBMS support graphics capability or an interface to a graphics package. Spreadsheet interface has also been announced by some vendors.

Though databases have gone through a considerable amount of technological improvement, distributed databases are not yet supported by any commercial vendor of UNIX-based DBMS. The facility to have distributed databases across machines could be very exciting, considering the rich environment that UNIX provides for communication among multiple computers.

5.13 Fourth Generation Systems

Fourth generation systems are becoming increasingly popular in the market today. What are fourth generation languages? Some experts in the area define them as nonprocedural languages like SQL and Datatrieve. A fourth generation system is an application development system that can replace the traditional approach to system implementation, which employs high-level languages like C and COBOL, with features such as a report writer, a forms management system, and support for a fourth generation language. A fourth generation system is easy for end users to use and the application development time is significantly reduced. Informix offers Informix-4GL, which is a fourth generation language that provides the same capabilities as a programming language like C or COBOL, and a lot more!

5.14 Selecting a DBMS

One of the major problems that a database designer can encounter during the project is to select the right DBMS. The best DBMS in the UNIX environment really depends on the application. Benchmarks have indicated that some DBMS are ideal for applications involving extensive inquiries, while others are more suitable for applications involving frequent updates. Many database packages are continually being enhanced with improved versions frequently available. For an application in need of a DBMS, the selection of a DBMS, based on existing DBMS studies, comments from users of any particular DBMS, and vendor literature, can be a confusing issue. A database package that lacked desired features a year ago may now have those features. The selection of a DBMS must be based on various factors, with each factor weighed to determine its importance based on the application under consideration. The next few sections discuss the factors that should be considered before selecting a DBMS.

5.14.1 Application Data Model

Some applications are inherently hierarchical. While hierarchical models can be represented using relational DBMS, the transformation can be inefficient. The DBMS should be able to support the data model that is represented by the application. Most DBMS support only the relational model. Unify is among the better-known DBMS that also support nonrelational models. If the DBMS is relational, it must provide all the features of relational models. Some of the features that may be missing include support for views, ability to handle null values, and adequate support to enforce data integrity.

5.14.2 Query Language

The query language that the DBMS supports to interface with the database is one of the most important factors to consider when selecting a DBMS. This issue is now simplified because most of the commercially available DBMS at this writing support SQL. The only notable exception is Ingres. In the future, a DBMS that does not support SQL may find itself ostracized from the UNIX DBMS family. Additional problems involve finding programmers having knowledge of a nonstandard query language.

In evaluating DBMS which support SQL, one must be careful in determining exactly which features of SQL are supported: there is always the likelihood of a clause or aggregate function missing, and that missing feature may be significant for the application at hand. Unify, for example, does not support the *create* command in its implementation, and some users may find it annoying to have to go through the menu interface to create a new table.*
Some missing features may not be important for some users and therefore a

---

*Unify DBMS, Release 3.2.

DBMS must be evaluated with the application in mind.

5.14.3 Host Language Interface

Host language interface is another important feature that deserves serious consideration during the selection of a DBMS. While all DBMS can be expected to have an interface to the C language, additional host language support can be important. The approach used in designing the host language interface should also be considered: some users like the approach followed by Ingres, while others may prefer to invoke function calls directly in their programs. A full support for the query language within the host language is a desirable feature. The host language interface must be user friendly and must interface with the forms package supported by the DBMS.

5.14.4 Query Execution Efficiency

If there is a single factor that should never be neglected in evaluating a DBMS package, it is the speed with which the queries are executed. The query optimizer associated with a DBMS must be able to use the best access method for satisfying the query. It must also have a module to perform a query transformation. The execution efficiency of a query often depends on the design of the database. In performing benchmark tests, care must be taken to be uniform in designing the databases across the DBMS being considered. The availability of good access methods very often determines the execution efficiency.

5.14.5 Report Writers and Forms Management

Unlike SQL, there is no standard report writer language that is being widely used. This makes evaluating report writers of different packages more difficult. In general, all report writers must support the features that were discussed in Section 5.10. In addition, it should be possible to use report writers on data from a flat file, on output from a query language, or on any relation belonging to the database. It must also provide a facility to redirect the report to a printer or a specified file. Creation of default reports is another desirable feature. The forms management package must be able to handle data validation, on-line help, and error messages for each type of data item, and it should have the ability to both update and query the database through forms.

5.14.6 Other Miscellaneous Features

The list of factors to be considered while evaluating a DBMS package is endless. The following are some additional features to be considered:

- It should be possible to reconfigure the database elegantly. For example, Unify stores the entire database in one file, and therefore changes to the structure of a single table often requires that the whole database be restructured.
- If security features are important for the application, the DBMS should support field-level security. Password features are also desirable.
- The DBMS must be able to support various data types, such as date, money, time, boolean, and serial, in addition to the standard data types integer, float, and character strings.
- The DBMS must be able to support search on UNIX regular expressions.
- The DBMS must have a rich set of functions at the query level.
- The DBMS must have a menu generator.
- In an environment where disk storage is important, it is important to have a DBMS that requires minimal disk storage.
- The DBMS must have a good recovery feature to ensure data integrity after a system crash.
- A good DBMS will allow for easy loading of data into the database from flat files. It will also provide a feature to dump tables from the database into flat files.
- The DBMS should allow multiple users to use the same database without it losing integrity or tying itself into a deadlock. This could be important for databases which have multiple users.
- The DBMS must also be supported on various hardware configurations. This is necessary if there is a likelihood of the hardware being upgraded or changed. It would be disastrous if the DBMS was not supported on the new hardware.
- The DBMS should offer good error messages. Informative messages are helpful for any software system, and DBMS are no exception to this rule. Unfortunately, some DBMS which are available commercially provide very cryptic error messages, and some provide error numbers rather than error messages!
- Some DBMS packages can handle a limited number of fields per record, records per file, or files per database. These limitations are normally not a barrier for most applications; however, it is always advisable to check into these restrictions.
- Technical support is a very important feature that is very often neglected during the evaluation phase. Technical support from some vendors is so poor that sometimes problems in using the software are

interpreted by evaluators as bugs! Regular training programs can be helpful to both vendors and users.

■ Most vendors provide trial copies. This trial copy should be tried by the potential user before any decision is made, especially one based on based on vendor-supplied literature.

Access to user groups, magazines, reviews of DBMS, and current users of the DBMS being considered can be very helpful in the evaluation process. Commercially available DBMS packages discussed in this chapter are continuously enhanced; new features are added and old drawbacks eliminated. The drawbacks of some of the DBMS packages discussed here may no longer be true.

6 Text Formatting Tools

UNIX provides a host of utilities for text formatting. These utilities are useful for producing high-quality documents on phototypesetters and conventional printers. The utilities are grouped into two categories: the actual software that drives the phototypesetters and the utilities that work as preprocessors for these drivers. *Troff* and *nroff* are the basic formatting utilities. *Troff* is suitable for driving phototypesetters while *nroff* is suitable for conventional printers. Though *troff* and *nroff* are very powerful for most formatting needs, novice users find it difficult to do more advanced document preparation, which may include drawing of tables and pictures, with *troff* or *nroff*. UNIX provides another set of utilities which function as preprocessors to these text formatters. The function of these preprocessors is to provide a high-level interface to the text formatting tools. *Tbl* is the preprocessor that is used extensively for drawing tables. *Pic* provides a mechanism for drawing simple pictures on a phototypesetter. *Eqn* is the mathematician's tool for typesetting mathematical characters and expressions on phototypesetters. Many printers presently support a language called POSTSCRIPT. Translators to translate *troff* output into POSTSCRIPT are also available. Several vendors also provide *troff* support for the HP LaserJet printer. This chapter discusses only those segments of these utilities that the author considers necessary for the creation of good documents by programmers and analysts.

6.1 Getting Started with Troff and Nroff

Troff and *nroff* are identical in most respects. The major difference is that *troff* commands, which provide an interface to the phototypesetter, will not function properly with *nroff*, which is suitable for communicating with conventional printers. With the advent of inexpensive laser printers, conventional printers may soon become obsolete, making personal publishing and printing a reality, so *troff* will be emphasized in this chapter.

Troff reads from the standard input and outputs to the standard output. *Troff* understands some of the basic requirements of a text formatter and will do these by default. Consider the simple, unformatted paragraph shown in Figure 6.1.

```
Now my story ends. I look back, once again, for the last time.
I see myself, journeying along the road of life. I hear the roar
of many voices, not indifferent to me as I travel on. What faces
are the most distinct to me in this fleeting crowd? Some kind
and some otherwise. I shiver as I ask this
question to my thoughts. The debate continues as more issues
arise and fill my mind until there is room for no more. The
overfilled mind cries. There is a nervous breakdown, the world
shatters. The betrayal continues and the betrayed starts
betraying. This is one journey that is not worth traveling.
I change my path. Soon, I am called a loser! This is the
story of one such loser. Born in  a free society where the
poor are as free to be hungry as the rich are to be excessive.
The alienation of the two becomes a bond in freedom! The
ultimate instinct is survival. The race is too fierce. There
is ample proof of the Darwinian principle of the survival of
the fittest.*
```

Figure 6.1 Unformatted Text

This unformatted input can be formatted by *troff* with some basic commands:

---

*Adapted from Charles Dickens' *David Copperfield*.

```
.ll 3i
.nh
.po 0.5i
```

When these commands are inserted at the beginning of the text file, they format the input text according to their functions. First, the *.ll 3i* command informs *troff* that the line length of the ouput text is to be set to three inches. The next command, *.nh*, refers to no hyphenations. *Troff* will try to put each word from the input text on the ouput line. When a word does not fit in fully on the line, this word has to be broken, unless the *.nh* command is present to eliminate hyphenation of words across line boundaries. The command *.po 0.5i* sets the page offset to half an inch. The function of this command is to set the left margin half an inch to the right of the left edge of the paper. The right margin is then set according to the page offset and the length of the line. These simple commands create the formatted text shown in Figure 6.2.

Now my story ends. I look back, once again, for the last time. I see myself, journeying along the road of life. I hear the roar of many voices, not indifferent to me as I travel on. What faces are the most distinct to me in this fleeting crowd? Some kind and some otherwise. I shiver as I ask this question to my thoughts. The debate continues as more issues arise and fill my mind until there is room for no more. The overfilled mind cries. There is a nervous breakdown, the world shatters. The betrayal continues and the betrayed starts betraying. This is one journey that is not worth traveling. I change my path. Soon, I am called a loser! This is the story of one such loser. Born in a free society where the poor are as free to be hungry as the rich are to be excessive. The alienation of the two becomes a bond in freedom! The ultimate instinct is survival. The race is too fierce. There is ample proof of the Darwinian principle of the survival of the fittest.

Figure 6.2 Formatted Text

Sometimes it is necessary to start writing on new lines. *Troff* treats each line as a single piece of continuous text unless one uses the *.br* command to force the start of a new line. The *.sp* command forces blank lines. The *.in* command is used to change the indentation at the left margin for all lines following the command. The *.ti* command is used to change the offset temporarily for the next line only. This is particularly helpful for starting a new paragraph. The *.ls* command is used to control the distance between two lines.

It is important to remember that there are various units that can be used to specify the arguments to these commands. In *nroff*, arguments are normally specified in number of characters or lines. *Troff* accepts various units, for example em, en, basic unit, inch, etc. Most of these are important to professional phototypesetters. For most people, it is sufficient to know the units explained in Table 6.1. The command *.sp 2c*, for example, will leave a gap of two centimeters between two consecutive lines, and the command, *.in 1i* will indent the text following this command by one inch. The *.ce n* command is used to center lines of text, where *n* specifies the number of lines to be centered. Most *troff* parameters can be changed with respect to their previous value by preceding the argument with the appropriate sign. Thus *.po +0.5i* will increase the page offset by half an inch.

TABLE 6.1 Commonly Used Units in Troff

Units	*Troff* indicator
i	Inch
c	Centimeter
p	Point = 1/72 inch
P	Pica = 1/6 inch

Let us look at a sample *troff* input which uses the commands explained so far to format a letter:

```
.in 3in
1212 Jackson Avenue
.br
Ratantown, NJ 07100
.br
.sp
August 12, 1986
.sp 2
.in
```

```
Mr. Jerry Mariott
.br
Nutan Consultants, Inc.
.br
1802 Shalan Avenue
.br
New York, NY 01001
.sp 2
Dear Mr. Mariott:
.sp
I am writing to you regarding your advertisement in the New York
Times dated Aug. 10, 1986. I am presently employed by a major
financial institution as a database analyst. I would like to be
considered for the position of project leader in your company.
.sp
I have enclosed my resume for your perusal. As you can see from
my resume, I have fairly diversified experience in the area of
database management systems, having worked with the major database
management systems currently available in the market.
.sp
I will be waiting eagerly for your response.
.sp 3
.in 3i
Sincerely,
.sp 2
John Doe
```

After we run *troff* to format this letter, it looks as it is shown in Figure 6.3.

6.1.1 Fonts and Point Sizes

Fonts are character types that allow users to produce documents with different levels of emphasis. They also serve to distinguish one segment of text from another. The most commonly used fonts are *italic*, roman and **bold**. Normally a fourth font, referred to as the special mathematical font, is also available.[*] The command *.ft* is used to change the font to be used in outputting the text. The letter B is used to specify the bold font, the letter I is used to specify italic font, and finally the letter R is used to specify the roman font. It is also possible to change fonts in the middle of a line by inserting the text sequence \fF where F is the name of the font to be used. The following text input illustrates the use of commands to change fonts:

---

[*]Additional fonts may also be available; check with your administrator.

1212 Jackson Avenue
Ratantown, NJ 07100

August 12, 1986

Mr. Jerry Mariott
Nutan Consultants, Inc.
1802 Shalan Avenue
New York, NY 01001

Dear Mr. Mariott:

I am writing to you regarding your advertisement in the New York Times dated Aug. 10, 1986. I am presently employed by a major financial institution as a database analyst. I would like to be considered for the position of project leader in your company.

I have enclosed my resume for your perusal. As you can see from my resume, I have fairly diversified experience in the area of database management systems, having worked with the major database management systems currently available in the market.

I will be waiting eagerly for your response.

Sincerely,

John Doe

Figure 6.3 Formatted Letter

```
.ft R
This line is in roman font.
.ft I
This line is in italic font.
.ft B
This line is in bold font.
.ft I
This part of the line is in italic and \fRthe remaining is in roman.
```

Let us run *troff* with the input file displayed above. The output of this *troff* run is shown here:

> This line is in roman font.
> *This line is in italic font.*
> **This line is in bold font.**
> *This part of the line is in italic and* the remaining is in roman.

Notice how the fonts can be changed within a line. This feature is very helpful for highlighting key words. Certain fonts are specified using two characters, for example, the **Helvetica-Bold** font is usually specified by the two letters *HB*.[*] These fonts can be changed within a line by using the command \f(*xx*, where *xx* is the name of the font. The left parenthesis is required when the font name is two characters.

6.1.2 Changing Point Sizes

The size of the output character can be changed by using the *.ps* command. The units are commonly specified in points, and there are normally 15 point sizes available. Like the commands to change fonts, it is also possible to change the size of characters in the middle of a line. The command \s is used for this. Here is a *troff* specification file to show how character size can be changed:

```
.ps 6
This line is in point size 6.
.br
.ps 7
This line is in point size 7.
.br
.ps 9
```

---

[*]This may vary depending on the implementation of the *troff* driver for the specific printer.

```
This line is in point size 9.
.br
.ps 10
This line is in point size 10.
.br
.ps 12
This line is in point size 12 and \s8 This line is in size 8.
```

This *troff* specifications file generates the following output:

This line is in point size 6.

This line is in point size 7.

This line is in point size 9.

This line is in point size 10.

This line is in point size 12 and This line is in size 8.

Once again we have been able to change the output format within a line.

6.1.3 Macros in Troff

Troff allows the use of macros. Macros in *troff* have the form:

```
.de MN
troff commands
..
```

The *.de* command defines a macro. The definition is terminated by a double dot (..). A macro can be invoked like any other command. All commands which are included in the macro definition are expanded by the macro invocation. A macro name can be one or two characters long. Macros can be used to group a frequently used set of commands into a simple command. Arguments can also be passed to macros. These arguments can be correctly interpreted within the macro by their position on the invocation line. Here is a sample macro that prints the first word in bold font on a fresh line and the remaining five words in roman font on the next line. Note the use of the escape characters to refer to the arguments used in the macro definition.

```
.de MC
.br
.ft B
\\$1
.ft R
\\$2 \\$3 \\$4 \\$5 \\$6
..
```

This macro can be invoked as

```
.MC Program Compute the Sum of Integers
```

which produces the following output:

Program
Compute the Sum of Integers

6.1.4 Environment Switching

Troff provides an environment that can be used to store various parameters such as page length, line length, partially filled words, and partially filled lines. These parameters can be saved by saving the environment itself. Processing can then start in a new environment. The old environment can also be restored when desired. The command *.ev* switches to the specified environment.* If no argument is given, the previous environment is restored. Environment switching is very useful for processing page breaks and diversions. This feature will be used in the next section to illustrate the processing of page breaks.

6.1.5 Traps and Page Breaks in Troff

Troff uses a default page length of 11 inches. This can be changed by the use of the *.pl* command. *Troff* continues to output lines of text until it senses the end of the page as defined by the page length command. It then skips to the next page and continues to output more lines of text. Clearly, this is not a very desirable feature, since often, at the top or bottom of a page, it is desirable to include some special processing like page numbers and/or titles.

---

*Most *troff* implementations have a limit of three environments.

Traps are used to process page headings and footings. Traps for processing page breaks have the general form

.wh *distance macro*

Distance is the vertical position on the page and can be either positive or negative. Positive distance is measured from the top of the page, and a negative distance is measured from the bottom of the page. A zero indicates the top of a page. *Macro* is the name of the macro to be invoked at the specified page position. Here is a simple *troff* specification text that uses a page length of three inches, prints text after skipping 0.5 inch from the top of the page, and leaves a margin of 0.5 inch at the bottom of the page:

```
.pl 3i
.ll 4i
.wh -0.5i BP
.de BP
.ev 1
.ll 4i
'bp
'sp 0.5i
.ce
Processing Page breaks
'sp 0.3i
.ev
..
.sp 1i
This is a sample text segment to illustrate the use of macros
for processing page headings and page footings. The macro
BP is invoked when the print position reaches 0.5 inch from the
bottom of the page. It skips another 0.5 inch from the top of the
page and prints a centered heading, \fIProcessing Page Breaks,\fR
for the purpose of illustration. As you can see, we have used a
new environment to process the page breaks. At the end of the
processing we return back to the old environment. The line length
has to be reset in the new environment. The use of a different
environment eliminates the problem of printing partially filled
lines at the top or bottom of a page.  Sometimes, page breaking
requires the use of another trap to be invoked at the top of a
page. In this example, we have used only one macro which is
invoked relative to the bottom of the page.
```

Try to run this *troff* file on your system using *nroff* or *troff*, and study the output. Try to understand the entire output format from the top, bottom, left, and right margins.

The attentive reader will recognize that the break commands in the previous example have been modified from .*sp* to '*sp* and from .*bp* to '*bp*. The break commands beginning with a . (dot) cause all input text that has been read into the buffer to be printed, so that the next input line can start on a fresh line. Clearly, this will have undesirable effects during page breaks, because it is an attribute associated with the environment. The last and the first line on each page will not be guaranteed to be completely filled. The '*sp* and the '*bp* commands eliminate this problem. The title length has to be specified in the new environment that is used to process page breaks. In general, the use of the break commands discussed here along with the use of a new environment should be used for processing page breaks. The use of a new environment during page breaks also eliminates problems associated with fill/no-fill modes, fonts, and point sizes that may be in effect when the page break is invoked.

6.1.6 Processing Titles

Titles are processed through the use of the .*tl* command. This command has the form

```
.tl 'left'center'right'
```

Left is the segment of the title that is left-adjusted, *center* is the segment of the title that is centered, and *right* is the segment of the title that is right-adjusted. This adjustment is done in the length of the title. The length of the title can be adjusted using the .*lt* command. The percent sign *(%)* is a *troff* register, that is used to print page numbers. The current page number itself can be changed using the .*pn* command. Let us provide a title to the previous *troff* output by rewriting the macro BP, as shown below:

```
.de BP
.ev 1
.ll 4i
'bp
'sp 0.5i
.ce
.lt 4i
.tl '%'Processing Page Breaks'%'
```

```
'sp 0.3i
.ev
..
```

This macro will generate a page title that looks like this:

1   Processing Page Breaks   1

The *.pn* command could have been used to change the page number to something other than 1.

6.1.7 Filling and Adjusting

Filling is the process of creating lines having as many words as can be accommodated, given the limitation of the length of the line. Adjusting is the process of spacing words within lines so that the right and the left margins are properly aligned. These features are automatically taken care of by *troff*. Sometimes these features are not desirable and have to be switched off. One common situation is when printing a program listing in the middle of documentation. Indenting, filling, and adjusting a program listing can destroy the readability of the program beyond imagination. The command *.na* is used to stop the adjusting feature and the command *.ad* is used to reactivate it. Similarly, the commands *.nf* and *.fi* are used to stop and restart filling. If the following program had to be listed in the middle of a formatted document, the text would look as shown below:

```
.na
.nf
#include <stdio.h>
main()
{
        int number1,number2;
        char string1[30];
        while (1)
        {
          eof = scanf("%d%d",&number1,&number2);
          result = number1 + number2;
          printf("%d\n",result);
        }
}
.ad
.fi
```

After printing the program, we reset the adjust and fill modes so that the following lines of documentation will be filled and adjusted.

6.1.8 Registers and Strings

Troff provides access to a set of registers, which can be either user-defined or predefined by *troff*. These registers are used to store numbers. A register name can be one or two characters long. Some basic arithmetic operations are possible on these registers. Number registers, as they are often called, are defined by the use of the command *.nr*. This command is followed by the name of the register, followed by an optional initial value, followed by an optional auto-increment or auto-decrement value. A register is accessed in the input text by the use of commands shown in Table 6.2.

TABLE 6.2 Interpolation of Register R

Input	Interpolated value
\nR	Contents of R
\n+R	R + auto-increment
\n−R	R − auto-decrement

A register name that is two characters long is accessed as \n(RR, where *RR* is the name of the register. If the incremented value of register *RR* is required, it is accessed as \n + (RR.

A string in *troff* is defined by the *.ds* command; therefore, the string *ST* can be made to have the value *TABLE NO* by the use of the command:

```
.ds ST TABLE NO
```

This string can be interpolated anywhere in the text by the use of the input sequence *(xx, where *xx* is the name of the string, as in *(ST . If the string name is only one character long, then the string can be interpolated by the input sequence * , as in *S .

Here is a macro that is a simplified version of the macro that was used for printing section headings for typesetting this book:

```
.de NS
.ft B
\\nC.\\n+S \\$1 \\$2 \\$3 \\$4 \\$5 \\$6 \\$7 \\$8 \\$9
```

```
.ft
..
```

In this macro, register C contains the chapter number. Register S contains the section number, which is incremented and then printed. The arguments to the macro specify the name of the section. To generate the chapter and section number, simply specify the name of the section along with the macro invocation, and *troff* will automatically increment the section number. Thus, if the current value of register C is 6, and if the current value of register S is 2, then

```
.NS Third section
.NS Fourth section
```

will generate

6.3 Third section

6.4 Fourth section

6.1.9 Diversions

Sometimes it is important to know the size of a processed segment of output before actually outputting it. These situations arise during the processing of tables, pictures, and footnotes, when one wants to avoid breaking them across a page. Diversions are used for storing these processed segments. Once processed, the horizontal and vertical sizes of the processed segment can be determined, and the segment can be output accordingly at an appropriate position. There are various commands associated with diversions. The *.di* command starts diverting the processed output into the specified diversion. This diversion can be ended by using the same command without any argument. Thus

```
.di DR
troff input
.di
```

will divert the output of *troff input* into the specified diversion *DR*. This diverted and processed output can be reproduced by invoking the diversion as follows:

```
.DR
```

Once diverted, the vertical size of this diversion is available in register *dn* and the horizontal size in register *dl*. Normally, one would check to see if the diverted output can be fitted into the remaining space of the page. If there is enough space on the page, the processed diversion is output, otherwise processing continues until a new page is encountered. The macro that is invoked for page breaks is modified to spit out any pending diversions. Similarly, diversions can be used for processing footnotes. See the example in the next section for more details.

6.1.10 Conditional Input

Sometimes it is desirable to print something only if a certain condition is satisfied. *Troff* provides the *.if* command, which checks for the condition and outputs text accordingly. There are many forms of conditions that are available. One of the conditions is to check whether the page number is even or odd. This feature was used in the *troff* input for this book, to generate different page titles on odd and even pages. The command *.if o* \{ *commands* \} will execute the specified commands if the page number is odd. Another use of the *.if* command is in the processing of diversions. The *.if* command can be used to check whether the diversion can be accommodated in the remaining portion of the page.

Some examples of the use of the *.if* command are:

```
.if e .tl 'EVEN PAGE'''
.if o .tl 'ODD'''
```

which will output different titles on odd and even pages, and

```
.if \nX>\nY \{
troff commands
\}
```

which will execute the specified *troff* commands only if the content of register *X* is greater than the content of register *Y*.

Let us write a set of *troff* macros to retain a block of text on a single page.

If there is not enough space on the present page, printing of input external to the block will continue. The diverted block will then be printed on the next page. The macros *BL* and *BE* are used to enclose the block of text. The new-page macro, *BP*, is modified to output pending diversions.

```
.wh -2i BP
.de BP
.ev 1
'bp
'sp 30p
.tl '%' Processing Page Breaks '%'
.ps
'sp 13p
.nf
.FG
.rm FG
.ev
..
.de BL \" This is a troff comment line; from \" to end of line
.br
.ev 2
.fi
.ll 3i
.di FG
..
.de BE
.br
.di  \" Note how the newline character is concealed in the .if
.if \\(dn<=\\n(.t \{ \
.nf
.FG
.rm FG
\}
.ev
..
```

This example illustrates many *troff* features which were explained in the previous sections. The *BL* macro initiates a diversion in fill mode, and the *BE* macro terminates the diversion. The *dn* register has the height of the most recent diversion, and the predefined *troff* register *.t* stores the distance to the next trap, which is set at the bottom of the page. The *.if* command is used to check whether there is enough space, for the diverted output, on the current page. Note how multiple commands for the if statements are enclosed within the \{ and \} marks. The page-break macro has been modified to print any pending diversions. To avoid the diversion being printed twice, it is removed after it is printed by the use of the .rm command. The .br commands are used to begin new lines where necessary.

6.1.11 Linear Motion and Lines

Local horizontal and vertical motion are possible in *troff* by the use of the \h'N' and the \v'N' commands respectively. N specifies the distance. It is always safe to specify the unit to override any default units; therefore, to move to the right by three inches, issue the command \h'3i'. Similarly, it is possible to move to the left by specifying a negative distance. Vertical motion upward is possible by using a negative N in the \v'N' command.

Troff also provides some commands to draw lines. Horizontal lines can be drawn by the use of the command \l'Nc'. The character c is used to specify the line drawing character. Similarly, \L'Nc' is used to draw a vertical line downward for a distance of N, using the character c to draw the vertical line. A negative value of N will draw the line upward.

6.1.12 Special Registers and Characters

Troff provides access to many non-ASCII characters and a host of predefined number registers, and these are tabulated in Tables 6.3 and 6.4 respectively.

TABLE 6.3 Special Non-ASCII Characters

Character	Input Sequence
Γ	\(*G
α	\(*a
β	\(*b
γ	\(*g
≥	\(>=
→	\(->
↑	\(ua
÷	\(di
○	\(ci

6.1.13 Include Capability of Troff

Troff offers a feature that includes an external file in the file that is currently being processed. This feature can be used by specifying the file to be included along with the *.so* command. To include the macro definition file named macros.file in the current input file use

```
.so macros.file
```

This feature is useful for including shared macro definition files without having to specify them on the command line each time *troff* is run.

6.1.14 Command-Level Options

Troff provides a series of command level options. The most commonly used options are $-o$, $-n$, and $-T$. The option $-o$ is used to specify the page numbers to be output, e.g., $-o3-23$ will output only pages 3 to 23. The $-n$ option is used to specify the starting page number. In the absence of this option, the first page will be numbered 1. The option $-T$ is used to specify the print device. Check with your system administrator for the available list of printers at your site.

TABLE 6.4 Important Predefined Registers

Register	Contents
%	Current page number
ln	Output line number
dw	Current day of the week
mo	Current month
yr	Last two digits of current year
dl	Width of last completed diversion
dn	Height of last completed diversion

6.1.15 Closing Thoughts

Troff is too big a language to be covered in a single section; however, the commands discussed here should enable the reader to produce high-quality documents. *Troff* is relatively old. Enhancements to *troff* have largely consisted of macros which make it more user friendly. With the use of preprocessors like *pic*, *eqn*, and *tbl*, *troff* is still a powerful tool for phototypesetting. These preprocessors are discussed in the following sections.

6.2 Tbl: Preparing Tables

Troff provides features for formatting and printing tables, but these features are not very convenient for novice users to handle. *Tbl* provides an easier method for printing tables in *troff*. *Tbl* commands can be very easily embedded in a *troff* specifications file. In this section, we will see the use of *tbl* for formatting tables of moderate complexity. The input specifications file is first passed through *tbl*. The output is piped to *troff*, and the output of *troff* can be piped to the local print spooler.

6.2.1 Getting Started with Tbl

A simple table consists of rows, columns and column headings. Columns may contain numeric or string data. A table may be centered or left-justified. The whole table may be enclosed in a box. The rows may be separated by lines. Similarly, columns may be separated from each other by vertical lines. A column heading may span several columns or the whole table may have a heading spanning all the columns. The general format of a *tbl* specification file and a sample tbl specifications file are shown in Figure 6.4.

```
.TS                            .TS
table-level options ;          box;
column-level options.          a a.
rows ....                      item11↑item12
      .                        item21↑item22
      .                        item31↑item32
.TE                            .TE
```

Figure 6.4 Tbl Specifications Format and Sample Tbl Specifications

The sample *tbl* specification file shown in Figure 6.4 generates the table shown below in Table 6.5.

TABLE 6.5 Simple Table

item11	item12
item21	item22
item31	item32

The *t* character is used in Figure 6.4 to indicate the tab character. It is the default column-separating character. This default character can be changed by the use of the table-level specification *tab (x)*, where *x* becomes the new character to separate column entries. The next section explains more table-level specifications. If the *tbl* specifications file is compared to the general format of the *tbl* specifications given in Figure 6.4, the following observation can be made. First, *box* is a table-level specification and is terminated by a semicolon. The column-level specifications are given in the next line and consist of two *a* characters separated by a single blank. This line is terminated by a period. Finally, the actual data that makes up the table is entered. Each line corresponds to a row. Columns are tab-separated. The *tbl* specifications are terminated by a *.TE* command.

6.2.2 Table-Level Specifications

Table-level specifications affect the whole table. We used the *box* specification to instruct *tbl* to enclose the whole table in a box. Other commonly used table-level specifications are shown in Table 6.6.

TABLE 6.6 Table-Level Tbl Specifications

Specification	Effect
allbox	Boxes the entire table and each row and column
center	Centers the entire table
expand	Expands the entire table to make it as wide as the current line length
tab(x)	Changes the column-separating character to x

Let us try to use one of these table-level specifications to box each item.

The modified *tbl* specifications file looks like this:

```
.TS
allbox;
a a.
item11⟋item12
item21⟋item22
item31⟋item32
.TE
```

The actual table that *tbl* draws after piping the output to *troff* is:

item11	item12
item21	item22
item31	item32

6.2.3 Column-Level Specifications

Let us look at the column-level specifications that *tbl* provides. In our example, we have only used the *a* specification to format each column. The *a* column format specifies that the column is an alphabetic column and that data in that column is to be left-adjusted. When there is more than one row specifying the column format, each data line corresponds to a row specification. The last column format specification line corresponds to the remaining rows in the table. Other commonly used column formats are explained in Table 6.7.

TABLE 6.7 Commonly Used Column Formats

Format	Description
r	Right-adjusted column entry.
c	Centered entry.
n	Numerical column entry.
s	The entry from the previous column continues in this column.

Let us have a spanned heading for the table. The table specifications file is rewritten as follows:

```
.TS
allbox;
c s
a a.
Spanned Heading
item11↙item12
item21↙item22
item31↙item32
.TE
```

The new table generated by *tbl* is shown in Table 6.8.

TABLE 6.8 Table with Spanned Heading

Spanned Heading	
item11	item12
item21	item22
item31	item32

6.2.4 Boxing Selected Columns

The *allbox* specification boxes the entire table and each row and column. It is possible to box only selected columns or even selected items. If the column-formatting characters are separated by a vertical bar (I), a vertical line is drawn separating the items in the two columns. Similarly, spanned horizontal lines can be created by having a line containing only an underline (_) or an equal sign (=). This will cause a line to be drawn equal to the full width of the table. It is possible to draw a line to extend the width of one column only to meet horizontal or vertical lines adjoining this column by having the column entry where this line is desired made up of the single character _ or =. Here is an example:

```
.TS
box;
c|s|s
a|a|n.
Spanned Heading
=
```

```
item11ʎitem12ʎ100
ʎ_
item21ʎitem22ʎ2
ʎ_
item31ʎitem32ʎ45
.TE
```

The actual formatted table is shown in Table 6.9.

TABLE 6.9 Table with Boxed Items

Spanned Heading		
item11	item12	100
item21	item22	2
item31	item32	45

6.2.5 Passing Troff Commands

Troff commands enclosed within a *tbl* specifications file are passed to *tbl* untouched. This facilitates changes in fonts and point sizes within the table. Let us get a bit more fancy and generate the table heading in bold font. The column headings are also centered in the columns.

```
.TS
allbox;
c s s
c c c
a a n.
.ft B
Spanned Heading
Column1ʎColumn2ʎColumn3
.ft R
=
item11ʎitem12ʎ100
item21ʎitem22ʎ2
item31ʎitem32ʎ45
.TE
```

The table is printed as shown in Table 6.10. Note how the table headings are printed in a different font from the items themselves. Also, the table-level specification *allbox*, along with the = line (for a line to span the entire table) has the effect of printing three lines at the specified position.

TABLE 6.10 Table with Varied Fonts

Spanned Heading		
Column1	Column2	Column3
item11	item12	100
item21	item22	2
item31	item32	45

It is also possible to specify different fonts for different columns. This can be done by appending *F*, where *F* is the font specification character, to the column-formatting key letter *f*. To print the second column in the previous table in bold, the *tbl* specification file will have to be rewritten as follows:

```
.TS
allbox;
c s s
c c c
a afB n.
.ft B
Spanned Heading
Column1↙Column2↙Column3
.ft R
item11↙item12↙100
item21↙item22↙2
item31↙item32↙45
.TE
```

The resulting table is shown in Table 6.11.

6.2.6 Columns with Blocks of Text

Tables in real life are often more complex than a single-line entry for each item. On many occasions, a block of text has to be entered in a column which

TABLE 6.11 Varied Column Fonts

Spanned Heading		
Column1	Column2	Column3
item11	item12	100
item21	item22	2
item31	item32	45

is associated with a single-line item in another column. *Tbl* provides a mechanism to enter such columns. A single contiguous column can be entered as follows:

```
previous columnℓT{
   block of
   text corresponding to
   a column
T}ℓnext column
```

Text entered within a *T{* and a *T}* constitutes a single column item that may span many rows. The width of this column can also be specified explicitly by using the *w* format and by enclosing the width in parentheses alongside the column format specifier. The following text will produce the table shown in Table 6.12:

```
.TS
box;
c|lw(2i)|lw(1.5i).
item1ℓT{
This is a block of text
that spans across more than
one row. All the text that is
enclosed in this block belongs
to only one column. The column
width is specified as 2 inches.
T}ℓT{
This is the third column
of the same row. It is also
the final column. A narrow
column width is specified
for this column
```

```
T }
  .TE
```

TABLE 6.12 Table with Column Blocks

item1	This is a block of text that spans across more than one row. All the text that is enclosed in this block belongs to only one column. The column width is specified as 2 inches.	This is the third column of the same row. It is also the final column. A narrow column width is specified for this column

Tbl provides features that can handle very complex tables. In this chapter, we covered the most commonly used features. Most programmers and analysts will find the features covered in this chapter sufficient for preparing technical documents; however, please refer to the bibliography at the end of this book for a more detailed source of information about *tbl*.

6.3 Drawing Pictures with Pic

Pic is a program for drawing simple pictures involving squares, circles, rectangles, arcs, etc. Like *tbl*, it is a preprocessor to *troff*. *Pic* commands are surrounded by a *.PS* and a *.PE*. The reader will notice the similarity with the use of the *.TS* and the *.TE* commands in *tbl* specifications. At the shell level, the format of the command to use *pic* is identical to that of the command to use *tbl*. If you are using *pic* and *tbl* specifications, you can pipe the output of *pic* into *tbl*. The output of *tbl* can be piped to *troff* and finally to the local print spooler, as shown below:

```
pic input-file | tbl | troff -Tdevice-name | lpr*
```

6.3.1 Getting Started

Let us draw a simple box followed by a circle followed by an ellipse. Let these figures be joined together by small lines. Here is a *pic* specification to draw this picture:

---

*On some systems, the print spooler is called lp.

```
.PS
  box; line;circle;line ;ellipse
.PE
```

The picture drawn by *pic* is shown in Figure 6.5.

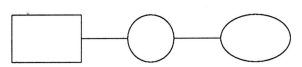

Figure 6.5 Simple Picture Drawn by Pic

6.3.2 Pic Building Blocks

Pic provides some building blocks for drawing pictures of various figures. The *pic* specifications file contains the description of each building block separated by a semicolon or a newline character. These building blocks have default parameters associated with them. The picture drawn by *pic* in the earlier section made use of these default parameters. The default values associated with these figures are shown below:

Figure	Default parameters
Box	Width : 0.75" Height : 0.5"
Circle	Diameter : 0.5"
Ellipse	Width : 0.75" Height : 0.5"
Arc	Radius : 0.5"
Arrow	Length : 0.5"
Line	Length : 0.5"
Move	Length : 0.5"

These parameters can be changed by the user to generate pictures having these basic figures in different sizes. We can now redraw the picture in Figure 6.5 using our own parameters. The modified *pic* specification file is as follows:

```
.PS
box width 1i height 1i; line 0.5i;circle rad 0.5i;
line 0.5i; ellipse height 0.25i length 0.5i
.PE
```

The picture generated by *pic* is shown in Figure 6.6.

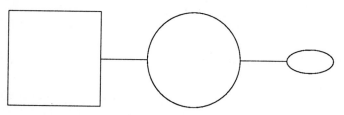

Figure 6.6 Picture with Specified Parameters

The entire picture can be scaled by using an argument on the .*PS* command line. This argument specifies the width of the picture. The height of the picture is scaled proportionately. Let us modify our *pic* specification file to scale our picture to a width of 3" as shown below:

```
.PS 3"
box width 1i height 1i; line 0.5i;circle rad 0.5i;
line 0.5i; ellipse height 0.25i width 0.5i
.PE
```

The scaled picture is shown in Figure 6.7. The parameters defined previously will be evaluated, and the figures will be drawn in the same proportions with respect to each other as they were in Figure 6.6, but the scale of the entire picture will be altered according to the arguments on the .*PS* command line.

6.3.3 Positioning Figures

Pic uses the standard cartesian system. It starts at 0,0, and it is possible to position the figure at the required coordinates by using the *move* figure. Moving to a position is like drawing an invisible line. *Pic* also allows the user

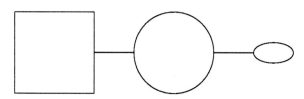

Figure 6.7 Scaled Picture

to place figures at any position using the *at* modifier. The position specified is used to locate geometrical center of the figure. The default direction of motion is from left to right. This direction can be changed using the following direction modifiers *right, left, up,* and *down.* The *pic* specification

```
.PS 1i 3i
box width 1i height 1i; move to 0.5i,-0.5i; down;line 1i;
box width 1i height 1i;
line 1i;box width 1i height 1i; move to 0i,-2.0i;
line left 1i; box width 1i height 1i;
.PE
```

produces the picture shown in Figure 6.8. Dotted lines can be drawn using the line modifier *dotted* and dashed lines can be drawn using the modifier *dashed.*

6.3.4 Drawing Arcs

Arcs are useful in generating figures which are not made up of simple straight lines. Arcs require three basic parameters: a direction, a start position, and a terminating position. The default direction of movement is counterclockwise. The *cw* modifier can be used to change the direction of movement to clockwise. The *from* attribute is used to specify the start position, and the *to* attribute is used to specify the terminating position. The commonly accepted template for a file figure can be drawn using lines and arcs. The *pic* specification file is as follows:

```
.PS
move to  1i,0i; line 1i; move to  1i,-0.5i;line right 1i
move to 1i,-0.5i;arc to 1i,0i; move to  2i,-0.5i;
arc to 2i,0i;
  .PE
```

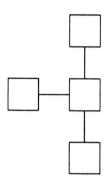

Figure 6.8 Using Direction Modifiers with Pic

These *pic* specifications generate the file figure shown in Figure 6.9.

Figure 6.9 Figure to Indicate a File

6.3.5 Macros in Pic

Pic allows the use of macros, which can be used to define figures which are not otherwise provided by *pic*. The syntax of a macro definition is:

define *name-of-the-macro* **X** *macro substitution* **X**

Macros also allow the use of arguments, and these can be referenced as $1, $2, ..., $9. The macro can be invoked by writing

```
name-of-the-macro(argument1,argument2,...,argument9)
```

Here is a macro definition for the file figure we drew in Figure 6.9. It takes as its first argument the *x*-coordinate of its top left corner, the second argument specifies the *y*-coordinate of its top left corner, the third argument specifies the width of the file template, and the height is fixed at 0.5 inch.

```
.PS
define FILE X move to  $1,$2;line $3; move to   $1,$2-0.5i;
line right $3; move to $1,$2-0.5i;arc to $1,$2;
move to  $1+$3,$2-0.5i; arc to $1+$3,$2 X
.PE
```

The macro is invoked as follows:

```
.PS
 FILE(1i,-0.5i,1i)
.PE
```

It produces the picture shown in Figure 6.10.

Figure 6.10 File Template Drawn Using a Macro

6.3.6 Processing Text

Text can be associated with any *pic* figure. The specification

```
.PS
box "centered" "text"
.PE
```

produces the simple box shown in Figure 6.11.

```
centered
text
```

Figure 6.11 Text Associated with a Pic Figure

Each line of text has to be entered in separate pairs of quotes. Text need not always be associated with a figure. It can be placed independently by using the *at* modifier. The position given specifies the center of the text. This can be changed by using the *ljust* and *rjust* modifiers. Here is an example to illustrate text processing in *pic*:

```
.PS
box at 2i,-0.5i;
"This is an example of text processing" ljust at 1i,-0.2i
.PE
```

The output produced by this *pic* specification is shown in Figure 6.12.

6.3.7 Miscellaneous Features

Pic provides some other features which are not covered in this chapter. These include setting variable values which can be used instead of numeric values. It is also possible to use expressions instead of actual numeric values. *Pic* can be used to draw splines through the use of the *pic* figure *spline*. *Pic* also keeps

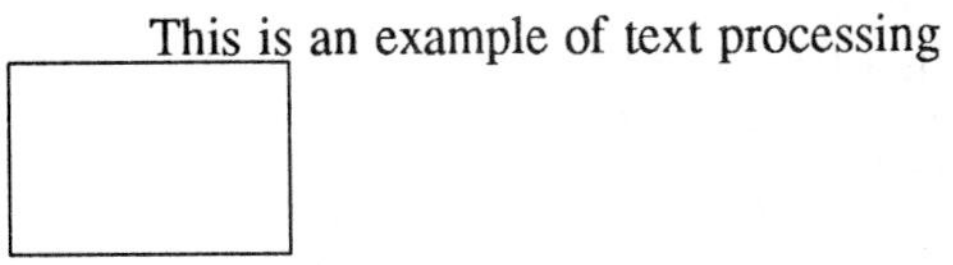

This is an example of text processing

Figure 6.12 Placing Text in Pic

---

track of the last figure drawn, and this can be referenced by using the attribute *last*. *Pic* provides an include facility, for example, it is possible to include the file incl_file, starting with the line *.PS* and ending with the line *.PE*, by using the *pic* command

```
.PS < incl_file
```

Troff commands can be used within *pic* specifications to change fonts and point size. The features of *pic* explained in this chapter are sufficient for a programmer or a analyst to draw flow charts, syntax graphs, and other illustrations.

6.4 Eqn: A Formatter for Mathematical Expressions

We have seen the use of *tbl* and *pic* for drawing tables and pictures. *Eqn* is another preprocessor to *troff* that is used for generating mathematical expressions. Like *tbl* and *pic*, *eqn* can help you avoid the possible frustration of working with *troff*. The preprocessor *neqn* is used for piping the output to *nroff* instead of *troff*. *Eqn* commands are enclosed within the lines *.EQ* and *.EN*. It provides features to generate mathematical expressions containing Greek symbols, fractions, matrices, subscripts, superscripts, etc. In this section, we will cover *eqn* features which generate mathematical expressions containing equations of moderate levels of complexity.

6.4.1 Getting Started

Let us generate a simple mathematical expression using *eqn*:

```
.EQ
z = x + y sup 2
.EN
```

This generates the following expression:

$$z = x + y^2$$

In the *eqn* specification file, the word *sup* was used to generate a superscript for *y*. Similarly, other words are available to generate mathematical expressions involving motions and sizes which would be hard to specify in *troff*.

Eqn allows the user to insert multiple spaces when inputting expressions but these spaces and newline characters are discarded when the expression is output. To force a space into an expression, the tilde (~) character can be used, as in the specification

```
.EQ
z~=~x~+~y sup 2
.EN
```

which outputs

$$z = x + y^2$$

One must be careful, however, because there are situations in which certain words must be surrounded by spaces. This is particularly true for the words *sub* and *sup*. Failure to do so will generate unexpected results. Let us look at one such example:

```
.EQ
z = x + y sup2
.EN
```

This specification produces

$$z = x + y sup 2$$

6.4.2 Special Eqn Words

Eqn uses a series of words for describing mathematical symbols. A small subset of these words and their *eqn* interpretations are listed in Table 6.13.

TABLE 6.13   Eqn Special Words

Word	Eqn Interpretation
sub	Subscript.
sup	Superscript.
over	Generate a fraction.
sqrt	Generate the square root symbol.
pi	Generate the symbol Π,
	to be interpreted as pi.
sum	Generate the summation symbol Σ.
int	Generate the integration symbol ∫.
prod	Generate the symbol Π,
	to be interpreted as a product.
inf	Output the infinity symbol ∞.
partial	Output the partial derivative symbol ∂.

Greek letters can be specified by writing the name of the letter, as in *omega* for the letter ω. *Eqn* can be forced to follow a user-specified grouping by using braces. Whenever you are in doubt, use braces to indicate the groups. Braces are particularly helpful to group items to be superscripted or subscripted and also in grouping fractions. When using constructions, such as summations, integrals, and limits, it may be necessary to use the *from* and *to* parts. If these parts contain any blanks, braces must be used for grouping. Here are some simple examples using the *eqn* words described in Table 6.13.

Input:
```
.EQ
int { u~partial v}~=~uv~-~int v partial u
.EN
```
Output:
$$\int u \; \partial v \; = \; uv \; - \; \int v \partial u$$

Input:
```
.EQ
```

```
(x -y) sup 2 (x sup 3 + y sup 3 ) over  x sup 2 - y sup 2 =
(x-y) (x sup 2 - xy + y sup 2 )
.EN
```
Output:

$$(x-y)^2(x^3+y^3\frac{)}{x^2}-y^2=(x-y)(x^2-xy+y^2)$$

Input:
```
.EQ
(x -y) sup 2 { (x sup 3 + y sup 3 ) } over { x sup 2 - y sup 2 } =
(x-y) (x sup 2 - xy + y sup 2 )
.EN
```
Output:

$$(x-y)^2\frac{(x^3+y^3)}{x^2-y^2}=(x-y)(x^2-xy+y^2)$$

Input:
```
.EQ
 K sub n = int from {omega t=0} to pi sin( omega t)
 + prod from x sub i=0 to n x sub i
.EN
```
Output:

$$K_n=\int_{\omega t=0}^{\pi} sin\,(\omega t)+\prod_{x_i=0}^{n}x_i$$

The error in the second example was intentional. This example highlights the disastrous results which can be expected if the braces are not specified for grouping. Adding redundant braces will not change the desired output, but failing to use a set where required can output totally unexpected expressions.

6.4.3 Formatting Matrices

Matrices can be output in *eqn* using the *eqn* word *matrix*. In addition, columns can be centered, right-adjusted, or left-adjusted, like in *tbl*, using the *eqn* words *ccol, rcol,* and *lcol.* Unlike *tbl, eqn* expects each column to have the same number of entries and the field must not be null. To output the matrix

xy_{i1} 123   *cat*

xyz_{i2} 23   *elephant*

x_{i3} 5   *tiger*

the following *eqn* specifications are required:

```
.EQ
matrix {
    ccol { xy sub i1 above xyz sub i2 above x sub i3 }
    rcol { 123 above 23 above 5 }
    lcol { cat above elephant above tiger }
        }
.EN
```

Each element of the column is separated by the word *above*.

6.4.4 Other Miscellaneous Features

It is possible in *eqn* to print enlarged braces by the use of the *left* and *right* commands to generate left and right braces respectively. Enlarged brackets, parentheses, and bars can be generated similarly. The expression

```
left { x over y~+~1 right }~=~ left { {x+y} over y right }
```

will generate

$$\left\{ \frac{x}{y} + 1 \right\} = \left\{ \frac{x+y}{y} \right\}$$

Eqn also provides features for changing fonts and point size. *Piles* can be generated which allow items to be piled on top of each other. Macro facilities are provided by the use of the *define* command. This facility allows a frequently used long string to be referred to by a short name. The *mark* command allows a series of equations to be lined up at a common point, normally an equal sign (=), and *lineup* can be used to position subsequent equations horizontal to this mark. *Eqn* will flag syntax errors in the input by the message *syntax error between lines line1 and line 2, file file1*, where the error is normally between lines *line1* and *line2*, or near there, and file1 is the name of the input file.

Finally, here are some more examples of *eqn*:

Input:

```
.EQ
X~=~{ U sup lambda~-~1 } over lambda~
.EN
```

Output:

$$X = \frac{U^{\lambda} - 1}{\lambda}$$

Input:

```
.EQ
Y~=~{ V sup delta~-~1 } over delta~
ln left | x over {ax + b} right |
.EN
```

Output:

$$Y = \frac{V^{\delta} - 1}{\delta} \ln\left|\frac{x}{ax+b}\right|$$

Input:

```
.EQ
f(x)~mark =~(~1~+~lambda~y) sup {{1 over lambda}~-1}
~ h((~lambda~ y~+~1~) sup {1 over lambda}).
.EN
.EQ
X~ lineup = ~lambda sup 2
.EN
```

Output:

$$f(x) = (1 + \lambda\ y)^{\frac{1}{\lambda} - 1} h((\lambda\ y + 1\ )^{\frac{1}{\lambda}}).$$
$$X = \lambda^{2}$$

Input:
```
.EQ
x~=~(~1 over b~)~v sup {delta~-~1}~[~lambda~(~{({v
sup delta~-~1~} over delta~) ~-~a } over b ~) ~+~1~] sup
{{1 over lambda}~-1~}
.EN
```

Output:

$$x = (\ \frac{1}{b}\ )\ v^{\delta-1}\ [\ \lambda\ (\ \frac{(\frac{v^{\delta}-1}{\delta})\ -\ a}{b}\ )\ +\ 1\ ]^{\frac{1}{\lambda}-1}$$

Input:
```
.EQ
int { sqrt { ax + b } over x } partial x~=~2 sqrt {ax +b}~+
~b int { {partial x} over {x sqrt {ax + b}}}
.EN
```

Output:

$$\int \frac{\sqrt{ax+b}}{x}\partial x\ =\ 2\sqrt{ax+b}\ +\ b\int \frac{\partial x}{x\sqrt{ax+b}}$$

In the above examples, braces have been used for grouping even when they were not required. Such an approach makes it easy to modify *eqn* specifications. In addition, it leaves no room for *eqn* to get confused!

6.5 Concluding Remarks: To Troff or Not To Troff

Troff has withstood the test of time. Initial versions of *troff* were useful only for the Wang Laboratories' C/A/T phototypesetter. With the success of the UNIX system, AT&T packaged *troff* with several preprocessors which were discussed in this chapter and called it the Documenter's Workbench. AT&T also made it available for other phototypesetters and called it *ditroff* or *device independent troff*. For a long time, the Documenter's Workbench was the only text formatting package available in the UNIX environment. This situation has now changed. Two other packages, *TeX* and *SCRIBE*, are gaining popularity among UNIX text formatters. Both these packages offer features which are comparable to those of *ditroff*. Differences exist primarily in the internal algorithms they use. With the recent boom in desktop publishing and the availability of inexpensive laser printers, many more text formatters will be available. For the time being, *troff* with its preprocessors, macro packages, and support for a variety of printers is still the best!

7 Data Communications

UNIX provides numerous utilities for basic data communication among various systems and users. This communication can be done over either dial-up or hardwired communication lines. There are primarily two important data communication utilities. They are *cu* and a group of programs that is referred to collectively as *uucp*. These two utilities share many features and files. *Cu* is used primarily to log on a remote system. *Uucp*, on the other hand, is used primarily to transfer files between UNIX systems which are in the *uucp* network. It is also used to issue a command from a local UNIX system to a remote system.

In this chapter we will look at the features and use of *cu* and *uucp*. Our intention is to provide some explanation about the use of these programs; we will not discuss implementation of either *cu* or *uucp*. Later in the chapter, we will discuss some other commonly used utilities for communication among users. A very brief discussion about distributed file systems is also included.

7.1 Uucp: Programs and Files

The term *uucp* is used to refer to a collection of programs. These programs also include a program called *uucp*! The most commonly used *uucp* programs are listed in Table 7.1.

TABLE 7.1 Commonly Used Uucp Programs

Uucp program	Function
uucp	Copy files from one UNIX system to another UNIX system.
uux	Execute a command on a specified system. Allows input and output files to be collected from different systems.
uuto	Send files from one UNIX system to another.
uupick	Accept or reject files sent to the user by *uucp*.
uunames	Display the names of the systems known to *uucp*.
uustat	Display the status of the *uucp* jobs and kill specified *uucp* jobs.

In addition, there are certain administrative programs, the most important of which are *uulog, uuclean, uutry,* and *uucheck. Uucp* operates in batch mode. Whenever a request is made, *uucp* spools the request for later transmission by a daemon. There are three basic daemons in *uucp,* namely *uucico, uuxqt,* and *uusched.*

Uucp also uses some directories and control files to store and receive information that may be necessary to execute *uucp* commands. The most important directories are */usr/lib/spool, /usr/spool/uucppublic,* and */usr/spool/uucp.* These directories may vary, depending on the version of *uucp* on your system. Important control files are L-devices, L-dialcodes, L.aliases, L.cmds, L.sys, and USERFILE. The contents of these files are also explained in the following sections.

7.1.1 Uucp: Getting Started

Unlike most other UNIX commands, *uucp* commands are not executed immediately. Instead, a sequence number is assigned to the job. Naturally, once you have given a command, you would like to know the status of the command, and this is done by the *uucp* command *uustat. Uuto* is used for sending files to a remote system. These files can be picked on the remote system by using the *uupick* command. *Uux* can be used to execute a command on a remote system. It creates the work, data, and execute files needed to execute commands on the remote computer. Let us use *uucp* to transfer file file1 from system sysa to system sysb:

```
uucp sysa!/mnt/user1/file1 sysb!/mnt/user2/file1
```

If */mnt/user1* is the login directory of *user1* on system sysa and if */mnt/user2* is the login directory of *user2* on system sysb, then the above *uucp* command can be rewritten as follows:

```
uucp sysa!~user1/file1 sysb!~user2/file1
```

Normally, the user directories cannot be written to. *Uucp* will fail to copy files if there are potential security violations. There is a directory on most UNIX systems which is often referred to as the *uucp* public directory. When it is not possible to write files to a remote system because the target directory cannot be written to, the *uucp* public directory can be used to receive the files. The *uucp* public directory is normally named */usr/spool/uucppublic*. The location of the *uucp* public directory is available in the *PUBDIR* variable of the *uucp* source. If your system has the *uucp* source available, *grep* the header file for the *PUBDIR* string, or contact your local UNIX guru or the system administrator, if you are not sure about the *uucp* public directory.

If the */mnt/user2* directory on system sysb cannot be written to, the *uucp* command given earlier would fail. The remedy to this is to transfer the file to the public directory of the remote machine. There is a potential problem associated with such a transfer, however, since the *uucp* daemons normally preserve the execute permission and assign permission 0666 to transferred files in the public directory. Therefore, these files are readable and even writable by every user on the remote system! To copy file1 from system sysa to the *uucp* public directory of system sysb, the following *uucp* command can be used:

```
uucp sysa!user1/file1 sysb!~/file1
```

This will copy file1 into the directory */usr/spool/uucppublic* on system sysb. It is also possible to copy the file into a directory in the public directory. Thus, the command

```
uucp sysa!user1/file sysb!~/dir1/file1
```

will create, if necessary, the directory *dir1* in the *uucp* public directory on the remote system and then copy file1 into that directory.

The syntax of *uucp* is identical to that of *cp*. In fact, it is possible to use *uucp* to transfer files on the same system. The *cp* command

```
cp file1 file2
```

is syntactically equivalent to

```
uucp file1 file2
```

When the name of a system is missing, *uucp* assumes the current system to be the name of the system. *Uucp* does not generate a job number for a strictly local transaction. The similarity between *uucp* and *cp* makes it very easy for novice users to use *uucp*. We have so far assumed, without explicitly stating so, that the user initiating the *uucp* command was logged on the source system and had read permission for the files to be transferred. For security reasons, it is difficult to access files by any path name on a remote machine. To fetch files by path names, it is more practical to ask the user on the remote system to send the files to you.

7.1.2 Using Shell Metacharacters

Uucp recognizes and expands shell metacharacters. These metacharacters have the same special meaning as the metacharacters in the *cp* command. For example, to copy all C source files from the login directory of user *user1* on system sysa into the directory *dirc* in the *uucp* public directory of system sysb, the following command can be used:

```
uucp sysa!~user1/*.c sysb!~/dirc
```

Other metacharacters recognized by *uucp* are ?, *, [, and].

7.1.3 Command Line Options

Uucp provides some command line options which can be used to control the action of *uucp*. The options described here are available on most systems. The $-d$ option is used to make all directories necessary to complete the *uucp* command. The $-f$ option overrides the default $-d$ option and should be used when you don't want *uucp* to make intermediate directories for copying files. *Uucp* runs a daemon program to actually copy the files. The daemon program may run at an unpredictable time, depending on the job queue and the availability of the target system. The files to be copied may be removed or modified during this time. *Uucp* provides the $-C$ option to copy the source files into the spool directory from where the *uucico* daemon can pick them up for the actual copy. The $-c$ option can be used to inform *uucp* that the files to be transferred are to be taken from the source directory. This suppresses the copying of files to the spool directory. The time of the actual copy is not known. The user may like to sequence another command after the transfer of files is completed. The $-m$ option sends mail when the copy is completed. The $-n$ option is used to notify the specified user on the remote system that a file was sent. The *uucp* command can itself be executed on a remote system. The $-e$ option is used to specify the system on which the *uucp* command is to be run. Later in this chapter, we will discuss the *uux* command which is used for remote execution of a command. Here are examples of some of the options:

```
uucp -m sysa!/mnt/dir/usrl/file3.c sysb!~/sh.c
```

This command copies the file called file3.c in directory */mnt/dir/usr1* from system sysa to the *uucp* public directory on system sysb as file sh.c. After copying the file, mail is sent to the sender. The command

```
uucp -m -nuser2 sysa!/mnt/dir/usrl/file3.c sysb!~/sh.c
```

is similar to the previous example, except that in addition to sending mail to the sender, it also sends mail to user *user2* on the remote system.

7.1.4 Uuto: Sending Files

The *uuto* command is used to send files to a specified destination. It uses the *uucp* facility to perform the transfer of the files. The source of files to *uuto* has the same syntax as the source for the *uucp* command. The destination is more restricted. The destination in *uuto* has the form:

```
system!user
```

where *user* is a valid login id on the remote system. When the copy is completed, the −*m* option can be used to send notice to the sender signaling that the copy is complete. *Uuto* also provides the −*p* option, which is similar to the −*C* option of *uucp*. This option copies the source files to the spool directory before the actual transmission. The files can be retrieved on the target system by executing the *uupick* command on the target system. If *PUBDIR* is defined to be */usr/spool/uucppublic*, *uuto* places the target files in the directory

```
/usr/spool/uucppublic/receive/user/source-system
```

where *user* is assumed to be a valid login id on the destination system and *source-system* is the name of the system from where the files were transferred. The name of the directory is derived from the destination specifications on the *uuto* command. When the transfer is completed, the recipient is notified by mail. If the −*m* option is given, as soon as the files arrive at the destination, the sender is also informed about the completion of the file transfer. The command

```
uuto -m /mnt/dir1/cy2.c sysb!user3
```

will copy file cy2.c from directory /mnt/dir1 on the local system, sysa, to the directory

```
/usr/spool/uucppublic/receive/user3/sysa
```

on system sysb.

7.1.5 Uupick: Picking Files from the Public Directory

Uupick picks up files sent to the user by the use of the *uuto* command. It searches the directory

```
/usr/spool/uucppublic/receive
```

If there are any entries in this directory for the user, *uupick* will print the following prompt for each entry:

```
from system system-name: [file file-name] [dir dir-name]
```

System-name is the name of the system from which the file was sent, *file-name* and *dir-name* stand for the name of the file and the name of the directory, respectively. *Uupick* then waits for the user response and takes action for each entry depending on the response:

newline	Do nothing to the present entry; skip to the next entry.
d	Delete the current entry.
m *dir*	Move the file to the specified directory *dir*.
a *dir*	Move all files sent from the system to the specified directory.
p	Display the file.
q	Quit the session.
^d(*control D*)	Same as q.
!	Escape to the shell; any command can be specified.
*	Print a summary of all the commands.

In the previous section we used the *uuto* command to send file cy2.c from system sysa to system sysb. If you are logged on system sysb, the *uupick* command can be used to move this file to the directory /mnt/dir2 as follows:

```
uupick
from system sysa : file cy2.c
?m /mnt/dir2
105 blocks
```

The size of the file is displayed in number of blocks. The block size used to calculate the file size is usually 512 bytes. It is also possible to pick files which have arrived from only specified systems by using the $-s$ option. The *uupick* command

```
uupick -s sysc
```

will prompt for entries which have arrived from system sysc only.

7.1.6 Uunames: Displaying Names of Systems

Uucp, *uuto*, *uupick*, and the other commands to be explained in this chapter need to know the names of the systems which are recognized by the *uucp* network. These system names can be displayed using the command *uunames*. This command is helpful when you are not sure about the spelling of a system name or when you need to check whether a system is on the *uucp* network. Here is an example:

```
uunames
sysa
labsys1
agscomp1
```

This example displays the names of the three systems which are accessible on the *uucp* network. The −*l* option can be used to display the name of the local system only, and the −*v* option is available to display a short description of the system. The −*v* option is only available if the description of the system exists in the ADMIN file. If this file is unavailable, the −*v* option is silently ignored. On some systems the *uunames* command is not available; however, a command called *uuname* can be used, and it is identical to the *uunames* command except that the −*v* option is not available.

7.1.7 Uustat: Inquiring the Status of Uucp Jobs

All *uucp* transfers do not take place immediately. As explained earlier, it is the *uucico* daemon that actually transfers the files across systems. The transfer may take several minutes or even hours, depending on several factors, for example, some systems can be accessed only on certain days, and some have restrictions regarding the time at which the system can be accessed. These factors, in addition to the inevitable possibility that the remote system may be down, make it difficult to predict the time of completion of a *uucp* job. The user may like to know the status of the *uucp* command that was executed. The −*m* option is normally available to send mail to notify the user of the completion of a job. *Mail* may also be sent if *uucp* had problems in executing the *uucp* command. The *uustat* command allows the user to query the status of the *uucp* commands and gives the option to kill commands initiated by the user. The information that *uustat* displays may depend on the *uucp* version. The most commonly displayed information includes the following:

Job number   This unique number identifies the *uucp* job. It can be used to kill the *uucp* command.

User   This is the name of the user who initiated the *uucp* job.

Size   This is the size of the file to be transferred. It is normally displayed in bytes.

System   This is the name of the remote system to which the file is to be transferred.

Command time   This is the time when the user initiated the *uucp* command. It also includes the date.

Status time   This is the time when the status of the *uucp* command was requested.

Status   This is the actual coded status of the command.

On some systems, the $-v$ option is available to print a verbose description of the status rather than printing just a code. The following command line options are most frequently used:

$-k$ Kill the specified job

$-j$ Display the status of the specified job; *all* may be used to display the status of all jobs.

$-s$ Display the status of all *uucp* jobs concerned with the specified target system.

$-o$ Display the status of all *uucp* jobs older than the specified number of hours.

These options are sometimes available in different forms. Check your local UNIX reference manual for any possible differences and also for other command line options available. If no options are given, *uustat* will display the status of all *uucp* jobs initiated by the user.

7.1.8 Uux: Execute Commands on a Remote System

Uux executes a command on a remote system and collects data files from various systems required to complete the execution of the command on the remote system. The syntax of *uux* is

> uux *[options] command-string*

Command-string is identical to a shell command string. The command and the other file names specified as arguments may be optionally preceded by *system-name!*, where *system-name* is the name of the local system or any remote system and must be included in the system names generated by *uunames*. If *system-name* is omitted, the local system is assumed. A valid file name is either a full path name, a path name preceded by *~user*, or just a simple file name. If it is a simple file name, it is prefixed by the current directory. If it is preceded by *~user*, then *user* is replaced by the login directory of the specified user. Here is an example:

> uux sysa!comm1 sysb!/data/dir1/file2 sysc!~user1/temp/file3 file4

This command will run the command *comm1* on system sysa. To complete the execution, it will require three data files. File file2 is fetched from system sysb. The entire path name for this file is specified on the command line. File file3 is fetched from system sysc. If */e12/dir3* is the login directory of user *user1* on system sysc, then file3 is fetched from the directory */e12/dir3/temp* on that system. Finally, file4 is fetched from the current directory on the local system where the *uux* command was initiated. The presence of an optional minus sign (−) on the command line causes the standard input to the *uux* command to be the standard input to the command to be executed using *uux*.

If one of the command line files is an output file, *uux* will naturally fail to get the file. To avoid this situation, output files should be escaped using parentheses. For example:

> uux sysa!comm2 sysb!/fir/dir1/inpfile \(sysb!/fir/dir1/outfile \)

will execute command *comm2* on system sysa. The input file inpfile is fetched from directory */fir/dir1* on system sysb, and the output file outfile is created on system sysb in directory */fir/dir1*. If meta characters are used in file names, it is safe to have the entire command string enclosed in quotes, as in the following example:

```
uux "sysa!comm3 sysb!/fir/dirl/fi? sysc!/fir/dirl/f2?"
```

For security reasons, the commands to be executed on a remote system are usually restricted. *Uux* generates a job number like the other *uucp* commands do. This job number can be used to inquire the status of the *uux* command using the *uustat* command. If the command string is a shell pipeline, only the first command can have a system name associated with it. The other commands in the pipeline will be executed on the system associated with the first command.

Uux does not execute the commands directly. The daemon *uuxqt* actually does the execution. In that sense, *uuxqt* is similar to the *uucico* daemon that is associated with the *uucp* command. The file transfers involved in the execution of the *uux* command are actually done by the *uucico* daemon.

7.2 Administrative Programs

The programs of the *uucp* family that we have studied so far are used directly by users whose sole purpose is to access different systems. The availability to all users of the *uucppublic* directory for writing and the availability of the system itself for execution of commands from remote systems makes the *uucp* software susceptible to many undesirable problems. A series of administrative programs are available to the *uucp* administrator for controlling access to the system and also to restrict use of the system by external users. These administrative programs will be discussed in the following sections.

7.2.1 Uulog: Displaying the Log File

Uucp maintains a log of usage for each remote computer the system communicates with. *Uulog* displays the content of this file according to the following options that may be specified:

- −s This option displays the log file for communication with the specified system only.
- −u This option displays the log file for communication initiated by the specified user only.

In the absence of the above options, the log for all systems and users is displayed.

7.2.2 Uuclean: Cleaning the Spool Directory

Uucp requests are spooled. Files are often copied first into the spool directory rather than directly into any user specified directory. The spool directory may also be used by inadvertent users for other, unrelated work. *Uuclean* scans the spool directory for old files and takes appropriate action to remove these unwanted files. These files may include mail which cannot be delivered or files which cannot be transferred due to unreachable systems. Number of days or hours may be specified as an option to remove only those files which are older than the specified number of days or hours. It is also possible to specify the name of the spool directory to be searched. An option also exists to send mail to the owner of each file being removed. Most files in the spool directory are owned by the owner of the *uucp* programs. *Uuclean* is normally started by a daemon.

7.2.3 Other Administrative Programs

The other important *uucp* administrative programs available are *uutry* and *uucheck*. *Uutry* tries to establish a connection with the specified system for the purpose of debugging. It actually invokes the daemon *uucico* to establish a connection with the remote system. *Uucheck* checks for the presence of the files and directories required by the *uucp* software.

7.2.4 Daemons Initiated by Uucp

Uucp daemons are processes that run in the background to execute the commands requested by *uucp* or *uux*. The three important daemons are *uucico*, *uuxqt*, and *uusched*. *Uucico* is probably the most important of the *uucp* daemons. It scans the spool directory to check whether there is a work file which describes the next activity to be performed. If it finds one, it will select the device used to establish a link with the remote system, perform the required login sequence, check permissions, and then execute the request if all's well. It will also update the log file. This daemon can be started by either *uucp*, *uux*, or by a system daemon such as *cron*. It is also possible to start this daemon directly, but such occasions arise only during testing. Finally, it can also be started by a remote system. If *uucico* is started by a remote system, it is said to be in SLAVE mode otherwise it is said to be in MASTER mode.

Uuxqt is another daemon that is used to effect remote execution of commands. It searches the spool directory for the required files that have been sent from remote systems. If the executable file is found, *uuxqt* tries to find out if the required data files are present. If the data files are present and have the necessary permissions, the L.cmds file is searched to check whether *uuxqt* has permission to execute the requested command. If all these validation checks are satisfied, *uuxqt* proceeds to complete the requested command.

Uusched actually schedules the queued work in the spool directory. It is started by the daemon *uudaemon.hour* which itself is started by the daemon *cron*. The function of *uusched* is to randomize the order in which *uucico* will pick up the remote system to be called.

7.3 Support Files

In addition to the executable files, the *uucp* family of programs require supporting data files. These files are required to supply *uucp* with the information required to establish links with remote systems. They also include files which specify the permissions for executing commands from remote systems. The contents of some of these files is the topic of discussion in the next few sections.

7.3.1 L.sys

The support file *L.sys* contains information needed by the *uucico* daemon to establish a link with the remote system. It provides data about the name of the remote computer, the type of the connecting device that should be used to establish a link with this system, the time when the system can be accessed, the speed at which this device communicates, and dialing information about the system. In addition, it also has information about the login procedure on the remote system. Each entry in the L.sys file has the form

Systemname Times Caller Class Device [Expect Send]...

Systemname is the name of the remote system with which the local system may try to communicate via the *uucp* network. *Times* is the time when the remote system can be contacted. This can be specified in many forms, including day of the week, time of the day, peak time, nonpeak time, etc. *Caller* is the device type used. *Class* is used to specify the baud rate. *Device* is normally the phone number to be called. Substitutions may take place depending on the entries in the L-dialcodes file, as explained later. *Expect* and *Send* correspond to the set of strings which form the login procedure to the remote system.

7.3.2 L-devices

This file contains information about devices that are used to establish a connection with the remote system. Typically, it has a field that indicates if the link to be established is a direct link to another computer or some other type of link. Other fields in this file have information depending on the type of link to be established. This includes the baud rate for dialers, the type of dialer, e.g., *hayes* for Hayes Smartmodem, and other information required for dialing outside systems.

7.3.3 L-dialcodes

This file has abbreviations that may be used in the phone number entries in the L.sys file. Each abbreviation has the format:
    <abbreviation><dial sequence>
For example, the entry
    ab 9=1900–
in the L-dialcodes file will expand the entry ab4828982 to 9=19004828982.

7.3.4 L.aliases

This file provides an alias for sitenames. It is used to refer to a system by another name. Entries in this file have the format
    real_name alias_name
This facility is particularly helpful when a sitename is changed temporarily.

7.3.5 L.cmds

Earlier we looked at the *uux* utility to execute commands on remote systems. Clearly, if users were allowed to execute commands freely on remote systems, there could be various security problems. To avoid these problems, the *uucp* software provides a mechanism to restrict the commands which can be executed on remote systems. The L.cmds file is used to implement this security mechanism. It contains the list of commands which can be executed on a given system by remote systems. Commonly allowed commands are the following:

rmail

rnews

ruusend

In addition, the *PATH* variable can be set in this file to help *uucp* locate the commands.

7.3.6 USERFILE

In addition to restricting the commands to be executed by remote systems, the directories which can be accessed by local and remote users can also be restricted. The file USERFILE contains this accessibility information. Each line in this file is of the form:

[loginname],[systemname]c[pathname][pathname]...

Loginname is a valid user name in the /etc/passwd file. *Systemname* is the name of the remote system. *Pathname* indicates the permissible paths for the specified login name and system name. If the *c* entry is present, the remote system will call the local system, after which the conversation is terminated. The local system will then immediately call the calling system back and start processing the request.

7.4 Cu: Connecting to a Remote Computer

Cu is used primarily to call other UNIX systems. Once you are logged on the remote system, you can use the system almost as if you were directly connected to the system. In addition, you can transfer files between the two systems. Several options are available on the command line. The commonly used options are explained below:

−s   This is the most commonly used option. It is used to specify the transmission speed. The default value is 300 baud. Other standard values are 110, 150,

	300, 600, 1200, 4800 and 9600.
−l line	This option is used to specify a device name to be used as the communications line. If this option is not specified, *cu* will search for an available line having the right speed. If the speed is not explicitly specified, *cu* will fetch it from an internal file which is used to store this information.
−d	This option causes diagnostic traces to be printed.
−n	If this option is specified, *cu* will request the phone number to be dialed by the user rather than taking it from the command line.
number	This is the actual telephone number to be dialed to establish the required connection. An equal sign may be used for secondary dial tones and a minus sign may be used for incorporating delays.
system	*Cu* and *uucp* share some common databases. It is possible to establish a connection with a remote system by specifying the *uucp* name of the system.

Here are some examples of establishing a connection with a remote computer using *cu*. The command

```
cu -s1200 9=12004824748
```

will call the specified telephone number and establish the required connection using a 1200 baud line. The command

```
cu systemb
```

will call the *uucp* system named systemb. Systemb must be a valid system name. The command

```
cu -l /dev/ttyRS dir
```

will establish a connection via a direct line using the specified device. Notice that no phone number is necessary. Once you have established a connection with the remote system, you will need a valid login name and password to actually log on the remote system. If you can log on the system successfully, all commands will be executed on the new remote system. Command lines starting with a tilde (~) have a special meaning: these command lines can be used to establish communication between the local and the remote system. We will refer to these commands as *cu* commands.

7.4.1 Transferring Files

Cu can be used to pick up files from the remote system. The *cu* command %*take* is used to copy a source file from the remote system to the local system. If the remote system prompt is −> and the local system name is locs, the following command will copy the file srcfile from the remote system to the local system:

```
->~[locs]%take srcfile
```

Notice that locs is actually echoed by *cu*. If the destination argument is omitted, the name of the copied file will be the same as the source file. If you are copying files which contain tab characters, be sure to execute the command *stty tabs* to ensure that tab characters are copied without expansion. The *cu* command %*put* is used to copy files from the local system to the remote system. The syntax of the %*put* command is exactly the same as the syntax of the %*take* command. It is possible to escape to the local system temporarily by using the *cu* command containing the single character "!". This *cu* command can be followed by any command that will be executed in a subshell on the local system. The command

```
~![locs]cat file1
```

will display the contents of file1 on the local system. The *cu* command %*break* can be used to transmit a BREAK to the remote system. The *cu* command containing the single character . (period) terminates the conversation with the remote system.

7.5 Communication among Users

UNIX also offers many utilities that are used for communicating among users. Perhaps the most popular of these is the *mail* utility, which is used for sending and receiving mail among users. *Postnews* is used to send news articles. Users can check to see if any news has arrived by using the *checknews* utility. News can be read by using the *readnews* command. The following sections describe the various features provided by these utilities.

7.6 Mail Processing

Unix provides mail utilities for users to send and receive mail. There are variations of these utilities on different UNIX versions. System V provides *mail* and *mailx*. *Rmail* is another variation, which allows users to send mail only. BSD UNIX supports *mail*, which has capabilities which are similar to *mailx* on System V. In the next few sections, we will look at some of the features of these mail-processing utilities.

7.6.1 Mail on System V

Mail on System V UNIX provides some basic capabilities to send mail to users and to read mail sent by users. No arguments are required to use *mail* to read incoming mail. *Mail* will print the user's mail in last-in, first-out order. After printing each message, *mail* will prompt with a question mark (?), waiting for the user response to decide the disposition of the message. Expected user responses and the disposition of the message are:

newline   Continue to display the next message if there is one, else quit the *mail* session.

+   Same as newline.

p   Print the message again.

s   Save the message in the specified file. If no file is specified, mbox is assumed.

w   Same as the *s* option but the header information is not saved.

m   Mail the message to the specified users.

d   Delete the current message.

q   Put the undeleted messages back in the mail file and quit the *mail* session.

!   Execute the specified UNIX command.

A sample session to read incoming mail is shown here:

```
mail
From user1 Mon Oct 20 22:23 EDT 1986
Received: by system1.UUCP; 20 Oct 86 22:23:28 EDT (Mon)
Date: 20 Oct 86 22:23:28 EDT (Mon)
From: user1 (Tare)
```

```
Message-Id: <8610210223.AA00482@system1.UUCP>
Apparently-To: user2

This is the actual message
This is the second line of the message
This is the third line of the message


?m user3
```

In this session, we mailed the incoming message to another user, *user3*. Incoming mail is normally stored in the directory */usr/mail*, or */usr/spool/mail*, or some other spool directory. If the user wishes to read from a different file, this file name can be specified on the *mail* command line, as shown below:

```
mail -f mbox
```

This command, used with the *-f* option, will read incoming messages from the file mbox. Other commonly used command line options for reading *mail* are *-p*, which causes mail to be printed without prompting for disposition, the option *-q*, which enables interrupts (normally interrupts only terminate the current message), and the *-r* option, which causes mail to be printed in FIFO (first-in, first-out mode).

7.6.1.1 Sending Mail

The *mail* utility can be used to send messages to another user by specifying the user on the command line; thus,

```
mail user3
This is the first line of the message to be sent
And this is the second and the last line
EOT (control-d)
```

will send the message to user *user3*. The same message could have been sent to both *user3* and *user4* by using the *mail* command

```
mail user3 user4
```

Usually it is more convenient to create the message using a standard editor and then redirect it using *mail*. *Mail* can be sent to a user on a remote system by prefixing the user name with the remote system name and an exclamation mark. To send the message in file mess.inp to user *user4* on system sys5, use the following command:

```
mail sys5!user4 < mess.inp
```

Mail will use *uucp* to send the message to the remote system; however, it will not use *uucp*, if the specified remote system name is actually the name of the local machine. The *uuname* utility can be used to check the names of valid system names recognized by *uucp*.

7.6.2 Mailx: An Interactive Message-Processing System

Mailx provides a very flexible environment and powerful features for processing mail. Some of the features of the standard *mail* utility discussed in the previous section are still available. In addition, *mailx* offers a wide variety of features, some of which are rarely used. Indeed, there are too many features to be listed here. In this section and in the following ones, we will look at some of the important features of this utility, leaving the interested reader at the mercy of the *man* command to look up the less-known features.

The functions of *mailx* can be classified into two categories. First, it can be used to receive incoming mail. Second, it provides a powerful environment to send new mail and to respond to mail from other users.

While reading incoming mail, *mailx* expects commands from the user and accordingly decides the disposition of the message. These commands have the general form

```
[command] [message list] [arguments]
```

Message list is used to refer to the list of space-separated message specifications. Frequently used message specifications include the following:

n   Message number *n*
$ The last message

*	All the messages
n-m	Messages from *n* to *m*
:d	All deleted messages
:n	All new messages
:r	Messages already read
:u	Unread messages
:o	Old messages

Many commands are available to manipulate the incoming *mail*. These can be used to get on-line help, to display incoming mail, to respond to arrived mail, and to save selected messages.

7.6.3 Mailboxes

Since we are talking about mail, you might have wondered, where is the mailbox? All incoming messages for the user called *user* are saved in the file */usr/mail/user.* During the processing of *mail*, it may be necessary to save these messages. Messages are normally saved in the file mbox in the user's home directory. In addition, various commands and shell variables are available to change this default behavior and have *mailx* interact with other files.

7.6.4 Reading Incoming Mail

The equal sign (=) command can be used to print the current message number. During the printing of the message it is sometimes desirable to suppress header fields. Header fields include the status and cc (*carbon copy*) list. The *ignore* command can be used to suppress the specified header fields. The *print* command is used to print messages by piping them through a pager like *pg* or *more*. To print the messages without any interaction with a pager, the *Print* command (with an uppercase P) can be used. If you wish to print only the first few lines of the specified messages, you can use the *top* command, which prints the first five lines of the message.

7.6.4.1 Saving and Deleting Messages

Incoming mail can be saved in a specified file by the use of the *copy* command. This command copies the specified messages but does not mark these messages as saved. The *Copy* command (with an uppercase C) is

---

/usr/spool/mail/user for BSD UNIX.

identical to the *copy* command, except that the name of the file in which the message is to be copied is derived from the name of the sender. The *delete* command is used to delete messages from the primary mailbox residing in the directory */usr/mail*. The *dt* command also deletes the specified messages, but in addition it prints the next message after the last deleted message. Incoming messages can be edited and subsequently saved using the *edit* command. The default editor is invoked and the specified messages are placed in a temporary file for the purpose of editing. Additional massaging of messages is possible by piping the messages through a shell command. The *pipe* command can be used for this purpose. The command

```
pipe 1-3 shcom
```

will pipe the first three messages through the shell command *shcom*. The *Save* command can also be used to save the specified messages in a specified file. If a file name is not specified, the sender's name is used as the name of the file. This command will mark the messages as saved. Messages can be saved in the specified file, without the header and with trailing blank lines deleted, with the use of the *write* command.

7.6.4.2 Miscellaneous Commands

While reading an incoming message, it is possible to respond to that mail with the *respond* command. The subject line of the response is taken from the message iself. The next section gives a more detailed description of sending mail. The *quit* or the *exit* command can be used to exit a mail processing session. On-line help is available with the *help* command, which displays a summary of commands. In addition, the *list* command prints a list of all commands available.

7.6.5 Sending Mail

Mail can be sent to a user or a group of users using the *mailx* command. Recipients are specified on the command line; thus, mail can be sent to user *user1*, as shown here:

```
mailx userl
```

A group name can be used instead of the user name. A group can be created by the use of the *group* command while in read message mode but it is more convenient to define groups in the startup file mailx.rc in the user home directory. This file is used to specify *mailx* commands which are to be executed upon entering the *mailx* environment. If the mailx.rc file has the command

```
group grpl userl user2 user3
```

then the *mailx* command

```
mailx grpl
```

will send the mail to users *user1*, *user2*, and *user3*.

In the earlier section where we discussed the use of the *mail* command, readers were advised to use the editor to create messages prior to mailing them. *Mailx* provides a very powerful environment for editing the mail to be posted. It first prompts for the subject of the mail. All lines entered after the subject line form the main body of the message. It is possible to escape this input mode by starting a new line with the tilde escape character ~. There are various commands which can be executed during this escape mode. Though they are sometimes referred to as tilde escapes, the escape character can be changed by setting the environment variable *escape* to the required character. This is particularly important if the user is logged on a remote system using *cu*. All lines starting with the tilde character will first be interpreted by the transmit process of *cu*. There is a mechanism to let *cu* pass the tilde command to the remote system uninterpreted. This can be done by using two tilde characters instead of one. The commonly used tilde escapes are discussed in the next section.

7.6.6 Tilde Escape Commands

The ~*!* escape command can be used to execute a shell command during the input mode. The command

```
~!date
```

will display the date. The output of the command is not appended to the mail. The ~h escape command is used to provide an additional prompt to change the header data, which includes subject, cc list, to list, etc. The subject alone can be changed using the ~s escape command. For example,

```
~s New Programmer
```

will change the subject line for the message to *New Programmer*. If the user is sending mail in response to incoming mail by using the *respond* command, the received message can be embedded in the reply using the tilde escape command ~f. This is particularly helpful if some of the targeted recipients have not received the embedded message. A message list can be specified along with the ~f command to embed any number of incoming messages in the outgoing mail. The user typing the input message cannot be expected to type the mail without any typing errors. There is also the possibility that the user may wish or need to incorporate changes in what has already been entered. Such situations require the use of an editor. The ~e command can be used to edit an existing message. It invokes the default editor on the current content of the message. The default screen editor, such as *vi*, can be invoked using the ~v command. After the editing session is complete, the user is once again placed in the normal input mode. New names can be added to the list of carbon copy recepients using the ~c command. At any point, the current message in its entirety can be displayed using the ~p command. Sometimes, users decide to terminate the messages they are writing before sending them, due to some recent change in a situation or to the whimsical nature of the user! When a partially entered message is interrupted and terminated abnormally, it is saved in the file dead.letter. If the user decides later to send an edited version of this killed message, it is possible to edit this partially saved message using the ~d command. Finally, the input mode can be terminated by the . (period) command, which posts the mail to the specified set of users. Here are two examples of the use of tilde escape commands:

Example 1:
```
mailx jdoe
Subject: Example of the use of tilde escapes
~!who
root    cons     Apr 19 07:03
rst     ttyd05   Apr 20 23:24
jdoe    ttyd06   Apr 21 22:18
!
```

```
~d
"/d4/tare/dead.letter" 12/423
~e
423
```
ed session
```
w
q
(continue)
~p
---------
Message contains:
To: jdoe
Subject: Example of the use of tilde escapes
```
Contents of the message
```
(continue)
.
(EOT)
```

Example 2:
mailx
```
mailx version 2.14 9/10/86 Type ? for help.
"/usr/mail/user1": 1 message 1 unread
>U  1 user2  Tue Apr 21 01:12  12/259 Mail from user2 to user1
?1
Message  1:
From user2 Tue Apr 21 01:12 EDT 1987
To: user1
Subject: Mail from user2 to user1
Status: RO


Hi user1!
Have you used the KWA utility developed by user3? I am told that it
provides all the features of awk but is much faster. Any comments?


? respond
To: user2
Subject: Re: Mail from user2 to user1
~f
Interpolating
(continue)
```

```
~c user3
Yes, it is a terrific utility. User3 has done a wonderful job of
putting some life into awk. It is much faster than awk.



(EOT)
```

In example 1, we first executed the shell command *who* to check the users who were then logged on the system. This was followed by the use of the *~d* escape command to include the dead.letter file in the message that was being composed. The *ed* editor was invoked to edit the message. Finally, the message was displayed using the *~p* command and the . (dot) command used to send the mail and end the *mailx* session. In the second example, *mailx* was invoked to read the incoming mail. *User1* decided to respond to the mail from *user2* by invoking the *respond* command. This initiated composition of a new message that was sent to *user2*. The subject line was copied from the message which was received. *User1* also decided to send a copy of the reply to *user3* by using the *~c* command. *User1* knew that *user3* had not received the original message and therefore decided to include the original message by using the *~f* escape command. Finally, the . (dot) command was used to end the *mailx* session.

7.6.7 Shell Variables

Several shell environment variables affect the processing of mail while using the *mailx* command. The shell variable *HOME* is used to locate the directory in which the default secondary file mbox and the startup file mailx.rc reside. The name of the startup file can be changed by resetting the shell variable *MAILRC* appropriately. The *askcc* variable can be set to prompt the user for a list of cc (carbon copy) names after the message is terminated. The *DEAD* variable stores the name of the file in which partially interrupted letters are stored. As discussed earlier, the escape character, which by default is set to the tilde character (~), can be changed by setting the shell variable *escape* to the new character. There are numerous other shell variables which can be changed to alter the environment in which *mailx* processes mail. A complete list can be found in the UNIX reference manual of your local UNIX system.

7.6.8 BSD and the Mail Utility

The default*mail package on the BSD version of UNIX is similar to the *mailx* utility of System V. There are some differences, but most of the features are common and a user familiar with the *mailx* package should find it relatively easy to make a transition to the *mail* utility of BSD.

7.7 Sending News Items

News items can be sent to various users using the *postnews* command. This command actually uses the low-level command *inews* to send the news to various users in the newsgroup. A newsgroup can be formed by using the *inews* command with the *−C* option. The *postnews* command first prompts for the title of the news item. This title is displayed to the receiver of the news item and makes it easy for the receiver to decide about its relevance. *Postnews* requires the user to enter the name of the newsgroup to which the item belongs and also the names of the group to whom the item is targeted. After these prompts are answered, the default editor is invoked where the news item can be entered. The file to be edited already has the header information entered. When the user terminates the editing session, the news item is broadcasted. Soon you are in the news!

7.7.1 Reading News Items

News items can be read using the *readnews* command. There are many command line options available to control the news items to be read. The *−l* option will output only the titles of the news items. The news items are ordinarily displayed with the oldest item first and the latest item last. This sequence can be reversed using the *−r* option. The *−a* option can be used to peruse news items that were posted after the specified date. Acceptable date formats include *mm/dd* and *mm/dd/yy*. If the year is omitted, it defaults to the current year. The user reference manual lists the complete set of command line options that are available.

After the first title is displayed, *readnews* will prompt and wait for the user response. Commonly used responses are

y   Print the current article and proceed
       to the next news item.

---

*In addition, old version 7 UNIX mail is available as */bin/mail*.

n   Skip to the next news item.

q   Quit the *readnews* session.

Here are some examples:

Example 1:

```
readnews -a 07/25
```

The command in example 1 will allow the user to read news items that were posted after July 25 of the current year. In the following session, the news items are read in reverse chronological order:

Example 2:

```
readnews -r
----------------------
 newsgroup group1.general
----------------------

Article 439 of 439, Wed 20:46.
Subject: New utility for tape processing
Path: systema!user7 (John Doe @ JDoe Computers, Inc, Trenton)
(12 lines) More? [ynq] y

A new utility has been developed in our research department for
efficient processing of tapes. This utility has many selection
features and provides a SQL-like  query interface. For more
information read the man page for the "tapequery" command.

Last article.  [qfr]q
```

The UNIX news feature is very convenient to use to share information among users about new developments and other topics that may be of general interest.

7.7.2 Checknews: Check for News Items

The *checknews* utility is useful to see whether there is a news item that has not been read by the user. In addition to the command line options of *readnews*, the following keywords can also be used:

e   Executes the *readnews* command if there is any news item to be read.

y   Indicates that there is at least one news item to be read.

n   Reports "No news" if there is no news item to be read. There is no response if there is at least one news item to be read.

q   Indicates that there is a news item by returning the appropriate value. A return value of 0 means there is no news and a return value of 1 means that there is at least one news item.

The command

```
checknews y
There is news
```

indicates that there is at least one news item to be read. This command should be included in a user's .login or .profile file.

7.8 Write: Write to Another User

Write is probably the most primitive form of communication between users. To use *write*, just use the command along with the login name of the user you wish to send a message to. If the user is logged on one or more terminals, whatever you key on the terminal will be written to the user's terminal. The message is finally terminated by the EOT (control D) character. What happens to the receiver's terminal? The message is displayed on the terminal, but it is preceded by the line

```
Message from <sender> on <terminal name> at <time>
```

It is very irritating to have a message appear on your screen when you are actively using your terminal for an important task. UNIX provides the *mesg* command, which can be used to enable or disable other users from sending such messages to your screen. The *mesg* command with the *y* argument enables other users to write to your terminal using the *write* command; the *mesg* command with the *n* argument disables other users from writing to your terminal. Various diagnostic messages are displayed when a user tries to write to users who are not logged on or to an invalid user or to users who have disabled other users from writing to their terminals.

7.9 Distributed File Systems

With the diversity of products and operating systems in the marketplace, the need to share information across different hardware and software systems is becoming increasingly critical. The ideal situation would be to have all computers run the UNIX operating system. The availability of standard networking utilities would then make it easy to link diverse applications into a single transparent distributed system. In reality, there are too many different file systems involved. A distributed file system provides access to different file systems residing on various hardwares. In addition, it provides savings in storage. If a distributed file system is capable of supporting a combination of different hardwares and operating systems, it is termed a heterogeneous distributed file system, otherwise it is called a homogeneous distributed file system. The two most widely known distributed file systems in the UNIX world are AT&T's RFS (Remote File System) and Sun Microsystems' NFS (Network File System). A discussion of RFS or NFS is beyond the scope of this book, but there is little doubt that with the advent of distributed processing, distributed file systems have a very bright future.

7.10 Concluding Remarks

The various utilities discussed in this chapter suffice for most data communication needs. Many users have a tendency to neglect news items and even incoming mail; however, it is a good practice to read the news items on your system regularly. If you have mail, you cannot afford to neglect it: it may be from your boss requesting that some important job be done. Failing to read it may cost you your job!

8 The Writer's Workbench

The Writer's Workbench is a collection of programs which have been provided for improving the writing style of writers. It provides programs that nearly eliminate manual proofreading of documents. The English language is far from the compiler writer's dream of a language that offers itself to be defined in a finite set of grammatical rules. The resultant language is therefore difficult to parse; however, some of the programs provided in the Writer's Workbench do not suffer because of the difficulty in parsing the English language. The program to check spelling is the most striking example of a process that is easily automated and not made difficult by the idiosyncracies of English.

The output of the Writer's Workbench programs is not always correct. Sometimes the suggested changes may not be required. The ability to distinguish a good writing style from a bad one ultimately (and fortunately) must be left to human intelligence. This is not a criticism about the programs that are available to electronically assist writing, but a warning to limit expectations.

All writing should be subjected to the rules of good writing style, to help make comprehension easy. We will use the Writer's Workbench programs with the basic assumption that the user is going to use the programs in a

UNIX environment with *nroff* or *troff* utilities to format the text, even though strictly speaking, this is not necessary. There are numerous programs available in the Writer's Workbench; programs which are considered necessary for writing good documentation will be discussed in this book. Each of these programs comes equipped with a variety of options, and those important for documentation writing are discussed. Each program is discussed separately, so that users can decide which programs they think are most relevant to their own writing.

If you do not have the Writer's Workbench system in its entirety, you may still have access to some of the programs discussed in this chapter. Spell is one such program that is widely available. The output of your programs may differ from the ones displayed in this chapter. The emphasis here is on the usage of the Writer's Workbench programs rather than on the rationale for the design of them. Readers interested in the rhetorical and psychological writing principles underlying the programs should refer to the bibliography at the end of the book. In particular, the paper by Nina H. Macdonald provides a close insight into their design.

8.1 Getting Started

The first step is to see if you have the Writer's Workbench (WWB) software installed on your UNIX system (you may have to set your *PATH* appropriately to access the WWB software), and if it is installed, check the version number of the system. The version number of the system can be displayed with the use of the *−V* option of the *wwb* command. For example,

```
wwb -V
WWB version 3.0: : :
```

states that you have version 3.0 installed. If you get the message

```
unknown WWB flag -V
```

then you may have an earlier version which can be checked with the *−ver* option. There are substantial differences between versions released before version 3.0 and the 3.0 version. The material covered in this chapter discusses version 3.0 and later versions.

8.2 Types of WWB Programs

The WWB programs can be classified into four groups. These groups consist of programs to

a. Give on-line help or suggestions.
b. Proofread documents.
c. Analyze the style of documents.
d. Customize the WWB environment.

8.3 On-Line Help

On-line help is available with the WWB system in two forms. First, on-line information is available to describe the WWB programs. Second, the WWB system provides on-line help with grammar, spelling, punctuation, and usage. In addition, the $-O$ option can be used with all the WWB commands to give a synopsis of the command line. A list of all the programs in the WWB system can be printed with the *wwbinfo* command, which is reproduced for you here:

```
wwbinfo

                    PROGRAM-FUNCTION TABLE


_____


            On-Line Help with WRITER'S WORKBENCH Programs

wwbaid..........describes programs and explains how to use them
wwbhelp word.....gives information about programs and functions
wwbinfo..........prints this PROGRAM-FUNCTION TABLE


            On-Line Help with Grammar, Spelling, Punctuation, and Usage

prosestnd........prints standards used by prose to evaluate documents
continrls........explains clear ways to present contingencies
punctrls........explains punctuation rules
spelltell word...finds the correct spelling of word
splitrls........explains split infinitives
```

tmarkrls.........explains correct use of trade/service marks
worduse phrase...explains correct usage of words and phrases

Programs for Proofreading

acro file........finds acronyms
consist file.....runs three consistency checking programs
 tmark file......finds inaccurate trade/service marks (uses tmarkdict)
 conscap file....checks for inconsistent capitalization
 conspell file...lists words spelled inconsistently (British vs. American)
proofvi file.....proofreads text and corrects errors interactively
                       (runs spellwwb, punct, double, and diction)
sexist file......finds sexist phrases and suggests changes (uses sexdict)
switchr file.....finds words used as both a noun and a verb
wwb file........runs proofr and prose
 proofr file.....runs five proofreading programs
  spellwwb file..checks spelling (uses spelldict)
  punct file.....checks punctuation
  double file....finds consecutive occurrences of the same word
  diction file...finds awkward phrases, suggests changes (uses ddict)
  gram file......finds split infinitives and wrong articles

Programs for Style Analysis

findbe file......prints file and highlights all forms of the verb "to be"
match file(s)....collates style-file statistics from different texts
morestyle file...runs four additional stylistic analyzes on text
 abst file.......evaluates text abstractness
 diversity file..measures variety of vocabulary with type/token ratio
 neg file........finds negative words, evaluates their overall effect
 topic file......reports frequent words to give an idea of the topic
org file........prints condensed version of text to show organization
parts file......assigns grammatical parts of speech to words
reroff file......puts mm/nroff macros back in an already formatted text
syl file........counts syllables of each different word in file
WWB file........runs proofr and prose
 prose file......gives detailed commentary about the style of a file
  style file....calculates and summarizes style statistics

Programs to Analyze Procedural Documents

continge file....analyzes treatment of contingencies in procedural text
murky file.......finds hard-to-understand sentences in procedural text

Programs to Customize Dictionaries and Standards

dictadd..........adds phrases to user's personal dictionaries:
     ddict - personal dictionary of awkward phrases
     sexdict - personal dictionary of sexist terms
     spelldict - personal dictionary of correct spellings
     tmarkdict - personal dictionary of trade/service marks
spelladd.........adds words to spelldict dictionary
mkstand..........calculates standards for prose from user documents

---

 Note: Indented commands are automatically run by the command that
immediately precedes them. Indented commands can be run singly as well.

The *wwbaid* program can be used to provide information about any specific
command. The list of WWB commands for which on-line help is available
from the *wwbaid* command is displayed here:

wwbaid cmds
★★

     WRITER'S WORKBENCH SYSTEM COMMAND NAMES

abst	findbe	prose	switchr
acro	gram	prosestnd	syl
conscap	match	punct	tmark
consist	mkstand	punctrls	tmarkrls
conspell	morestyle	reroff	topic
continge	murky	sexist	worduse
continrls	neg	spelladd	WWB
dictadd	org	spelltell	wwbaid
diction	parts	spellwwb	wwbhelp
diversity	proofr	splitrls	wwbinfo
double	proofvi	style	

The *wwbaid* program provides help on various topics associated with the command. The most commonly used topics are

description   Provides a brief description of the command usage
example   Provides an example of the command usage
options   Explains the various options associated with the command

To display the description of the *acro* command, the command

```
wwbaid description acro
```

will display the following:

```
acro -- description


    The acro command locates acronyms in your text.  Acronyms are
    words formed from the first letter(s) of each significant part of
    a compound term, such as MADD for Mothers Against Drunk Drivers,
    or GM for General Motors.  acro lists each acronym found in the
    text and shows how many times it was used.  Next, each sentence
    in which an acronym was used is printed, with the acronym
    distinguished from other words by brackets and stars.

    When you give acro more than one input file, it will
    complete its report on one file before beginning to
    analyze the next.
```

To list an example of the usage of the *acro* command, use the following
command, which will result in the example provided:

```
wwbaid example acro
acro -- example


        Consider the excerpt below from a file named "games."

                The race was close, but she moved ahead to win a
                Medal for the USA team.

        The command:
                acro games
```

```
will print:

acro -m m games
        The following acronyms are used in file "games":
        1 USA

        Acronyms appear on the following lines of "games":

        beginning line 1 games
        The race was close, but she moved ahead to win
        a Medal for the *[USA]* team.
```

The *wwbhelp* program gives information about any topic associated with writing and grammar. For example, if the user wishes to retrieve the names of the WWB programs that cover the topic of adjectives, the following command can be used:

wwbhelp adjective

which will display

```
adjectives, labeled..............................parts file
verb-adjective ratio.............................prose file
        ...........................wwb file
```

Additional search is possible by specifying related topics when the word prompt *word?* appears. A *q* entered in response to the word prompt will terminate the *wwbhelp* session.

8.3.1 On-Line Help for Writing

The WWB system provides a set of programs which provide on-line help with grammar, spelling, punctuation, and usage, which will be covered in the following sections.

8.3.1.1 Worduse: Help with Words and Phrases

The program *worduse* explains the correct use of words and phrases. It can be used as

```
worduse word
```

where *word* is the word or phrase on which some help is being sought. One can seek help on the usage of the word *affect* as shown below:

```
worduse affect
        AFFECT: EFFECT:   AFFECT is used  most  often  as  a  verb.
        (Used  as  a  noun, AFFECT does appear rarely as a technical
        term in psychology, where it means "an emotion.") Used as  a
        verb, AFFECT means to influence, to pretend, to assume.

        EFFECT is used as both a noun and a verb.  As a noun, EFFECT
        means  result; as a verb, it means to cause, to bring about,
        to accomplish.

                VERB:   If you choose the better grade of lumber,
                        it will affect the final cost.

                VERB:   She affected an air of indifference.

                NOUN:   Seeing the accident had a depressing effect
                        on all of us.

                VERB:   The committee effected significant changes in
                        company policy.

When the prompt "word?" appears type any more words
you want information about.
When you wish to stop, type q.

word? q
```

As you can see, it is possible to retrieve information about the usage of more than one word in a single *worduse* session. As in most WWB programs, a *q* terminates the session.

8.3.1.2 Spelltell: Help with Spelling

When doing any sort of writing, we often encounter words whose spellings we are not very sure about. Traditionally, writers have resorted to the dictionary to clarify doubts about the spelling of words. The *spelltell* program can usually provide the correct spelling of the word in question. The command to use is

```
spelltell misspelled-word
```

where *misspelled-word* is the word whose correct spelling is required. Here is an example:

```
spelltell necessary
necessary
corect
correct
Hit return key
corrects
```

In this session, we first check for the correct spelling of the word *necessary*. The *spelltell* program cleverly reports the correct spelling of this word. After reporting the correct spelling, it silently expects the user to enter the next word. For the purpose of demonstration, we asked *spelltell* to report the spelling of the word *corect*. After reporting the correct spelling, an empty string was given as the next input by simply hitting the return key. *Spelltell* reports the next possible match for the incorrectly spelled word. In the current session, it displays the next word, *corrects*.

How does *spelltell* check for the correct spelling? It assumes that the first letter of the incorrectly spelled word is correct. It then applies a pattern-matching algorithm to find the length of the longest matching common subsequence between the input word and the dictionary entry. When there are multiple words which are equally close to the input, the shortest will be returned first. This was demonstrated using the misspelled word *corect* when the word *correct* was returned before the word *corrects*.

8.3.1.3 Punctrls: Help on Punctuation Rules

Punctrls provides help on punctuation rules. It does not need any options or words on the command line to do so. It simply prints a set of some standard punctuation rules, as follows:

```
punctrls
```

1. Periods and commas <u>always</u> go inside double quote marks.

   EXAMPLE: "I want to go to the fair," he said.

   The only allowable exception is a single character
   in quotes, e.g., use a tilde "~".

2. Semicolons and colons <u>always</u> go outside double quotes.

   EXAMPLE: He knew what was meant by "hardcopy"; he didn't
   know about "software."

3. Question marks and exclamation marks go inside or outside
   double quote marks depending on the sentence sense.

   EXAMPLE: "Where are you going?" he asked.
             What is meant by the word "firmware"?

4. When a quote ends with a question mark that ends a clause
   and a comma would normally appear at the end of the clause,
   it is standard to leave the comma out. (The first example
   sentence under item 3 illustrates this.)

5. When using single quote marks instead of double quote marks,
   the same rules apply. (Single quotes are considered
   incorrect, except inside a quotation enclosed in double
   quotes.)

6. When a sentence is enclosed in parentheses, the period goes
   inside the closing parenthesis.

   EXAMPLE: (This is a sentence.)

7. If the words inside parentheses do not constitute a sentence, but are at the end of the sentence, the period goes
   after the closing parenthesis.

   EXAMPLE: This is a sentence (but not this).

8. No commas, semicolons, or colons should appear before a left parenthesis. If such punctuation is needed, it is placed after the phrase in parentheses.

   EXAMPLE: After eating salt (sodium chloride), he threw up.

9. Dashes never occur next to commas, semicolons, blank spaces, or parentheses.

   EXAMPLE: Before World War I--but not afterwards--Iceland was a part of Denmark.

Most of these rules are applied to your writing by the WWB program *punct*.

8.3.1.4 Splitrls: Help on Split Infinitives

Splitrls is the WWB program which provides on-line information about split infinitives. Like the *punctrls* program discussed in the previous section, it does not require any options to display this information. The information provided by this command is shown below:

```
splitrls
        An infinitive is a verb form that contains the word "to."
Examples include:

1.  to make
2.  to pursue
3.  to eat
4.  to be going

        An infinitive is said to be split when a word or phrase
occurs between "to" and the verb.  Possible split infinitives
include:

1.  to often make
2.  to quickly pursue
3.  to immediately eat
4.  to soon be going

        There is nothing ungrammatical about split infinitives; usu-
ally, however, they are awkward.  If the meaning of the phrase is
```

clear without the split infinitive, by all means don't use it.
There are cases, however, where the meaning is not clear
unless the infinitive is split. For example a and b do not mean
the same as c.
a. Really to understand calculus, you must do the exercises.
b. To understand calculus really, you must do the exercises.
c. To really understand calculus, you must do the exercises.
In such cases, many grammarians will tell you it is acceptable to use the split infinitive. It is usually possible, however, to change the form of the sentence as in examples d and e,
and keep some readers from downgrading you.
d. Really understanding calculus requires your doing the exercises.
e. To understand calculus fully, you must do the exercises.

Several WWB programs look for split infinitives. These programs will be discussed later.

8.3.1.5 Continrls: Help on Presenting Contingency Rules

The *continrls* program provides information about clear ways to present contingencies. The output of this program is:

```
continrls
                    Presenting Contingencies
        Research shows that contingencies presented in block paragraphs
        are often harder to follow than contingencies presented in
        non-paragraph forms.  Suggested non-paragraph forms include
        IF-THEN lists, IF-AND-THEN contingency tables, and logic trees.
        IF-THEN List Example

                _____
                | IF the light is|   THEN                   |
                |_____|_____|
                | red            |   stop                   |
                |_____|_____|
                | yellow         |   proceed with caution|
                |_____|_____|
                | green          |   go                     |
                |_____|_____|


        ⊕ Use an IF-THEN list  when  you  have  one  decision  to
```

display.

IF-AND-THEN Contingency Table Example

	IF		AND		THEN	
	the traffic light is red		–		stop	
	the traffic light is yellow		there is traffic		proceed with caution	
			there is no traffic		go	
	the traffic light is green		–		go	

⊕ Use an IF-AND-THEN contingency table when you have two decisions in succession to display.

Logic Tree Example

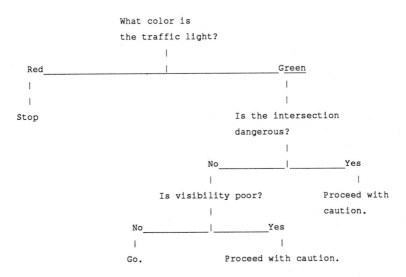

⊕ Use a logic tree for three or more consecutive decisions.

The output explains the possible ways of expressing contingencies. In the first example, we have only one decision to make, so we can use an IF-THEN list. Programmers will not need much explanation or help in understanding the output, which suggests possible ways of expressing contingencies clearly.

8.3.1.6 Prosestnd: Print Standards Used by Prose

Prose is the WWB program that describes the writing style characteristics of input text. It checks to see if scores on certain style variables fall within a given range for documents of a specified type. *Prosestnd* prints the range of scores for these style variables which *prose* considers acceptable for the specified type of document. The *prose* program describes style characteristics of a document. Commonly understood document types are educational and technical. The −*u* option can be used with the *prosestnd* program to specify the type of document. Thus −*u t* tells *prosestnd* to print acceptable scores for a technical document and a −*u e* option prints the acceptable scores for educational documents. Let us print the acceptable scores for technical documents:

```
prosestnd -u t
These are desirable ranges for technical documents based
on 30 technical documents judged good by technical managers:

Kincaid readability grades:....................  >10.1 to 15.0 years
Average sentence length:.......................  16.7 to 25.3 words
Average length of content words:...............  5.8 to 7.0 letters
Percentage of short sentences:.................  29.2% to 38.0%
Percentage of long sentences:..................  11.7% to 18.9%
Percentage of simple sentences minus
the percentage of complex sentences:...........  -24.2% to 30.1%
Percentage of compound sentences plus
the percentage of compound-complex sentences:..  5.7% to 35.2%
Passives should be fewer than:.................  28.6%
Verb-adjective ratio should be higher than:....  0.35
Nominalizations should be fewer than:..........  4.2%
Expletives should be fewer than...............  5.7%
```

Prosestnd printed the acceptable ranges of 11 style scores for technical documents.

8.3.1.7 Tmarkrls: Correct Use of Trademarks and Service Marks

Tmarkrls prints information about the correct use of trademarks and service marks. Two other WWB programs, *consist* and *tmark*, identify trademarks that are incorrectly used in the input text. Here is the output of the *tmarkrls* program:

tmarkrls

Trademarks and service marks are any words, names, symbols, or devices used to identify and distinguish a product or service from those manufactured or sold by others. The rights to a trademark or service mark can be lost if the mark is used improperly. The rules for the correct use of trademarks and service marks are listed below.

1. Always use a trademark or service mark as an adjective modifying the common name of the product or service.

    EXAMPLE: UNIXTM operating system
    (mark) (common name)

2. Always make the trademark or service mark typographically distinct.

    EXAMPLE: WRITER'S WORKBENCHTM Software

    In addition to using all capital letters, a mark may be made distinctive by using boldface type, by enclosing it in quotation marks, or by italicizing it.

3. Always show the reader if the mark is registered. Use the registered mark symbol (an R enclosed in a circle) or an asterisk with a footnote to designate a registered trademark or service mark the first time it appears in the text.

    EXAMPLE: WE* 32000 Microprocessor

    * WE is a registered trademark of AT&T.

4. Never use a registration notice for unregistered marks. Instead, the first time a mark appears in the text, use an asterisk with a footnote or the letters "TM" to show that a trademark (or "SM" to show that a service mark) is an unregistered mark.

    EXAMPLE: VAX* 11/780 computer

* VAX is a trademark of Digital Equipment Corporation.

5. The "TM," "SM," and registered mark symbols can only be used when the author or the author's employer owns the trademark or service mark. All others must use a footnote naming the mark's owner. (See example 4.)

8.4 Programs for Proofreading

In the earlier sections, we used WWB commands to get on-line help for writing documents. Once the document is prepared, the next step is to proofread and analyze it. Various programs are provided by the WWB program to proofread and analyze the completed document. These programs are the topics of discussion in the following subsections.

8.4.1 Preparing Input Text

The document to be proofread by WWB programs can be either a *nroff* or *troff* file with possible *ms* or *mm* macros or a simple formatted file. The WWB programs would be very confused when analyzing text which contains macros if it was not possible for them to recognize formatting commands and interpret text accordingly. Programs which analyze text at the sentence level are particularly sensitive to the presence of macros and formatting commands in the input text. These programs include *parts, mkstand, morestyle, murky, style, switchr, topic,* and the program *wwb* itself.

WWB provides the *deroff* command to interpret the macros and the nonsentence text associated with them; thus, input to *eqn, tbl,* footnotes, and the like are skipped from the input text. In addition, all lines to be centered are excluded from analysis. There are several problems associated with *deroff* processing. Perhaps the most serious problem occurs when *deroff* eliminates most of the input text! It is therefore advisable to run *deroff* and check the output before running other WWB programs. *Deroff* must be told which macros were used by the use of the $-m$ option. For example, *deroff* $-m$ *m* will expect *mm* macros in the input text. By using *deroff* explicitly and separately, the user is aware of the text segment that was skipped by *deroff* and can make temporary changes in the document to rectify the situation.

After the WWB analysis is completed, the original macros which were removed or changed can once again be included appropriately.

Another problem arises while processing formatted text. The formatted text with centered headings, tables, equations, etc., cannot be handled appropriately by some of the WWB programs. These programs require an unformatted text as their input. *Reroff* reads a formatted file and outputs an unformatted file with the appropriate *mm* macros included. Each line is interpreted differently depending on various factors, like its left margin, its right margin, initial special mark, font, etc. Of course, *reroff* cannot duplicate the original unformatted input file and has many limitations which are well documented in the WWB user's guide.

8.4.2 Commonly Used Options

Most of the proofreading and analysis programs share some common options. The −*V* option, which was discussed earlier with the WWB program for determining the version number of the WWB software, is also available with most of the other commands. The −*O* option gives the synopsis of a command. The −*m* option is used to specify the formatting macros in the input file; thus, −*m m* specifies that the input file has *mm* macros, −*m s* specifies a file with *ms* macros, and the −*m n* option can be used to specify that the input file is already formatted and that *reroff* must be run on it. The −*l* option produces a verbose output with explanations and suggestions about whatever area of writing is being examined by the program you are running. The −*s* option gives a terse output and should be used by experienced users; the default option is −*l*. The −*i g* and the −*i n* options can be used to skip or include list items in the input text as defined by the *mm* macros. The option −*i g* is the default option. Many WWB programs require appropriate dictionaries to perform their analysis. The simplest example is the *spelltell* program, which requires access to the dictionary of words. The location of the dictionary used by the command can be displayed by the use of the −*d* option. When used with the *spelltell* program, the output

```
spelltell -d
spelltell dictionary directory: /usr/add-on/wwb/lib/spelltell
```

informs us that the dictionary used by *spelltell* is located in the directory */usr/add-on/wwb/lib/spelltell*.

Let us look at some of the proofreading programs.

8.4.3 Spellwwb: Check Spelling Errors

Spellwwb is probably the most commonly used program in the WWB software. It examines each word in the input text and tries to match it against the list of words in the dictionary. If it cannot find an exact match, it tries to derive the closest possible match from the words in the dictionary by using its own set of rules. If both attempts fail, it reports a spelling error. If the −*l* option is active, it will also suggest possible correction. Here is an example:

```
cat spell.example
If a software product sells the most, it must be the best, right?
Not neccessarily. This belief becomes a self-perpetuating fallacy:
retailers   stock   and   recommend   what   will   sell    best,    many
consultants specialize in areas where there is work, and magazines
keep   readers   informed   about   products   that   most    of    their
subscrbers use.

spellwwb spell.ex
spellwwb -l spell.ex

Possible misspellings of non-capitalized words in spell.ex
with suggested corrections
neccessarily: necessarily
subscrbers: Scribners

If any of these words are spelled correctly, later type
                spelladd word1 word2 ... wordn
to have them added to your spelldict file.
```

Spellwwb has correctly detected the two spelling errors in the input text, but it has failed to report the correct change for the second error.

The −*b* option checks for British spellings. The following example demonstrates the −*b* option:

```
cat spell.ex2
The colour graphics used in the movie produced a spectacular effect.

spellwwb -s -b spell.ex2
spellwwb -s -b spell.ex2
color
```

If a word is correctly spelled but is reported as an error by *spellwwb*, it should be added to the dictionary to prevent further erroneous messages. *Dictadd* and *spelladd* are the WWB programs which are provided for this purpose. They are explained later.

8.4.4 Acro: Finding Acronyms

Acro locates acronyms in the input file and prints a frequency count of all acronyms used in the input. It prints the sentence containing the acronym and highlights the acronym with asterisks and brackets. Here is an example:

```
cat acro.ex
The UNIX Operating System is becoming increasingly popular on
both  micros and minis. Various software packages are currently
under development to run on this operating system. The  VAX series
of computers has made it the most popular operating system in the
academic environment.

acro acro.ex
acro -m m acro.ex

This program searches for acronyms in a text file.
It will also find words that are printed in capital letters.

Your readers may be unfamiliar with the acronyms that
appear in your document.  Check the first time each is
used and make sure it is fully defined.


The following acronyms are used in file "acro.ex":
   1 UNIX
   1 VAX

Acronyms appear on the following lines of "acro.ex":

beginning line 1 acro.ex
The *[ UNIX]* Operating System is becoming increasingly popular
on  both  micros and minis.

beginning line 3 acro.ex
The  *[ VAX]* series of computers has made it the most popular
```

```
operating system in the academic environment.

file acro.ex: number of lines 5 number of phrases found 2
```

8.4.5 Punct: Check Punctuation

Punct detects punctuation errors in the input text. It also gives a count of the number of double quotes, single quotes, apostrophes, left parentheses, and right parentheses. When errors are detected by *punct*, the line with the errors is printed. In addition, *punct* prints the line number and the line with a correction. A file called pu.*file* is also created which has all the punctuation errors changed appropriately; *file* is the name of the input text file. Most of the punctuation rules followed by *punct* are listed by the *punctrls* program. Let us look at some punctuation errors in the following text:

```
cat punct.ex
She said "To me parting is a painful thing".
 I took  her  hand in  mine,  and   we    went
out  of   the   ruined  place. as the morning
mists had risen long ago when  I first   left
the   house,,  so  the   evening  mists  were
rising  now, and in all  the  broad   expanse
of   tranquil   light they showed  to  me,  I
saw  no  shadow   of  another  parting  from
her.
```

Here is what *punct* reports:

```
punct punct.ex
punct punct.ex

2 double quotes and 0 single quotes
0 apostrophes
0 left parentheses and 0 right ones

line 1
OLD: She said "To me parting is a painful thing".
NEW: She said "To me parting is a painful thing."
line 3
```

```
OLD: out   of   the   ruined   place. as the morning
NEW: out   of   the   ruined   place. As the morning
line 5
OLD: the    house,,   so   the   evening   mists   were
NEW: the    house,   so   the   evening   mists   were


The changed version of your text is in your file named pu.punct.ex.
Do you want to save it? (y or n)
y
pu.punct.ex has been saved


For more information about punctuation rules, type:
         punctrls
```

Punct has detected three punctuation errors. First, it has found a period outside a double quote mark in the first line. In the third line, it detected a sentence starting with a lowercase letter. Finally, it reported the presence of two consecutive commas in the fifth line of the text. *Punct* creates a new corrected file with the name of the input file and a prefix of *pu.* and gives the user the option to save it. If the errors detected by *punct* are genuine, then saving the corrected file can save some time in editing the original file.

8.4.6 Double: Detect Same Consecutive Words

Double is the WWB program which finds consecutive occurrences of the same word. It does not report consecutive occurrences of single-character words unless the word is *a*. When it finds a double word, it prints it and the line number of the first occurrence of the double word, as shown below:

```
cat double.ex
Conjunctions   are   normally   used   to   join
two   words   or   sentences.   "Because"   is one
of the commonly   used   conjunctions.   This
is   a   rare occurrence of a sentence starting
with a conjunction.  A   sentence   should   not
start   with   the   word   "because,"   because
because is a conjunction!
double double.ex
double double.ex


For file double.ex:


because because appears beginning line 6
```

The consecutive occurrences of the word *because* are reported by the *double* program along with the line number on which the first word occurs.

8.4.7 Diction: Locate Wordy Sentences

Diction locates all sentences that contain incorrect or wordy phrases. In addition, it also locates some sexist terms. After locating the suspicious phrase, it encloses the phrase in asterisks and brackets and also prints the line number in which the phrase occurs. Finally, it prints some suggestions about replacing the text. Let us look at an example:

```
cat dict.ex
The   proliferation  of  PCs,   multiplicity   of
software  packages, and lack of a   common user
interface have created a great deal of growing
demand   for end-user training and support that
is   outstripping   the   capabilities   of   most
organizations.   As   can   be   seen   from   the
numerous small   training   houses   set   up   by
many    entr^preneurs,    this   has   resulted in
training of a poor quality. Another additional
problem which management is concerned about is
improperly used and   unused PCs.

diction dict.ex
diction -l dict.ex

beginning line 1 dict.ex
The proliferation  of  PCs,   multiplicity  of software   packages,
and lack of a common user interface have created
*[ a great deal of ]* growing demand  for end-user training and
support that is outstripping the capabilities of most organizations.

beginning line 9 dict.ex
*[ Another additional]* problem which management is concerned about
is improperly used  and    unused  PCs.

file dict.ex: number of lines 11 number of phrases found 2

Please wait for the substitution phrases
```

```
------------------- Table of Substitutions  --------------------

PHRASE                    SUBSTITUTION

a great deal of: use "much" for " a great deal of"
another additional: use "another" for " another additional"

-----------------------------------------------------------------
```

In this example, *diction* has located two phrases which are incorrectly used. They are *a great deal of* and *another additional*. *Diction* suggests that these phrases should be substituted with *much* and *another*, respectively. *Diction* looks for phrases in the file *ddict* in the WWB library directory. In addition, it can also be made to look at a user-specific *ddict* file. The *ddict* program can be used to create and update this file, as explained in Section 8.8.

8.4.8 Gram: Find Misused Articles and Split Infinitives

Gram reports misused articles (*a* or *an*). It also locates split infinitives, which are words or phrases between *to* and a verb. Here is an example:

```
cat gram.ex
Many computer users are  realizing  that   one
operating  system  may   not   be  enough for a
computer.  They   are   now   exploring   the
possibilities  of  two  concurrent  operating
systems which can co-reside  in  the   system.
This  often  involves  the use of a operating
system like UNIX, which is now being accepted
as   an   industry   standard,  with  a vendor-
specific  operating  system.  However,   some
users  are  anxious to quickly point out that
UNIX has  a  very  small  percentage  of  the
software  market  in  terms  of the number of
CPUs on which it is installed.

gram gram.ex
gram gram.ex
Possible grammatical errors:
In gram.ex:
```

```
article error: "a operating" should be "an operating" about line 8
split infinitive: "to quickly point " about line 12

For information on split infinitives type:
                    splitrls
```

There were two grammatical errors detected in the input text. These errors and possible substitutions are also explained by the *gram* program.

8.4.9 Tmark: Locate Incorrectly Used Trademarks

Trademarks and service marks are names identifying a vendor or a service organization. These names should always be used as adjectives. *Tmark* identifies erroneous use of these words and highlights these words with the use of asterisks and brackets. The line number is also printed. *Tmark* searches for each word in two system dictionaries and one user dictionary. The user dictionary of trademarks can be created and updated by the use of the *dictadd* program, as explained later. Here is an example:

```
cat mark1.ex
The UNIX operating system is very popular on minicomputers.
Many vendors support at least some version of UNIX on their
popular line of minicomputers.

tmark -s mark1.ex
tmark -s tmark1.ex

For the first trademark dictionary:

file tmark1.ex: number of lines 3 number of phrases found 0

For the second trademark dictionary:

beginning line 1 tmark1.ex
Many vendors support at least some version of *[ UNIX ]* on their
popular line of minicomputers.

file tmark1.ex: number of lines 3 number of phrases found 1
```

Let us correct it and pass the input to *tmark* once again:

```
cat tmark2.ex
The UNIX operating system is very popular on minicomputers.
Many vendors support at least some version of the UNIX
operating system on their popular line of minicomputers.

tmark -s tmark2.ex
tmark -s tmark2.ex


        No misused trademarks or service marks found.
```

Tmark is actually one of the three consistency checking programs in the WWB system. *Conscap* and *spell* are the other two programs and these are discussed in the following sections.

8.4.10 Conscap: Check for Consistent Capitalization

While writing long technical documents, one can easily lose track of consistency in capitalization. Consider the following paragraph:

```
cat conscap.ex
One of  the  major  differences  in  the  4.1
Berkeley   version   and   the  4.2  Berkeley
version  of Unix is that the former  supports
file   names  having  a  maximum length of 14
characters while the file name length in  the
latter  is  flexible.  Other versions  of UNIX
also  support  file  name   lengths   of   14
characters.

conscap -m n conscap.ex
conscap -m n conscap.ex


For file conscap.ex:
The following words were capitalized inconsistently:

 Number of
 Occurrences            Word

        1               Unix
        1               UNIX
```

The $-m$ n option was used to inform *conscap* that the input file is already formatted and does not contain any macros. In this example it was not required, because there are no sentences or phrases which indicate titles or headings. It was used to remind the readers of the availability of the $-m$ option on most WWB programs.

Conscap has detected the inconsistent capitalization of the words Unix and UNIX. It also gives a count of these words.

8.4.11 Conspell: Consistency in Spellings

Conspell locates inconsistent use of British and American spellings in the input file. Let us look at a sample text segment:

```
cat conspell.ex
From prehistoric  times, people have   always
been      fascinated    by   color.    From
paintings  with  different  colors  to  color
movies, color  has been  a  major  factor  in
people's imagination, fantasy, and dreams. In
the   computer    era,  one often comes across
terms like colour monitor,  colour  graphics,
etc.


conspell conspell.ex
conspell conspell.ex


Some words have two spellings: one preferred in American English
(for example, "color"), and the other preferred in British English
("colour"). Mixing British and American spellings in a document
can distract readers from your message.


Your document, conspell.ex,
uses some British and some American spellings of words.
If you are writing for an American audience, change all the
British spellings of words to their preferred American spellings.

The words spelled with American spellings are the following:
color
colors
```

```
The words spelled with British spellings are the following:
colour
```

The inconsistent use of British and American spellings of the word color is reported by *conspell* in this session.

8.4.12 Sexist: Report Sexist Terms

Sexist examines each word in the input text and tries to locate a match in the sexist phrase dictionary. It then reports any words which match. In addition, it detects inconsistent use of sexist terms, like *ladies and men*. Stereotypic words like *chairman* are also reported. Here is an example:

```
cat sexist.ex
Many women and boys  in  colleges  prefer  to
pursue a career in programming because of the
various challenges opened in  this  area  and
also   because   the   demand   for  programmers
continues to rise at a very steady pace.  The
chairman   of   the   department  of  computer
science at a  major  technological  institute
recently reported that more women are seeking
to pursue  a  career  in programming now than
ever before.

sexist sexist.ex
sexist -l sexist.ex

beginning line 1 sexist.ex
Many *[ women ]* and boys in colleges prefer  to pursue a career
in programming because of the various challenges opened in  this
area  and also   because   the   demand for  programmers continues
to rise at a very steady pace.

beginning line 5 sexist.ex
The *[ chairman ]*   of   the   department  of  computer science
at a  major technological institute recently reported that more
*[ women ]* are seeking to pursue a career in programming now than
ever before.

file sexist.ex: number of lines 11 number of phrases found 3
```

```
Please wait for the substitution phrases


------------------    Table of Substitutions    --------------------

PHRASE                    SUBSTITUTION

chairman: use "chair, coordinator, chairperson" for "chairman"
women: use "OK for particular women, or female classes" for "women"
women: use "average workers, average wage earners"
       for "working women"
women: use "wage-earning women" for "working women"


--------------------------------------------------------------------
```

Note how sexist terms have been highlighted by asterisks and brackets. The *sexist* program also suggests substitutions. The −*s* option can be used to exclude suggestions about substitutions.

8.4.13 Switchr: Find Words Used as Nouns and Verbs

Some words can be used as both nouns and verbs. Sometimes these words are used inappropriately and can confuse readers. *Switchr* finds such words and reports on them. Consider the following example, in which the word *list* has been used as both a noun and a verb:

```
cat switchr.ex
It is normally convenient to list  a  program
along  with  its  line  numbers. This  is
particularly important if you are  trying  to
debug  the  program, and  if  the debugger is
capable of debugging at  source  code  level.
List  is  one  of  the  UNIX utilities  which
produces  a  source  listing  with  the  line
number information.

switchr switchr.ex
switchr -l -i g -m m switchr.ex

Based on the results of a parts of speech analysis, switchr finds
```

the words   in a document   that are used as both a noun and a verb.
Although this is not necessarily a problem, it may be confusing to
the reader.

For file switchr.ex, these words are:

 list

beginning line 1 switchr.ex
It is normally convenient to *[list]*   a program along   with
its   line   numbers.

beginning line 6 switchr.ex
[List] is   one   of   the   UNIX utilities   which produces
a   source   listing   with   the   line number information.

file switchr.ex: number of lines 8 number of phrases found 2

The words in file "switchr.ex"
that were used as both a noun and a verb
are stored in file "sw.switchr.ex."

Do you want to save it? (y or n)
> y
sw.switchr.ex has been saved

Switchr derives its name from *switch*ing grammatical *r*oles. After highlighting
the words which are used as both nouns and verbs, *switchr* stores these words
in a file named sw.*input-file*, where *input-file* is the name of your text file.
This file can be saved by responding with a *y* to the prompt *Do you want to
save it? (y or n)*.

8.4.14 Proofvi: Proofreading and Interactive Editing

We looked at the use of the various proofreading programs in the previous
sections. The majority of these programs require that the user edit the file after
making a note of all the errors. *Proofvi* is the WWB program that goes a step
further. It can be made to run in the foreground as well as in the background;
the latter is the default mode. It runs the WWB programs *spellwwb*, *punct*,
double, and *diction*. All errors detected while these programs are running are
stored in a file named ref.*input-file*, where *input-file* is the name of the input

text file.

After completing the proofreading process, *proofvi* sends mail to the user indicating that it is now time to invoke the *proofvi* program again. This time *proofvi* displays the file almost like *vi*, the UNIX screen editor. All errors are highlighted. In addition, it provides a menu that describes the current error and suggests changes, and even offers the user a choice to correct the error quickly by accepting the suggested change. A subset of the *vi* editor commands are also available to the user to correct the errors in the file. Consider the following file:

```
cat proofvi.ex
If a software product sells the most, it must
be   the   best,   right?  Not neccessarily. This
belief becomes   a   self-perpetuating   fallacy:
retailers    stock    and    recommend   what   will
sell     best,    many consultants specialize in
areas   where there is work, and magazines keep
readers    informed    about     products      that
most     of    their subscrbers use.
```

This file was used in an earlier example to demonstrate the use of the *spellwwb* program. There are two spelling errors in this file, and these are the only *proofvi* detectable errors in the text. Let us run *proofvi* on it:

```
proofvi proofvi.ex
proofvi proofvi.out
The proofvi program is now  looking for  errors in your file
proofvi.ex; it will send you mail when it is finished.  Wait
until you get the mail to continue.
```

After some time, it will display the following message:

```
From Tare Fri Nov 28 22:10 EST 1986
Your reference file, ref.proofvi.ex, has been completed.
To run the interactive part of proofvi now,
exit the mail program and type
        proofvi proofvi.ex
```

To satisfy our curiosity, let us look at the reference file:

```
cat ref.proofvi.ex
! wwb, 11/28/86-22:10:21 , ex8,  533617803
: proofvi.ex : 1, 28, 1, 39, /neccessarily/ : S 1
: proofvi.ex : 7, 18, 7, 27, /subscrbers/ : S 2
```

This file is used by *proofvi* during the editing session. The user really need not know anything about it. It has codes for error types and also the line number of the line on which the error occurred. Let us invoke *proofvi* on the input file to edit the errors:

```
proofvi proofvi.ex
If a software product sells the most, it must
be  the  best,  right?  Not neccessarily. This
belief becomes  a  self-perpetuating  fallacy,
retailers   stock   and   recommend   what   will
sell   best,   many consultants specialize in
areas  where there is work, and magazines keep
readers   informed   about   products   that
most   of   their subscrbers use.
~
~
~
~
~
~
-------------------------------------------------------
:a Add to personal dictionary    :c Correct spelling with corrector
:g Globally change word          :t Type new word here
:i Ignore this word for rest of this file.

Ctrl-N Go to next error.                   SPELLING
                                           neccessarily
file proofvi.ex: 2 items found 2 remaining
```

The words in bold font are the error words, which are highlighted on the screen. The available menu options to correct these errors are also displayed. Most of these are self-explanatory. In the present example, it is a spelling error that is to be corrected. The *:c* option can be selected to correct the spelling error. Let us select this option. The bottom of the screen is redrawn and looks as shown here:

```
-------------------------------------------------------
CR -- See next possibility
y  -- Use this word as correct spelling            Correction
g  -- Use this word globally as spelling           necessarily?
q  -- Quit correcting -- not finding right spelling
```
FIND CORRECT SPELLING

The cursor is positioned on the question mark after the correct spelling guessed by the *spellwwb* program, which happens to be *necessarily*. This is the correct spelling of the misspelled word and the word can therefore be replaced by responding with the character *y* to the prompt. The screen is then updated to reflect the new spelling, and then ^N (control-N) can be typed to move the cursor to the next error.

The menu appearing at the bottom of the screen changes, depending on the type of error being highlighted. The menu to correct double word errors will look slightly different from the menu to correct spelling errors; however, the basic logic and the steps involved remain the same for all the menus. It is possible to end the session without completing the entire editing process by using the *vi* commands *:wq* or *ZZ*. Terminating a session prematurely will result in an updated reference file, so one can restart editing the input file without repeating the corrections completed in an earlier session.

Proofvi can also update the appropriate user dictionaries at the user's request.

8.5 Style Analysis Programs

In previous sections, we looked at the programs which can be used for proofreading any text. WWB also provides a series of programs for analyzing the style of a document. Additionally, programs are available to assign grammatical parts of speech to words, to count the number of syllables of each word, to print a condensed version of the input, etc. The following sections briefly describe these programs. Some technical writers may not find these programs of significant value in revising documents; however, these programs are discussed briefly in the following sections so that you will know of their existence.

8.5.1 Parts: Assign Grammatical Parts of Speech

Parts parses the input text and assigns a grammatical part of speech to each input token. It categorizes the input into one of the 13 word classes: noun, verb, article, adjective, adverb, conjunction, preposition, interjection, auxiliary verb, pronoun, subordinate conjunction, to be, and possessive. Needless to say, with the complexity involved in English grammar, it is very difficult to parse the language, and *parts* gives erroneous results in some cases.

8.5.2 Topic: A Program to Guess the Topic

Topic scans the input text and maintains a count of all the nouns and adjective-noun pairs in the input. After scanning the entire file, it outputs the 20 most frequently used nouns and adjective-noun pairs. The most frequently used item is printed first. If two items have the same count, they are printed in reverse alphabetical order.

8.5.3 Org: Print Condensed Version of the Input

Org reads an input file containing *mm* macros or an already formatted text file. If the text is already formatted, the −*r n* options must be used. *Org* identifies and prints the headings and the first and last sentence of each paragraph. It excludes tables, equations, footnotes, displays, and lists from the input text.

8.5.4 Neg: Find Negative Words

Normally, good documents should not contain a large percentage of negative words. WWB uses this as one factor in determining the quality of a document. *Neg* prints the negative words along with the number of times each word occurred in the input text. It also prints the sentences containing the negative words and highlights the negative words by enclosing them in brackets and asterisks. It recognizes negative words by comparing each word in the input with the list of words in the dictionary of negative words which is maintained in the file neg.d in the WWB library directory.

8.5.5 Abst: Evaluate Text Abstractness

Abst analyzes a document for abstractness. It compares each word in the input file with the words in the dictionary of abstract words. This dictionary is located in the file abst.d in the WWB directory. Like the *neg* program, it reports a percentage, in this case, it is the percentage of input words which are abstract. It also gives the user the option to save the list of abstract words found in the document in the file prefixed with *ab.*. Once the abstract sentences are identified, the writer can add appropriate explanations to clarify the abstract segments of the document.

8.5.6 Diversity: Compute Vocabulary Diversity

Good vocabulary has traditionally been associated with good writing ability. A measure of the richness in vocabulary is the ratio of the total number of distinct words used to the total number of words in the text. This ratio is known as the diversity ratio and is reported by the *diversity* program. Certain words like "to," "if," "which," and "but" are excluded in the computation. With the −*l* option, the program also explains the importance of diversity in the text and how the *diversity* ratio is computed.

8.5.7 Syl: Count Syllables of Each Word

Syl reads the input text and prints the number of syllables in each word. The output consists of a list of words ordered by the number of syllables in the words. Within this order all words are ordered alphabetically; thus, all one syllable words will be printed first, followed by all two syllable words, and within each class all words are sorted alphabetically.

8.5.8 Style: A Style Analyzer

Style reports various writing style characteristics of a document. It has numerous options to control its output. *Style* reports four readability scores: Kincaid Formula, Automated Readability Index (ARI), Coleman-Liau Formula, and Flesch Reading Grade Level. Each score is evaluated based on a different formula, for example, the Kincaid formula is calculated as follows:

11.8 * (syllables per word) + 0.39 * (words per sentences) − 15.59

When used with the −*a* option, *style* will print all sentences with their readability scores. *Style* prints a summary table of sentence length and structure, word length and usage, verb type, and sentence openers. When used with the −*e* option, *style* will print sentences that begin with an expletive.

The $-n$ option can be used to print sentences that contain a nominalization used as a noun. Passive words can be printed with the $-p$ option. The $-L$ option can be used to print sentences having more than the specified number of words. Similarly, the $-S$ option can be used to print sentences shorter than the specified number of words. Combinations of these options can be used to give a verbose output about the style characteristics. The *prose* program also describes the writing style of a document, but it produces the output in prose form.

8.6 Wwb: The Program Itself!

Wwb runs the *proofr* and the *prose* programs. These programs in turn run *spellwwb*, *punct*, *double*, *diction*, *gram*, and *prose*. *Wwb* is a program that suffices as a proofreading and analysis tool for most technical documents.

8.7 Murky and Continge

Murky and *continge* are programs which are used to analyze procedural text. *Continge* analyzes the wording of decision points in procedural documents and is particularly helpful for analyzing legal documents. It reports the count of contingency words, such as "if," "when," "except," and "whenever." It also reports sentences which contain poorly worded contingencies.

Murky uses the output from the *style* program to report sentences with passive verbs, long sentences, sentences with long words, and sentences with poorly worded contingencies.

8.8 Customizing WWB Environment

Many WWB programs require dictionaries to find certain types of words. The *spellwwb* program is probably the most frequently used WWB program that uses such a dictionary. The dictionary used by this program has a limited number of words. If a word in the input text cannot be located in this dictionary, *spellwwb* will report an error, even if the word is correctly spelled. The remedy to this problem is to add words which are frequently used, but not found in the WWB dictionary, to the user's own personal dictionary file. Programs which require a dictionary and which can look for words in the user's personal dictionary are *proofr*, *diction*, *sexist*, *spellwwb*, *tmark*, and the *wwb* program itself. The names of the dictionaries and the programs which use these dictionaries are listed in Table 8.1.

TABLE 8.1 WWB Personal Dictionaries

Dictionary	WWB Program
$HOME/lib/wwb/ddict	spellwwb
$HOME/lib/wwb/sexdict	sexist
$HOME/lib/wwb/spelldict	spellwwb
$HOME/lib/wwb/tmarkdict	tmark

In the following session, the two words *multiprocessor* and *server* are added to the dictionary which is used for checking spellings:

```
dictadd
Which of these files do you want to make entries in?
(To quit at any time, type "q".)

     1 - /mnt/tare/lib/wwb/ddict
     2 - /mnt/tare/lib/wwb/spelldict
     3 - /mnt/tare/lib/wwb/sexdict
     4 - /mnt/tare/lib/wwb/tmarkdict
     5 - dictionary-file

At the prompt, type 1, 2, 3, 4, or 5
>2
When you see the prompt, "word?", type in a word you want the
WRITER'S WORKBENCH system to consider correctly spelled.
Type a "q" when you want to quit this program.
word? multiprocessor
word? server
word? q
```

As you can see from the example, it is possible to add words or phrases to the other personal dictionaries. *Spelladd* is another program that is used to add words to the spelling dictionary. It enables the user to enter a large number of words into a single file and then augment the dictionary appropriately. If new-words-file is a file containing a list of words to be added to the spelling dictionary, then the dictionary is augmented by the following set of commands:

```
spell new-words-file >> $HOME/lib/wwb/spelldict
spelladd
```

The purpose of the first command is to eliminate the possibility of adding a word to the dictionary if that word is already present. The second command actually runs the UNIX utilities *sort* and *uniq* on the dictionary.

8.9 A Final Note

"Life is the art of drawing sufficient conclusions from insufficient premises."[*] The Writer's Workbench software was probably written with this philosophy in mind. It draws conclusions from the limited logic and information built inside the software. It is a good tool which can be used by the technical writer to improve both style and comprehension level of any document. With the advent of artificial intelligence and with more sophisticated and faster computing environments, it may one day be possible to approximate the human mind with machine logic. While that day is very far away, the writing process itself can never be automated. It works well with computer languages but it stops there! The beauty of the human mind is that it is sometimes undisciplined! Let it remain that way!

---

[*]Samuel Butler, *Note Books*, 1912.

9 Miscellaneous Utilities

The preceding eight chapters discussed some of the most important utilities in the UNIX environment. Those chapters included utilities which could be grouped by usage. There are many other utilities which are useful for different purposes, and they will be discussed in this chapter. The Curses package is useful to the programmer as a set of screen-handling functions in C programs. The *tar* and *cpio* utilities are used to archive files. *Ar* is useful for archiving and maintaining libraries. On-line calculators are available on the system in the form of the *bc* and the *dc* utilities. The *stat* group of commands provide some programs for elementary statistical analysis.

9.1 Curses

Programming projects can be classified roughly into two categories: those which involve a direct interface with the nonprogramming users and those which are used by software developers. The interface with the nonprogramming users must be user-friendly, because one cannot expect these users to understand the intricacies of the software. DBMS often provide screen handlers to help with the development of user-friendly interfaces. In the absence of screen-handling packages, the task of manipulating the screen rests solely in the hands of the programmer. The Curses package provides a high-level interface to the programmer, which enables the programmer to handle the screen by means of function calls in the C program. In addition, the programmer is freed from having to worry about the specific characteristics of many different models of terminals. The Curses library, with its database of terminal characteristics, deals with those low-level issues.

9.1.1 Getting Started

The Curses package must be informed about the terminal that is being used. This can be done by setting the UNIX shell variable *TERM*. A screen consists of lines and columns. Although most screens have 24 lines and 80 columns, programs must not make this assumption, but must make use of the variables *LINES* and *COLS*, which define the current screen size. These variables are defined by the Curses function *initscr*. All programs must also include the line

```
#include <curses.h>
```

at the beginning of the program. This should be in addition to other file inclusions that may be used in the program (except the stdio.h file, which is automatically included with the curses.h file). The program must be compiled and linked with the Curses library to create the executable program. Let us write a simple program using the Curses library to draw a box around the edges of the screen:

```
#include <curses.h>
main()
{
        int lines,columns,i;

        /* Initialize */
        initscr();
        clear();

        /* draw the vertical lines */
        for (i=0;i<LINES;++i)
        {
          move(i,0);
```

```
        addch(' | ');
        move(i,COLS-1);
        addch(' | ');
    }

/* draw the horizontal lines */
    for (i=0;i<COLS;++i)
    {
        move(0,i);
        addch('-');
        move(LINES-1,i);
        addch('-');
    }

/* update the screen */
    refresh();

/* End screen updating */
    endwin();
}
```

The *initscr* function is used to initialize the screen-manipulating parameters and modes. The *move* function is used to move the cursor to the required position on the screen. The row and column numbers start from zero in the upper left hand corner of the screen. Once the cursor is moved, any character can be output using the *addch* function, or any string can be output with the *addstr* function. The *addstr* function will be used in the next example. Finally, the screen itself can be updated to reflect the changes in the screen by using the *refresh* function. The function *clear* can be used to clear the screen. Before exiting the program, it is necessary to use the *endwin* function to reset the terminal settings. The program itself must be compiled with the *-l* option to link it with the Curses library, as in the following command:

```
cc  scrl.c -lcurses
```

When the program is executed, the screen looks as it is shown in Figure 9.1. In all the examples in this chapter, we will use the same screen size.

Now that we have started, let's try to use some more Curses functions. Curses is an ideal package for developing screen forms for displaying prompts and reading user input. It provides functions to display data in fancy modes like reverse video, blinking, underlined, etc. Let us write a program to generate a simple form to prompt for a name and a five-character id number.

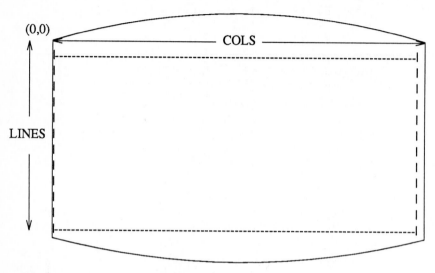

Figure 9.1 Box around the Screen

If the id number is not five digits long, an error message will be displayed at the bottom of the screen. After every entry, the cursor will move to a prompt that asks the user if more entries are to be entered. A "y" response will move the cursor to the name prompt for the next record; any other response will terminate the program. The prompts and the error messages will be displayed in reverse video mode. In addition, a beep will be heard just before the display of the error message. All valid entries will be stored in the file outfile. Here is the code for our program:

```
#include <curses.h>
main()
{
        FILE *fpout,*fopen();
        char response[24];
        fpout = fopen("outfile","w");
        initscr();
        clear();
        attron(A_STANDOUT);
        move(2,2);
        addstr("NAME : ");
```

```
move(3,2);
addstr("NUMBER  :  ");
move(4,2);
addstr("MORE(y/n)  :  ");
attroff(A_STANDOUT);
refresh();
while(1)
{       move(2,9);
        clrtoeol();
        getstr(response);
        fprintf(fpout,"%s",response);
        while (1) {
          move(3,11);
          getstr(response);
          move(LINES-1,0);
          clrtoeol();
          if (strlen(response) != 5)
          { move(LINES-1,0);
            beep();
            addstr("Invalid student number, enter again");
            refresh();
          }
          else {
                fprintf(fpout,"%s0,response);
                break;
          }
        }
        move(4,14);
        getstr(response);
        if (response[0]=='y')
                continue;
        else
                break;
}
        endwin();
}
```

Many features of the Curses package were used in this example. First, the
attron function was used to set special character attributes. The argument to
this function specifies the character attribute. The most commonly used
attributes are A_UNDERLINE, A_REVERSE, A_BOLD, A_DIM, A_BLINK,
and A_STANDOUT. Combinations of these attributes can be specified using
the C language logical *OR* (I) operator. These attributes are associated with a

character and can be turned off by using the *attroff* function. The syntax of the arguments to *attroff* is identical to the syntax of the *attron* function arguments. The *clrtoeol* function is used to clear the screen from the present position to the end of the line. The *beep* function sounds a bell on the terminal. The *getstr* function is used to read a line from standard input up to a newline character. This function also handles the erase and kill characters set by the user. Another input function is *getch* which reads a character at a time.

9.1.2 Setting Terminal Modes

Curses provides a set of functions that are useful for setting the terminal modes. The default modes depend on the terminal characteristics and the mode that was set when the program was started. Curses provides functions to read data from the terminal. These functions may pass the characters read to the program only after a newline character is encountered. This can be changed by putting the terminal in CBREAK mode. The *cbreak* and the *nocbreak* functions can be used to put the terminal into and out of CBREAK mode. Another pair of functions, *raw* and *noraw*, provide the same capabilities; however, when the terminal is set in the RAW mode by the use of the *raw* function, some of the signal-generating characters are passed through uninterpreted. The *nl* and the *nonl* functions control the translation of newline characters to carriage returns and line feed characters on output and the translation of the return key to newline on input. Disabling these translations results in faster cursor motion.

The current modes of the terminal can be saved using the *savetty* function and can be restored by a subsequent call to a *resetty* function. All intermediate settings done during these two calls are nullified. The *echo* and the *noecho* functions control the echoing (that is, the displaying on the screen) of characters typed by the user. Echoing is usually stopped while a user is entering a password.

Here is a program that prompts for a password. The user is given 10 chances to enter the password. If the user fails, the program terminates with the message *Too many attempts!*. On entering the wrong password, the user gets the error message *Invalid password, try again*. If the user is successful in entering the correct password, the program secured.program is run. Echoing is disabled while the user enters the password. The program code is as follows:

```
#include <curses.h>
main()
{
        char string[25];
        int count;

        /*** initialize   ***/
        initscr();
        clear();

        /*** display the Password prompt ***/
        move(2,1);
        addstr("Enter Password : ");
        refresh();

        /*** disable echoing ***/
        noecho();

        /*** Loop while the user gets the correct password  ***/
        /*** in ten attempts                                ***/

        while(1)
        {
                getstr(string);
                ++count;
                if (strcmp("passwd",string)==0)
                {
                        /*** enable echoing again ***/
                        echo();
                        endwin();
                        system("secured.program");
                        exit(0);
                }
                if (count>10)
                {
                        move(LINES-1,0);
                        addstr("Too many attempts!");
                        refresh();
                        endwin();
                        exit(0);
                }
                else
                {
```

```
move(LINES-1,0);
        addstr("Invalid password, try again");
        refresh();
        sleep(2);
        clrtobot();
        move(2,18);
        refresh();
      }
    }
  }
```

This program illustrates the use of setting and resetting the echoing character feature. The *clrtobot* function is similar to the *clrtoeol* function, but instead of clearing to the end of a line, it clears the screen from the right of the cursor position down to the bottom of the screen.

9.1.3 Formatted Input and Output

In the previous sections we studied the use of the *getch*, *addch*, *getstr*, and *addstr* functions. These functions are useful for handling unformatted input and output to and from the terminal. Curses provides variations of the *printf* and *scanf* functions to put formatted input and output for a terminal under the control of the Curses routines. The *printw* function can be used to output formatted text; its syntax is identical to the syntax of the *printf* function. Similarly, the *scanw* function can be used to read formatted data from the standard input.

9.1.4 Manipulating Displayed Text

Curses also provides a set of functions to manipulate the contents of the screen. The *insch* function can be invoked to insert a specified character to the left of the current position of the cursor. The *insertln* function can be called to insert a blank line above the current line. The *deleteln* function is used to delete the line under the cursor. All other lines below the cursor are moved up one line. The *delete* function can be called to delete the character under the cursor. All characters to the right of this character are moved to the left by one character. The following function illustrates the use of some of these functions:

```
func1()
{
int i,j, Atoa;
char ch;
Atoa = 'a' - 'A'; /*** ASCII offset between 'A' and 'a' ***/
for (i=0;i<LINES;++i)
        {
        for (j=0;j<COLS;++j)
                {
                move(i,j);
                ch =inch();
                if (ch >= 'A' && ch <='Z')
                        {
                        ch += Atoa;
                        delch();
                        insch(ch);
                        }
                }
        }
refresh();
}
```

What does this function do? It converts all uppercase letters on the current screen to lowercase letters. The rest of the screen is left untouched. The function *inch* returns the character at the current position of the cursor so the character can be examined. The function *func1* loops through all the positions on the screen, checking for the existence of any uppercase letters. If one is found, it is first deleted using the *delch* function. The addition of *Atoa* to the numeric value of the ASCII representation of an uppercase letter converts it to a lowercase letter. This new translated character is subsequently inserted in the current position by the *insch* function to produce the desired effect.

9.1.5 Windows

Curses provides a data structure that facilitates the use of a part of the actual physical screen as if it were the full screen. This user-defined segment of the screen is referred to as a window. A window defined in Curses cannot be larger than the physical screen. The window data structure itself consists of a two-dimensional array of characters, a set of attributes associated with each character, and other related items. Windows can be created by the use of the *newwin* function. This function requires the number of lines, the number of columns, and the start coordinates of the new window as its arguments. Windows are useful for giving users two different screen images to work with. Most of the functions to manipulate the standard screen that we have been using so far have parallel functions available which are applicable to window manipulations. Window-handling functions have a *w* prefixed to them. In addition, they take an additional first argument which refers to the window to be manipulated.

The following program uses one window to display the part description of the specified part number and another overlapping window to display supplier name for the specified supplier number. Specifying the letter *c* as a part number or a supplier number changes the window. Specifying a *q* quits the session. Here is the program:

```
#include <curses.h>
int win_ind;
WINDOW *win_parts,*win_supp;
char part_no[25][8],part_desc[25][25],supp_no[25][8];
char supp_name[25][25];
main()
{

        FILE *fp_parts,*fp_supp,*fopen();
        int eof=2,i;
        fp_parts = fopen("parts.file","r");
        fp_supp  = fopen("supp.file","r");
/*** Initialize the parts and suppliers array from the files ***/
        while(1)
        {
          eof = fscanf(fp_parts,"%s%s",part_no[i],part_desc[i++]);
          if (eof == EOF) break;
        }
        eof =2;
        i=0;
        while(1)
        {
          eof = fscanf(fp_supp,"%s%s",supp_no[i],supp_name[i++]);
          if (eof == EOF) break;
        }

        /***** initialize the two prompts for the two windows *****/
        initscr();
        win_parts = newwin(0,0,0,0);/*If x or y dimension is 0,  */
        win_supp  = newwin(0,0,0,0);/*it is set to LINES or COLS */
```

```
        wmove(win_supp,0,0);
        waddstr(win_supp,"Supp no : ");
        wmove(win_parts,0,0);
        waddstr(win_parts,"Part no : ");
        wmove(win_supp,1,0);
        waddstr(win_supp,"Supp name : ");
        wmove(win_parts,1,0);
        waddstr(win_parts,"Part desc : ");
        wmove(win_parts,LINES-1,0);
        waddstr(win_parts,"Enter c to change window and q to quit");
        wmove(win_supp,LINES-1,0);
        waddstr(win_supp,"Enter c to change window and q to quit");
        win_ind =1;
        while(1)
        {
                switch (win_ind)
                {
                case 1 :
                        parts();
                        break;
                case 2 :
                        suppliers();
                        break;
                }
        }
}

/**** function to manipulate the parts window ****/
parts()
{
    int i,found;
    char in_part[8];
    touchwin(win_parts);
    wmove(win_parts,0,10);
    wgetstr(win_parts,in_part);
    while ((strcmp(in_part,"q") != 0) && (strcmp(in_part,"c") !=0))
        {
                found = -1;
                for (i=0;i<25;++i)
                {
                        if (strcmp(in_part,part_no[i])==0)
                        {
                                found = i;
```

```
                            wmove(win_parts,1,12);
                                    wclrtoeol(win_parts);
                                    waddstr(win_parts,part_desc[i]);
                                    wmove(win_parts,1,10);
                                    wrefresh(win_parts);
                                    break;
                            }
                    }
                    if  (found == -1)
                    {
                            wmove(win_parts,1,12);
                            wclrtoeol(win_parts);
                    }
                    wmove(win_parts,0,10);
                    wgetstr(win_parts,in_part);
        }
/*** if q quit the session ***/
    if (strcmp(in_part,"q")==0)
    {
        endwin();
        exit(0);
    }


/*** if c change the window ***/
    if (strcmp(in_part,"c")==0)
    {
        win_ind =2;
        return(0);
    }
}


/*** function to manipulate the suppliers window ***/
suppliers()
{
    int i,found;
    char in_supp[8];
    touchwin(win_supp);
    wmove(win_supp,0,10);
    wgetstr(win_supp,in_supp);
    while ((strcmp(in_supp,"q") != 0) && (strcmp(in_supp,"c") !=0))
    {
        found = -1;
        for (i=0;i<25;++i)
```

```
        {
                if (strcmp(in_supp,supp_no[i])==0)
                {
                        found = i;
                        wmove(win_supp,1,12);
                        wclrtoeol(win_supp);
                        waddstr(win_supp,supp_name[i]);
                        wmove(win_supp,1,10);
                        wrefresh(win_supp);
                        break;
                }
        }
        if  (found == -1)
        {
                wmove(win_supp,1,12);
                wclrtoeol(win_supp);
        }
        wmove(win_supp,0,10);
        wgetstr(win_supp,in_supp);
    }
    if (strcmp(in_supp,"q")==0)
    {
        endwin();
        exit(0);
    }
    if (strcmp(in_supp,"c")==0)
    {
        win_ind =1;
        return(0);
    }
}
```

When using the *wrefresh* function with overlapping windows, only the segments of the window which were changed after the last *wrefresh* was invoked are refreshed. This is done to optimize the refresh; however, overlapping windows may write on the shared part of the screen and this will not be reflected in the optimized *wrefresh*. The call to *touchwin* assumes that the whole window was changed, so it rewrites the whole window. It is therefore advisable to use *touchwin* to refresh overlapping windows.

The program first initializes the two windows. The *win_ind* variable is used to keep track of the next window to be displayed. The *parts* function manipulates the window for displaying part description for the specified part number. The *suppliers* function manipulates the window for displaying the supplier name for the specified supplier number.

A window can be deleted using the *delwin* function. A window can be moved using the *mvwin* function. The function invocation:

```
mvwin(win1,3,5);
```

will move the *win1* window so that the upper left corner starts at the third row, fifth column.

9.1.6 Miscellaneous Functions

The Curses functions that have been used so far are the most commonly used functions; however, there are numerous other functions that are also provided for various needs. If the special debugging library *dcurses* is available on your system, then the calls to *traceon* and *traceof* may be used to turn tracing on for only that segment of the program that is enclosed between these two function calls. Curses also provides some low-level functions which can make a program small but which may not have screen optimization features. A few sets of merged functions are also available to combine move and output operations into a single function call. For example, the function call *mvaddch(12,4,'a')* will output the single character *a* at coordinates y=12 and x=4. The *keypad* function is used to provide special treatment to function keys.

9.2 Calculator Tools

The *bc* and the *dc* utilities can be used as desk calculators. Computers were not designed to be used as calculators alone, but it is very convenient to have access to a calculator on the system. Of course, it is always possible to write a C program to perform the desired calculations, but who wants to write a program to compute arithmetic expressions? *Dc*, an acronym for desk calculator, performs arithmetic on expressions expressed in reverse polish notation (RPN). The average UNIX user may not be familiar with RPN, so *bc* is a preprocessor to *dc* which is available to manipulate expressions in infix (or algebraic) notation, which is more commonly understood. In the following sections, the use of *bc* and *dc* as a calculator is discussed.

9.2.1 Dc: A Desk Calculator

Dc provides arithmetic computations on expressions which are expressed in RPN. If a file is specified, *dc* starts reading from it; otherwise, it reads from the standard input. Once the file is read *dc* starts reading from the standard input. It understands the following binary operators:

$$+ - / . \% \char`\^$$

The caret character (^) is used to express exponentiation.

Simple *dc* expressions are made of numbers and the above operators. Numbers may be integers or they may contain decimal points. Negative numbers must be preceded by an underscore (_). The stack itself can be manipulated using the basic stack manipulation commands shown in Table 9.1.

TABLE 9.1 Dc Stack-Manipulating Commands

Command	Operation
f	All values on the stack are printed.
p	The top value on the stack is printed.
c	The stack is emptied.
d	The top value on the stack is duplicated.
v	The top element is replaced by its square root.
q	Exit the *dc* program.

Here are some simple examples:

```
dc   #compute the value of: 12+24
12 24 +
P
36
q
```

```
dc   #compute the value of: (12*32) * ((32–12)²)
12 32 *
32 12 -
2 ^
*
P
153600
q
```

Dc also allows partial results to be stored in registers or stacked on other stacks. These registers, or stacked values, can be recalled and pushed on the present stack. The command *sn* pops the top element of the stack and stores it in the named register *n*. The command *Sn* pops the top element of the stack and pushes it on the named stack *n*. The command *lx* pushes the value stored in register *x* on the top of the main stack. The command *Lx* pops the top element of the stack *x* and pushes it on the main stack. The following example illustrates the use of registers:

```
dc #compute the value of: (32*42) + (12*10) - (12*11)
32 42 *
sa
12 10 *
sb
12 11 *
sc
la lb +
lc    -
P
1332
q
```

Dc provides additional miscellaneous operations; however, the requirement to express the arithmetic expression in RPN is not convenient for most users. Let's see how the *bc* utility can be used to compute the results of arithmetic expressions using infix notation.

9.2.2 Bc: Another Calculator

Bc is actually a preprocessor to *dc*. It allows arithmetic expressions to be expressed directly in infix, or algebraic, notation and is therefore more user-friendly than *dc*. It reads from the specified input file first and then from the standard input. It provides features that can be used for doing a lot more than just arithmetic computations. It provides statements which are reminiscent of the C language. In this section, we will be looking at some of the basic useful features of *bc*. The inquisitive reader should refer to the user reference manual for more details. The following example illustrates the use of *bc* for a simple computation. The expression was evaluated earlier using *dc*.

```
bc  #compute the value of: (32*42) + (12*10) - (12*11)
(32*42) + (12*10) - (12*11)
1332
quit
```

Bc also provides the sqrt function to compute square roots and the *-l* option provides access to the math library, which includes the sine, cosine, log, and other functions. Let us use *bc* to compute an arithmetic expression involving square roots:

```
bc  #compute the value of: (32+12) - √(12*32) / (131+12)
(32+12) - sqrt((12*32)/(131+12))
43
quit
```

In the above example, it is obvious that the computed result has lost its precision. *Bc* does not retain any digits to the right of the decimal point unless it is specifically informed to do so by the variable *scale*, which can be assigned some value accordingly before the computation is started.

```
cat exprfile
scale=4
(32+12) - sqrt((12*35)/(131+12))

bc exprfile
42.2863
```

The exprfile has two statements. These statements are separated by a newline character. *Bc* statements can also be separated by semicolons. If a statement consists of just an expression, the expression is evaluated and the result is displayed. Variables can be brought into existence by the use of single lowercase letters. Expressions can be assigned to these variables. Other statements supported by *bc* are

```
expr
{stat;....stat}
if (expr)
while (expr) stat
for (expr;expr;expr)
break
```
null stat
```
quit
```

where *expr* is any expression and *stat* is any statement. These statements can be used to write C-like programs like the following:

```
cat bcfile2
n=10
s=4
r=1
for(i=1;i<n;i++) r=r*i
r
quit

bc bcfile2
362880
```

This program computes the factorial of the initial value of *n*, which in the example was set to 10.

9.2.2.1 Functions in Bc

Functions can be defined in *bc* by using the *define* statement. Function definitions have the following syntax:

```
define f(a){
statement;
statement;
return(r)
}
```

The character *f* is the name of the function, and it can only be a lowercase letter. The character *a* is the argument to the function. There can be more than one argument; arguments are separated by commas. It is not necessary to return a value in a function; therefore, a function return can have either of the following syntax:

```
return
return(r)
```

All *bc* variables are global to the program, but automatic variables can be declared in functions to last only while the function is active. All automatic variables are initialized to zero when the function is invoked. The *auto* statement can be used to declare automatic variables. This statement must be the first statement in the function. A *bc* program using a function to compute the average of the two numbers 45 and 100 is shown here:

```
scale=2;
n=45;
m=100;
define a(x,y) {
auto z;
z=(x+y)/2;
return(z);
}.
a(45,100);
quit
```

Only 26 functions can be declared in a program, because of the restriction of using only single lowercase letters as function names. Variables and functions can have the same name.

9.2.2.2 Miscellaneous Features

Most of the C operators can be used in *bc* statements. One-dimensional arrays can also be used in *bc*, and they have a syntax similar to arrays in the C language. *Bc* also provides variables that can be set to interpret the input and output data in different radix. The *ibase* variable can be set to initialize the radix of the input data and the *obase* variable can be set to initialize the radix of the output data. This feature can be used to convert numbers from one radix to another.

9.3 Archiving Files

Traditionally, archiving utilities were provided to store files that are not currently in use. These files would be archived on tapes or floppy disks and restored when they were required again. The *tar* utility provided by UNIX is useful for storing files on tape and restoring these files again when the need arises. The *cpio* utility is useful for similar purposes.

During the development of a system, many functions are shared by different programs. These functions can be compiled, grouped together, and stored into a single archive file. This archive file can be used by the link editor during the compilation. *Ar* is the utility that provides the facility for creating such archives.

9.3.1 Tar: A Tape File Archiver

Running out of disk space is an age-old problem faced by most programmers. The temptation to run a *rm* −*rf* command to erase files should be resisted during such situations. It takes a lot more time to create files than to destroy them! What is the alternative? Backup the disk! Once you have a backup copy you can run the *rm* −*rf* command even if you don't know what the −*rf* options do! If you are fond of running a *rm* command, then you better know how to use the *tar* utility. *Tar* is the programmer's tool to store files on tapes and restore them when required. If you wished to store all the files in your current directory and its subdirectories on a tape mounted on a drive designated as /dev/mt/1h, here is how you would do it:

```
tar cf /dev/mt/1h
```

Simple! This can save you a lot of trouble if you inadvertently remove a file. The syntax of *tar* is:

```
tar function-selector [options] [files]
```

The *function-selector* controls the primary action of *tar*. The optional parameters can be used to provide additional information to *tar*. Finally, the files to be extracted from the archive or the files to be archived are specified. In the example, *c* is the primary function selector and *f* is the additional parameter specified. The *c* function selector is used to create a new tape file. The optional parameter *f* is used to specify that the next argument, /dev/mt/1h, be used as the name of the archive. A dot (.) in the example indicates that all files in the current directory are to be archived.

A − (minus) as the name of the archive causes *tar* to write to the standard output or read from the standard input. Commonly used archive or device names have the form /dev/mt/*nd*, where *n* is the tape drive number, and *d* is the tape density, which can be *l*, *m*, or *h* for low (800 bpi), medium (1600 bpi), or high (6250 bpi) density respectively.

Having stored the files on a tape, how do you extract these files from the tapes? The following command extracts all the files from the tape mounted on the tape drive designated as /dev/mt/2h and copies these files to the current directory:

```
tar xf /dev/mt/2h
```

If it is not necessary to extract all the files on the tape, then the names of the required files should be specified, as in

```
tar xf /dev/mt/2h file1 file2
```

which will extract only files file1 and file2.

9.3.1.1 More Options

The following additional primary options are used by *tar*:

r   The specified files are written at the end of the tape.

t   The names of all the files on the tape are listed.

u   Normally the specified files are written on the tape even if they are already on the tape. This option specifies that a file is to be added only if it is not already present or if it was modified after it was copied to the tape.

Tar also provides a set of additional options that can be used to control its action. They are:

v   This option provides output consisting of the name of each file preceded by the primary option. This lets you see the file names as the files are written to or read from tape.

w   This option provides an interactive session with *tar*. Before taking any action, *tar* prints the name of the file and the action to be taken, then waits for the user input. If the user response starts with a y, the action is executed, otherwise the action on the file is neglected and *tar* continues with the next file.

b   This option is used to specify the blocking factor.

The default blocking factor is one. When writing lots of data to tape, it is common to use a blocking factor of 20.

m· By default, *tar* restores the modification times as files are copied onto tape. Using this option causes *tar* to restore files as if they were modified during the execution of *tar*.

o Files extracted from a tape retain the user and group id as they appear on the tape. This option overrides this default action and causes the group and user id to be that of the user running *tar*.

9.3.1.2 Some Examples

To display verbose information about the files on the archived tape mounted on device /dev/mt/1h, you would use the following command (sample output follows the command):

```
tar tvf /dev/mt/1h
rw-rw-r--2407/1011    5730 Sep  2 10:00 1986 c0.c
rw-rw-r--2407/1011   56488 Sep  2 10:00 1986 c2.c
```

The *v* optional parameter is used above to display the information about the tapes on the file in verbose mode. This information is displayed in the same format as the output of the *ls* −*l* command. In addition, the numerical user id and group id of the file owner is displayed. This option is used to check that the appropriate version of the files has been retrieved. It is also handy for monitoring the writing or reading of *tar* tapes.

Here is an example of using *tar* in interactive mode:

```
tar wxf /dev/mt/1h c?.c
x c0.c :y
x c1.c :n
```

Here *tar* displays the action to be taken on the file. The *x* displayed indicates that the file is to be extracted. *Tar* then waits for the user response. A response starting with a *y* means that the file is to be extracted. Any other response means that the file is to be omitted from the *tar* command. In the above session, only the c0.c file is to be extracted.

9.3.2 Cpio: Copy Archives In and Out

Cpio is used to read a list of file or path names and to copy these files to the standard output in a special format. *Cpio* can also be used to extract these files from the formatted file. It is very useful when many small files (perhaps in several directories) need to be moved as a group from one machine to another. *Cpio*, in effect, bundles all of the files into one package. The package can be moved as a single unit and then unbundled in its new location.

There are three main options accepted by *cpio* and they are $-o$, $-i$, and $-p$. In addition, many keywords are provided to control the action of *cpio*. *Cpio* can also be used to archive files on a tape. The $-o$ option is used to read the names of files from the standard input and redirect these files into a single file. The default output file is the standard output. The output file also stores status information about the input files. The $-i$ option is used to extract specified files from a *cpio* formatted file. The $-p$ option is used to read a list of file or path names from the standard input and copy these files into the output directory.

9.3.2.1 Creating Cpio Files

Cpio files can be created using the $-o$ option. *Cpio* expects a list of file or path names from the standard input. It organizes these files into a single file. The status of the files is also copied. The output file size is an integer multiple of 512. It has trailer records with the string *TRAILER!!!* in them. The following example copies the files /ds5/us1/rprt/c4 and /ds5/us1/rprt/*.c into the tape file /dev/mt/1m

```
ls /ds5/us1/rprt/c4 /ds5/us1/rprt/*.c | cpio -o > /dev/mt/1m
392 blocks
```

Cpio displays the number of blocks in the output file. The v option can be used to display a verbose output of *cpio* action. It displays the names of the files as they are written to tape. It is good practice to also use the c option to write the *cpio* header information in ASCII characters. This permits portability, so that a *cpio* file created on one machine can be read on another machine. The B option can be used to control block size when the output is directed to a tape file. The a option is used to reset the access times of the files after they have been copied. Here is another example:

```
ls /ds5/usl/rprt/*.c | cpio -ova /dev/mt/1m
/ds5/usl/rprt/ nice.c
/ds5/usl/rprt/bkp.c
/ds5/usl/rprt/debug.c
/ds5/usl/rprt/filters.c
/ds5/usl/rprt/getpwent.c
/ds5/usl/rprt/m1.c
/ds5/usl/rprt/m2.c
/ds5/usl/rprt/match.c
/ds5/usl/rprt/passwd.c
o/ds5/usl/rprt/try.c
/ds5/usl/rprt/yacc.c
/ds5/usl/rprt/ymdhms.c
392 blocks
```

The names of the files were generated by the use of the *v* option.

9.3.2.2 Extracting Files from Cpio Archives

The −*i* option can be used to extract files from a *cpio* archive. Let us extract files m1.c and m2.c from the *cpio* archive file created in the previous example:

```
cat /dev/mt/1m | cpio -i m*.c
112 blocks
```

Several options are available to control the files to be extracted. Depending on the current directory, it may be necessary to create new directories during the extract process. By default, *cpio* will not create new directories. The *d* option can be used to create new directories if required. The *t* option can be used to print a table of contents of the input archive file. The following *cpio* command prints a verbose output describing the contents of the archive file arout:

```
cat arout | cpio -itv
153 blocks
100664 rst      5978  May 29 17:42:26 1986  ../m1.c
100664 rst      6034  May 29 17:44:35 1986  ../m2.c
100664 rst     65969  Sep  6 13:40:18 1986  c4
153 blocks
```

Normally, files are not replaced if a file with the same name exists and has a more recent modification time. The *u* option is used to unconditionally replace files. To unconditionally extract files m1.c and m2.c from the archive file arout, use the following command:

```
cat arout | cpio -iu ../m?.c
153 blocks
```

Note that the pattern defines the full path name as it appears in the archive. Multiple patterns can also be specified, as in

```
cat arout | cpio -iu ../m1.c c4
153 blocks
```

which will extract files ../m1.c and c4.

Cpio can be used with the *f* option to copy all files except those that match the specified patterns. The command

```
cat arout | cpio -if c4
153 blocks
```

will copy all files from the *cpio* archive except file c4. The *m* option can be used to retain the previous modification time. The *r* option can be used to rename the extracted files interactively. The file can be skipped by responding with a null line. Here is an example:

```
cat arout | cpio -iru
Rename <../m1.c>
mn1.c
Rename <../m2.c>
<null line>
Skipped
Rename <c4>
cx
153 blocks
```

Only files ../m1.c and c4 were extracted from the archive. It is important to note that not only were the file names changed in the above example but in the case of ../m1.c, the target directory was also changed. *Cpio* did not extract the file ../m2.c, because a null line was specified as the new name of the file.

9.3.2.3 Using the Pass (−p) Option

When used with the −p option, *cpio* reads a list of path names of files from the standard input and copies these files into the specified directory. Some of the options discussed earlier can be used to control the copying of files. Here is an example:

```
pwd
/usr1/dst1

ls -l dir2
total 0

ls  /usr1/dst/m1 /usr1/dst/m2 | cpio -pdu dir2
36 blocks

find dir2 -print
dir2
dir2/usr1/dst
dir2/usr1/dst/m1
dir2/usr1/dst/m2
```

The *d* option was used to create directories as necessary. The *u* option was used to copy the files unconditionally. Note how the files were copied into the new directory. The *find* command was used to display the entire hierarchy of the dir2 directory.

Unlike the −*i* and the −*o* options, the −*p* option copies the files relative to the specified directory and not to the standard output. The following example shows how the files are copied relative to the destination directory if the full path names are not specified for the input files:

```
pwd
/usr1/dst1/dir1

ls
file1 file2 file3 dir3
```

ls ../f*.c
```
file4.c
```

ls ../f*.c file1 /usr/dst1/dir1/file2 | cpio -pud dir3
```
247 blocks
```

find dir3 -print
```
dir3
dir3/usr/dst1/dir1/file2
dir3/file1
```

ls f*.c
```
file4.c
```

Note that the input file ../f*.c is copied in the current directory because all path names originate from the destination directory.

9.4 Ar: Archiving and Maintaining Libraries

Most software projects involve the development of functions which can be used by the different modules in the system. It is therefore convenient to store the object code of these functions in a single file. Changes to the functions can then involve maintaining only one file. SCCS can be used to maintain these archives. *Ar* is the UNIX utility used to archive and maintain these libraries. The syntax of the *ar* command is:

ar *options keywords archive-file file1 file2 ...*

Archive-file is the name of the final archive and file1, file2, etc., are the names of the component files that are stored in the archive. Various options and keywords are available to control the action of *ar*. These options are discussed in the following sections.

9.4.1 Adding Files to the Archive

Adding files can involve creating a new archive or adding these files to the existing archive. The following command creates a new archive named arch1 to store files func1.o and func2.o in *ar* format:

```
ar r arch1 func1.o func2.0
ar: creating arch1
```

A new archive arch1 is created. New files can now be added to this archive using the same option:

```
ar r arch1 func3.o
```

The archive arch1 was already present; therefore, *ar* did not recreate the archive but added the new file to the archive. If the file is already present in the archive, it is replaced by the new file. The *u* optional keyword is used to add a file only if it has a modification time later than the archive itself. Ordinarily, new files are added at the end of the archive. This default can be changed by using the *a* or *b* option to place the file after or before the specified file. The *i* option is synonymous to the *b* option; therefore, to add the file func4.o after the file func2.o, use the *ar* command as follows:

```
ar rua func2.o arch1 func4.o
```

The archive arch1 now has four files. They are func1.o, func2.o, func3.o, and func4.o.

9.4.2 Listing the Status of the Archive

The names of the files stored in the archive can be listed using the *t* option. If file names are specified along with this option, only the names of these files are listed; otherwise, the names of all the files in the archive are listed. The following command lists the names of all the files in the archive arch1:

```
ar t arch1
func1.o
func2.o
func3.o
func4.o
```

When the *v* option keyword is used with the *t* option, a verbose description of the contents of the archive is given, as follows:

```
ar tv arch1
rw-rw-r--2407/1011      33 Sep  5 00:02 1986 func1.o
rw-rw-r--2407/1011      35 Sep  5 00:02 1986 func2.o
rw-rw-r--2407/1011      15 Sep  5 00:10 1986 func3.o
rw-rw-r--2407/1011      20 Sep  5 00:32 1986 func4.o
```

The output is identical in format to the verbose output of the *tar* utility. It has the numerical group and user id along with an output reminiscent of the *ls* −*l* command.

9.4.3 Deleting a File from the Archive

Any component file can be deleted from the archive using the *d* option. The command

```
ar d arch1 func2.o
```

deletes the file func2.o from the archive arch1.

9.4.4 Printing and Extracting Files

Any file from the archive can be printed using the *p* option. To print the first four lines of the file poem2 from the archive poems, use the following command:

```
ar p poems poem2 | head −4
I wandered lonely as a cloud
That floats on high o'er vales and hills
When all at once I saw a crowd,
A host, of golden daffodils*
```

To extract the component files from an archive, the *x* option is used. The component files func1.o and func2.o can be extracted from the archive arch1 by using the following command:

---

*William Wordsworth, *Daffodils*.

```
ar x arch1 func1.o func2.o
ar: func2.o not found
```

Ar extracts the file func1.o but reports that the file func2.o was not found in the archive. We had deleted it from the archive using the *d* option.

9.4.5 Using Ar Libraries with the C Compiler

Libraries created by the use of the *ar* utility can be shared by various programs. In order to link a program that uses a function which has been compiled and archived in a library created by *ar*, use the name of the archive on the *cc* command line, for example,

```
cc some_prog.c archlib1
```

which will link the required functions from the specified library archlib1. This feature is particularly useful to group functions together in an archive for a specific use, for example, the standard math library is normally stored in the library /usr/lib/libm.a. To compile a C program which uses this library, the following *cc* command is used:

```
cc another_prog.c -lm
```

which is an abbreviation for

```
cc another_prog.c /usr/lib/libm.a
```

Most link editors which are invoked by the C compiler are capable of multiple passes over an archive; however, if the link editor is not capable of multiple passes, then the order of the archived files within the library becomes important. The utility *lorder* can be used to generate the correct order in which the files are to be archived within the library. *Make*, the utility for maintaining programs, recognizes the *.a* suffix as a library archive.

9.4.6 Other Options

Ar provides other miscellaneous options which can be used to exert additional control over *ar*. The *c* option suppresses the message that is displayed during the creation of the archive. The *q* option is used with the *r* option to *q*uickly add files without checking to see if the file is already present in the archive. This reduces the time it takes to add new files to the archive. The *m* option is used to move the files within the archive.

9.5 Stat: Elementary Statistics

Stat is a collection of statistical commands useful for generating basic statistical results from a sequence of numbers. The sequence of numbers is also referred to as a vector. Each element of the vector can be either an integer or a real number. The letter *e* can be used to signify base 10 exponentiation. Sample elements of a vector include the following:

```
45    45.12    4534.45e+12
```

Stat command files are normally stored in the directory /usr/bin/graf. Some of the *stat* commands can be executed in the normal environment by setting the *PATH* variable. Executing the *graphics* command will set the *PATH* variable to include the required directories. It also executes a new shell and changes the primary prompt to the caret character (^). After executing the required *stat* commands, the EOT character should be typed to restore the environment. *Stat* commands are organized into four groups. They are

      1. Transformers
      2. Summarizers
      3. Translators
      4. Generators

These commands are discussed in the following sections.

9.5.1 Transformers

Transformers transform the input vector into an output vector of the same length. The elementary transformers are listed below:

abs	Generate an output vector consisting of the absolute values of the input vector.
ceil	Round all input numbers up to the next integer.
cusum	Generate a vector consisting of the cumulative sum up to the element.
floor	Round each element down to the previous integer.
list	List vector elements delimited by the specified string.
log	Assign each output element the log of the input number. The base can be specified.
root	Compute the specified root of each element.

Other transformers available are af, exp, gamma, mod, pair, power, siline, sin, and subset. If *vectinp* is the input vector which contains the following elements:

```
cat vectinp
12.23   23.11 25.65 1.5e2.3 34 35 15 16 12 13 12.45
```

then the square root of each element can be computed as follows:

```
graphics
^  root -c3 -r2 vectinp
3.49714        4.80729        5.06458
12.2474        0.547723       5.83095
5.91608        3.87298        4
3.4641         3.60555        3.52846
^^D (control D)
```

The $-c$ option is commonly used which specifies the number of columns to be printed in the output. The $-r$ option is used to indicate the required root. Similar options are available for the other transformers.

9.5.2 Summarizers

In transformers, each element of the output vector has a direct one-to-one correspondence with the input element and is dependent only on the input element. Summarizers act on all the elements of the input vector, and the value of each element of the output depends on all the input elements. *Stat* provides the following summarizers:

bucket	Break the input into buckets.
cor	Compute the correlation coefficient given the file containing the base vector.
hilo	Find the highest and the lowest values in the vector.
lreg	Compute the linear regression.
mean	Compute the arithmetic mean.
point	Compute and output the point from the empirical cumulative density function expressed as a fraction, number, or a percent.
prod	Generate the internal product.
qsort	Sort the input vector.
rank	Rank the elements of the input vector.
total	Compute the sum of the elements of the input vector.
var	Compute the variance.

The following example illustrates the use of the summarizer *mean* to compute the arithmetic mean of the elements of vector *vectinp*:

```
^cat vectinp
12.23   23.11 25.65 1.5e2.3 34 35 15 16 12 13 12.45
^mean vectinp
29.0617
```

The elements can be added together using the summarizer *total* as follows:

```
^total vectinp
348.74
```

9.5.3 Translators

The *stat* group of commands also provides a set of functions to generate graphic pictures from the input vectors. These commands are called translators. The following set of translators are generally available:

bar	Build a bar chart.
hist	Draw a histogram.
label	Label the axis of the generated graph.
pie	Build a pie chart.
plot	Plot a graph.
title	Title a graph or a vector.

Your terminal must be able to interpret the output of these commands to draw the required pictures. The output is in Graphical Primitive String (GPS) format, which is a representation of the drawing. Device filters are available to read a GPS-described drawing and to display the picture on the graphical device. The following command will draw a histogram on a Tektronix 4014 terminal for the vector *vectinp2*:

```
^hist vectinp2|td
```

9.5.4 Generators

Generators are used to generate a sequence of numbers satisfying the specified generator command. The following generators are available:

gas	Generate additive sequence.
prime	Generate prime numbers.

rand   Generate random numbers.

Unlike the previous *stat* commands, generators do not require an input vector. By default, 10 numbers are generated, but more can be generated by the use of the −*n* option. Prime numbers can be generated as shown below:

```
^prime
2 3 5 7 11
13 17 19 23 29
```

Programmers often require random numbers to test their programs. *Rand* can be used to generate these numbers. To generate 15 random numbers in the range from 0 to 1, use the following command:

```
^rand -l0 -h1 -n15
0.513855       0.17572        0.308624       0.534515       0.947601
0.171722       0.702209       0.22641        0.494751       0.124695
0.0838928      0.389618       0.277222       0.368042       0.983429
```

The −*l* and −*h* options are used to specify the lower and upper boundaries for the random numbers.

9.5.5 Stat: Concluding Remarks

Stat provides a very elementary mechanism to generate statistical results. The various *stat* commands discussed in this chapter have provision for some options which allow programmers to have more control over the output. Despite these options, *stat* is not powerful enough to satisfy the needs of the average statistician. Various statistical tools have been developed to run in the UNIX environment. Perhaps the most popular is S.[*] It may not be the ultimate tool for statistical analysis but is definitely one of the best tools for the statistician working in the UNIX environment.

---

[*]Available from AT&T Technologies Software Sales.

Exercises

Chapter 1:

Let file1 be:

```
a11  12  a13  John Doe
a21  22  a23  Nikki McEnroe
a31  32  a33  Pat Rickster
a41  42  a43  Bob Herbst
```

and file2 be:

```
a11  12  b13  b14
b21  33  b23  b24
a31  32  b33  b34
b41  42  b43  b44
```

1. Write a *join* command to output the *join*ing of two files based on the first field of each file.
2. What will the following command output?
   join −a 1 −j1 1 −j2 1 file1 file2
3. Write a *sed* script to output only those lines from file1 which have the letter *B* in them.
4. Assuming that the fields are tab-separated, write an *awk* script to print the total number of items in the second column of file file1.
5. Select an appropriate filter to make each two consecutive lines of a single file run together to form one line in the output file. If the input is file1, the output will be:
   ```
   a11  12  a13  John Doe a21  22  a23  Nikki McEnroe
   a31  a32  a33  Pat Rickster a41  a42  a43  Bob Herbst
   ```

6. Using filters, display the count of the number of tab characters in the input file.

7. Use appropriate filters to merge two unsorted files. The output of merging files file1 and file2 would be:

```
all  12  a13  John Doe
all  12  b13  b14
a21  22  a23  Nikki McEnroe
b21  33  b23  b24
a31  32  a33  Pat Rickster
a31  32  b33  b34
a41  42  a43  Bob Herbst
b41  42  b43  b44
```

8. Use appropriate filters to write a shell script to convert a number from one number system to another.

9. Using filters, reverse the order of lines in file file2. The output would look like this:

```
b41  42  b43  b44
a31  32  b33  b34
b21  33  b23  b24
all  12  b13  b14
```

10. Use *awk* to output the count of words in a file starting with a specified letter. The letter is to be specified on the command line.

Chapter 2:

1. If you were assigned the task of porting one of the debuggers to another UNIX system, which debugger would be the easiest to port? Why?

2. Consider a program which expects a series of integers as input but terminates when it encounters a specific integer. Write a shell script using *dbx* and filters to generate integers and print the value of the integer along with an appropriate message when the program terminates. All other messages should be suppressed.

3. What is the significance of the −*g* option during the compilation phase? Why is this option not required while using *ctrace*? Is code that is generated using this option optimized? Can you optimize this code without recompiling the program?

4. Write a utility that will convert a number specified in one number system to a number in another number system using any one of the debuggers.

Chapter 3:

1. Write a C program using *lex* to read input text and:

a. Insert a blank between period-separated words, for example, *cat.The* would be output as *cat. The*.

b. Output those sentences that are longer than 20 words.

c. Display warning messages about words which are capitalized inconsistently in the input text, e.g., Unix and UNIX.

2. Write a C program using *lex* to:

a. Scan real numbers as defined by FORTRAN 77.

b. Truncate and translate real numbers to their integer values and replace the original numbers accordingly.

3. Using *yacc*, *lex*, and C, write a language processor to parse a language defined by the following grammar:

start	--->	begin *statement* end;
statement	--->	if (*expression*) *statement*
statement	--->	*var = constant*;
constant	--->	*digit	constant digit*
digit	--->	0|1|2|3|4|5|6|7|8|9
expression	--->	*var*
var	--->	*letter	letter var*
letter	--->	a|b|c|d|e|f

4. Write an error-reporting routine for the parser in exercise 3 which reports the type of error before aborting the parsing process.

5. Improve the code for the parser in the previous exercise to include error recovery routines so that the parser can report more than one error in the input.

6. Write a calculator using *yacc* and *lex* to perform arithmetic computations on expressions involving integers, (,), +, −, *, and /. The program should be able to read an expression and print the result. Proper error messages should be displayed to indicate any errors in parsing.

7. Consider the following grammar:

start	--->	a start b start| b start a start|

where *a* and *b* are terminal symbols. Write *yacc* specifications for this grammar. Can you convert this grammar to be left recursive? When you run *yacc* on this grammar, it will report a shift/reduce conflict. Locate this shift/reduce conflict in the y.output file.

8. Write a C program using *yacc* and *lex* that will accept only strings of 0's and 1's in which every zero is immediately followed by at least one 1.

9. Give a *m4* macro definition which will generate C code to check for the equality of the numerical value of the two arguments passed to it.

10. Give a set of *m4* macro definitions to compute the arithmetic value of any expression composed of the words MULTIPLY, DIVIDE, ADD, and SUBTRACT and any integer. For example, the output text for *5 MULTIPLY 7 ADD 2* will be 37.

Chapter 4:

1. If fin1.c and fin2.c are *touch*ed, what commands will the following makefile generate:

    final : fin1.o fin2.o

    cc -o final fin1.o fin2.o

2. Library archive libs1.a has two function members defined, f1 and f2. These were archived by using the *ar* command as follows:

    ar r libs1.a f1.c f2.c

    Subsequently, a *lex* specifications file plex.ll was written which used these functions. The file fin.c contained the *main* function that invoked the *lex* generated function *yylex*. Write the shortest possible makefile to maintain the dependencies in these programs.

3. For the SCCS file shown in Figure 4.3, draw the SCCS structure after a *comb* is applied to it.

4. Write a utility that runs *lint* on a C program and introduces the warning messages in the program as comments after the appropriate lines. Other warning messages should be commented at the end of the program.

5. Can you have *make* run *lint* each time before running the C compiler? If so, how?

6. If C program files to *m4* are designated by the suffix *.M*, write *make* rule(s) to convert any *.M* file to a *.c* file.

Chapter 5:

Consider the parts relation:

part_no	quantity	color

and the supplier relation:

supp_no	part_no

1. Write a QUEL statement to print the average of the quantity field.

2. Write a QUEL statement to print the total quantity by color. The output would look like this:

    red   12

    green   100

3. Write a QUEL statement to print the names of all suppliers who supply green colored parts.

4. Write a QUEL statement to display the part number of parts which are supplied by more than one supplier.

5. Write SQL statements to perform the same tasks as the QUEL statements in exercises 1 to 4.

6. Write an SQL query to print the supplier names of all parts whose average quantity in stock is more than 200.

7. Write an EQUEL program to read a file containing a list of part numbers and supplier numbers and print all relevant information about these parts and suppliers. Assume that part numbers are prefixed by the letter P and supplier numbers are prefixed by the letter S.

8. If you were using the UNIFY DBMS, which data access method would you use to access or structure an inherently hierarchical application?

9. Which is the best access method for searching for a range of values, B-trees or hashing?

Chapter 6:

1. Write *troff* commands to output titles with a centered page number and different left-justified titles on odd and even numbered pages. Make appropriate assumptions about page attributes.

2. Write a *troff* macro which can be used to number section headings. This macro when invoked as

     .MC This is a new section

will produce

     1.1 *This is a new section*

The first part of the section is fixed by a register, presumably the chapter number. The second part of the section number is incremented by one to produce a series of consecutively numbered section headings whenever the macro is invoked. Improve the macro to start sections on new pages whenever there is not enough space on the current page to accomodate the section heading and at least two more lines.

3. Use *tbl* to generate the following table:

HEADING1		SPANNED HEADING
column1	column2	column3
d11	12	This is a block of text that is input to *tbl*. Note how the left and the right margins within the column have been properly adjusted. The width of this column is 2 inches.
d12	45	This is the next row for the same column. It also has the same format as the first row. Once again note the justification of the margins within the column.

4. Use *pic* to draw the following diagram:

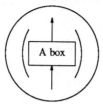

5. Use *eqn* to generate the following mathematical expression:

$$E(V^k) = \int (\delta (b (\frac{x^\lambda - 1}{\lambda}) + a) + 1)^{\frac{k}{\delta}} h(x)\, dx$$

6. Use *troff* to draw the following picture:

(Hint: Use the ■ character to draw vertical lines.)

Chapter 7:

1. Write a *uucp* command to copy all the files in the directory */mnt/wave* on system sysa to the *uucppublic* directory on system sysb.

2. List the names of the *uucp* support files which are most important for enforcing security in the *uucp* software.

3. Write a utility using filters that will send mail to a user only if the user is currently logged on the system. It will return with an appropriate message if the user is not currently logged on the system.

4. If *some_comm* is a UNIX command that expects two file names as command line arguments, and if one of these files is opened by this command in write mode and the other in read mode, write a *uux* command to execute this command on system sys1. The file to be read in input mode is resident on system sys2, and the output file is to be created on system sys1.

5. What would be a typical usage for the *mailx* startup file mailx.rc?

Chapter 8:

1. Use the dictadd program to add the word *VAX* to the list of trademark words in the user dictionary of trademarks.

2. Use the *topic* program to guess the topic of the following text:

Currently, WWB is available for the AT&T computers. It is available in slightly different versions for other computers. Portions of WWB are also available for the XENIX operating system. WWB requires more than a megabyte of space. In addition, when you are using the *proofvi* program of WWB, it is necessary that you work with a terminal with at least 24 lines and 80 columns.

3. Name the WWB program(s) required to do the following:

  a. Provide a measure of vocabulary richness.

  b. List punctuation errors in the input text.

  c. List spelling errors in the input.

  d. List wrong articles used.

  e. Display words with inconsistent capitalization.

4. Most WWB programs produce a long version of the output. How can this option be changed to produce a short version of the output?

5. Use the *parts* program of the WWB software to find the version number of the software.

6. Use *yacc* and/or *lex* to write the following utilities:

  a. Detect words starting with a vowel and change the article associated with this word to "an" only if the article used before it was "a".

  b. Introduce a blank between words separated by a period. The words must be alphabetic and the second word must begin with an uppercase letter.

Chapter 9:

1. Enhance the Curses program in Section 9.1.5 to display an error message in reverse video mode if the input supplier number or part number is missing.

2. Develop a simple utility to make a tape copy of a *tar* archive given two tape drives. One drive would have the source tape and the other would have the target tape. Provide a file selection capability to copy only the specified files.

3. Write *dc* statements to compute the value of the following expression:

$$((32 * 43)^2) * ((412 - 112)^2)$$

4. Write *bc* statements to compute the result of the following expression:

$$\sum_{i=0}^{5} sin(30*i)$$

5. Use *stat* commands to generate an output vector consisting of the square root of the absolute value of the input vector.

Bibliography

Books

Rebecca Thomas and Jean Yates, *A User Guide to the UNIX System*, Berkeley, California: Osborne/McGraw-Hill, 1985.

Henry McGilton and Rachel Morgan, *Introducing the UNIX System*, New York: McGraw-Hill, 1983.

Brian Kernighan and Rob Pike, *The UNIX Programming Environment*, Englewood Cliffs, New Jersey: Prentice-Hall, 1984.

UNIX User's Reference Manual—Check your local UNIX system documentation.

UNIX Programmer's Reference Manual—Check your local UNIX system documentation.

Ann Nicols Lomuto and Nico Lomuto, *A UNIX Primer*, Englewood Cliffs, New Jersey: Prentice-Hall, 1983.

The Bell System Technical Journal, July-Aug. 1978.

Brian Kernighan and Dennis Ritchie, *The C Programming Language*, Englewood Cliffs, New Jersey: Prentice-Hall, 1978.

Alfred V. Aho, Ravi Sethi, and Jeffrey D. Ullman, *Compilers, Principles, Techniques, and Tools*, Reading, Massachusetts: Addison-Wesley, 1985.

Alfred V. Aho and Jeffrey D. Ullman, *The Theory of Parsing, Translation, and Compiling, Vols. I and II*, Englewood Cliffs, New Jersey: Prentice-Hall, 1972-1973.

UNIX Programmer's Manual, Vols. 1 and 2, New York: Holt, Rinehart and Winston, 1983.

Richard A. Becker and John Chambers, *S—An Interactive Environment for Data Analysis and Graphics*, Belmont, California: Wadsworth Advanced Program Books, 1984.

Stephen G. Kochan and Patrick Wood, *UNIX Shell Programming*, Hasbrouck Heights, New Jersey: Hayden, 1985.

Mark Sobell, *Building Applications Using a 4GL*, Sunnyvale, California: Sobell Associates, 1986.

Brian Kernighan and P. J. Plauger, *Software Tools*, Englewood Cliffs, New Jersey: Prentice-Hall, 1976.

Chapter 1

William N. Joy, *An Introduction to Display Editing with Vi*, Berkeley Software Distribution UNIX Programmer's Manual.

Walter Zintz, New tools for programming productivity, *UNIX/World*, Vol. 4, No. 5, May 1987.

Alfred V. Aho, Brian W. Kernighan, and Peter J. Weinberger, *Awk—A Pattern Scanning and Text Processing Language*, Bell Laboratories, Murray Hill, New Jersey, 1978.

Dale Dougherty, Awk: A not so awkward tool, *UNIX/World*, Vol. 4, No. 5, May 1987.

Lee E. McMahon, *SED—A Non-interactive Text Editor*, Bell Laboratories, Murray Hill, New Jersey, Aug. 1978.

Elizabeth Vaughan, Pattern matching with regular expressions, *UNIX/World*, Vol. 4, No. 3, March 1987.

Chapter 2

T. A. Cargill, Debugging C programs with the Blit, *Bell Laboratories Technical Journal,* Vol. 63, No. 8, Part 2, Oct. 1984.

Bill Tuthill, Debuggers – Part I, *UNIX/World,* Vol. 4, No. 1, Jan. 1987.

Bill Tuthill, Debuggers – Part II, *UNIX/World,* Vol. 4, No. 2, Feb. 1987.

Samuel J. Leffler and William Joy, Using ADB to debug the UNIX kernel, *UNIX System Manager's Manual, 4.3 Berkley Software Distribution, Virtual VAX-11 Version,* June 1986.

J. F. Marazano and S. R. Bourne, *A Tutorial Introduction to ADB,* Bell Laboratories, Murray Hill, New Jersey, May 1977.

Chapter 3

M. E. Lesk and E. Schmidt, *Lex–A Lexical Analyser Generator,* Bell Laboratories, Murray Hill, New Jersey.

Stephen C. Johnson, *Yacc–Yet Another Compiler-Compiler,* Bell Laboratories, Murray Hill, New Jersey.

S. C. Johnson and M. E. Lesk, Language development tools, *Bell System Technical Journal,* Vol. 57, No. 6, Part 2, July-Aug. 1978.

W. L. Johnson, J. H. Porter, S. I. Ackey, and D. T. Ross, Automatic generation of efficient lexical processors using finite state techniques, *Comm. ACM,* Vol. 11, No. 12, pp. 805–813.

K. C. Tai, Syntactic error correction in programming languages, *IEEE Transactions on Software Engineering,* Vol. SE-4, No. 5, pp. 414–425.

Chapter 4

S. C. Johnson, *Lint–A C Program Checker,* Bell Laboratories, Murray Hill, New Jersey, July 1978.

Stuart I. Feldman, Make–A program for maintaining computer programs, *UNIX Programmer's Manual, Supplementary Documents I,* 4.3 BSD, April 1986.

Marc J. Rochkind, The Source Code Control System, *IEEE Transactions on Software Engineering*, Vol. SE-1, pp. 364-370, Dec. 1975.

Walter F. Tichy, An introduction to the Revision Control System, *UNIX Programmer's Manual, Supplementary Documents I*, 4.3 BSD, April 1986.

Rebecca Thomas, Advanced SCCS: How to make SCCS and Make work together, *UNIX/World*, Vol. 1, No. 5, Oct. 1985.

Brian Kernighan and Dennis Ritchie, *The M4 Macro Processor*, Bell Laboratories, Murray Hill, New Jersey, July 1977.

Chapter 5

C. J. Date, *An Introduction to Database Systems*, Vols. I and II, Reading, Massachusetts: Addison-Wesley, 1983.

UNIFY, *Programmers' Manual*, Unify Corporation, 1985.

UNIFY, *Reference Manual*, Unify Corporation, 1985.

INFORMIX-SQL, *Reference Manual*, Relational Database Systems, Inc., 1986.

INFORMIX-SQL, *User Guide*, Relational Database Systems, Inc., 1986.

Joe Kalash, Lisa Rodgin, Zelaine Fong, and Jeff Anton, Ingres Version 8, Reference Manual, *BSD 4.3 UNIX Programmer's Manual, Supplementary Documents*, Vol. 2, May 1986.

Chapter 6

Joseph F. Ossanna, *NROFF/TROFF User's Manual*, Bell Laboratories, Murray Hill, New Jersey, 1977.

Brian Kernighan, *A TROFF Tutorial*, Bell Laboratories, Murray Hill, New Jersey, 1978.

Lorinda Cherry and Brian Kernighan, *A System for Typesetting Mathematics*, Bell Laboratories, Murray Hill, New Jersey, Aug. 1978.

M. E. Lesk, *Tbl—A Program to Format Tables*, Bell Laboratories, Murray Hill, New Jersey, Jan. 1979.

Brian Kernighan, *PIC–A Graphics Language for Typesetting User Manual*, Bell Laboratories, Murray Hill, New Jersey.

Peggy Judd, Troff: A text software boon for scientific authors, *UNIX/World*, Vol. 2, No. 4, Feb. 1985.

Peggy Judd, Troff: A text software boon for scientific authors, *UNIX/World*, some corrections to the above article, May 1985.

Brian Kernighan, PIC–A language for typesetting graphics, *Software Practice and Experience*, Vol. 12, No. 1, pp. 1–21, Jan. 1982.

Christopher J. Van Wyk and C. J. Van Wyk, A Graphics Typesetting Language, *SIGPLAN Symposium on Text Manipulation*, Portland, Oregon, June 1981.

Sandy Emerson, The trouble with Troff, *UNIX Review*, Vol. 2, No. 5, Aug. 1985.

Chapter 7

Mark J. Hatch, Michael Katz, and Jim Rees, AT&T's RFS and SUN's NFS, *UNIX/World*, Vol. 2, No. 11, Dec. 1985.

Gary Sager and Bob Lyon, Distributed file system strategies, *UNIX Review*, Vol. 3, No. 5, May 1985.

D. A. Nowitz and Carl S. Gutekunst, Installation and operation of Uucp, *UNIX System Manager's Manual, 4.3 BSD UNIX*, Aug. 1986.

D. A. Nowitz, *Uucp Implementation Description*, Bell Laboratories, Murray Hill, New Jersey, Oct. 1978.

Bruce Borden, Mail in the electronic age, *UNIX Review*, Vol. 3, No. 7, July 1985.

David J. Cardinal, File Server offers transparent access to design tools, *Computer Design*, June 1985.

Chapter 8

UNIX System *Writer's Workbench User's Guide*.

Steve Rosenthal, Prose with style, *UNIX Review*, Vol. 2, No. 5, Aug. 1985.

Nina H. Macdonald, The Writer's Workbench: Rationale and design, *The Bell System Technical Journal*, No. 6, Part 3, July-Aug. 1983.

P. S. Gingrich, The Writer's Workbench: Implementations, *The Bell System Technical Journal*, No. 6, Part 3, July-Aug. 1983.

Michael Donohue, Vexations of the sexist, *UNIX Review*, Vol. 2, No. 5, Aug. 1984.

Steve Rosenthal, Putting Text in its place, *UNIX Review*, Vol. 2, No. 5, Aug. 1985.

Harry Avant, AT&T's Writer's Workbench, *UNIX/World*, Vol. 3, No. 8, Aug. 1986.

Chapter 9

Kenneth C. R. C. Arnold, Screen updating and cursor movement optimization: A library package, *UNIX Programmer's Manual, 4.2 Berkeley Software Distribution, Supplementary Documents*.

Aaron Marcus, UNIX and GKS in a new age, *UNIX/World*, Vol. 1, No. 5, Oct. 1985.

UNIX System, Graphics Guide, Western Electric.

Robert Morris and Lorinda Cherry, *DC−An Interactive Desk Calulator*, Bell Laboratories, Murray Hill, New Jersey, Nov. 1978.

Robert Morris and Lorinda Cherry, *BC−An Arbitrary Precision Desk-Calculator Language*, Bell Laboratories, Murray Hill, New Jersey, Nov. 1978.

Index